Christopher Stuart Patterson

**The United States and the States under the Constitution**

Christopher Stuart Patterson

**The United States and the States under the Constitution**

ISBN/EAN: 9783337187743

Printed in Europe, USA, Canada, Australia, Japan

Cover: Foto ©ninafisch / pixelio.de

More available books at **www.hansebooks.com**

# THE

# UNITED STATES

### AND THE

# STATES

## UNDER THE CONSTITUTION.

BY

CHRISTOPHER STUART PATTERSON,

OF THE PHILADELPHIA BAR.

PHILADELPHIA:
T. & J. W. JOHNSON & CO.,
535 CHESTNUT STREET.
1888.

# PREFACE.

This book has not been written to give expression to any theories, either in politics or in law. Its only purpose is to show by a classification and an analysis of the judgments of the Supreme Court of the United States, what the relations of the United States and the states are under the Constitution, as judicially construed by the court of last resort.     C. S. P.

CHESTNUT-HILL.

9 April, 1888.

# TABLE OF CONTENTS.

### CHAPTER I.

#### THE RELATION OF THE STATES TO THE UNITED STATES AND TO EACH OTHER.

1. The sanction of the Constitution.
2. The indissolubility of the Union.
3. The autonomy of the states.
4. The delegated character and limited powers of the government of the United States.
5. The Federal supremacy.
6. The restraints upon the states.
7. The force and effect of the preamble to the Constitution.

### CHAPTER II.

#### THE IMPLIED POWERS.

8. The necessity of their existence.
9. Their constitutional recognition.
10. The test of the relation of the means to the end.
11. Illustrations of the exercise of the implied powers.
12. The legal tender question.
13. The possible scope of the legal tender cases as authorities.

### CHAPTER III.

#### TAXATION.

14. Taxation defined and limited.
15. Taxation by the United States.
16. Direct taxation.
17. The requirement of uniformity.
18. Exemption of state agencies from taxation by the United States.
19. Charges which are not taxes exempt from constitutional restraints.

20. Taxation by the states.
21. The expressed restraints upon state taxation.
22. The implied restraint upon state taxation resulting from the federal supremacy.
23. Taxation of national banks.
24. State taxation as affected by the prohibition of the impairment of the obligation of contracts.
25. State taxation as affected by the grant to Congress of the power of regulating commerce.

## CHAPTER IV.

#### THE REGULATION OF COMMERCE.

26. The constitutional provisions.
27. The history of the commercial clause.
28. Commerce defined.
29. The regulation of commerce defined.
30. The general distinction between the powers of the United States and of the states over commerce.
31. Navigable waters.
32. Title to the soil under navigable waters.
33. The regulation of navigation.
34. The regulation of subjects of commerce.
35. The taxation of ships.
36. Duties on tonnage.
37. The taxation of the water transportation of passengers.
38. The taxation of goods in interstate commerce.
39. Discriminating taxation against products and manufactures of other states.
40. The taxation of exports by the United States.
41. State taxation of imports and exports, and inspection laws.
42. Improvements of navigation.
43. Dams and bridges.
44. Ferries.
45. Wharves and piers.
46. Pilotage.
47. Quarantine and sanitary regulations.
48. Port dues.
49. Port regulations.
50. Preferences of ports.
51. Interstate railway transportation.
52. Railway tolls.
53. The police regulation of railways.
54. State taxation of interstate transportation by railways.
55. Telegraphs
56. Commerce with the Indian tribes.

## CHAPTER V.

### THE IMPAIRMENT OF THE OBLIGATION OF CONTRACTS.

57. The prohibition affects only laws passed by states.
58. The term "law" defined.
59. Judgments of state courts not conclusive either as to the non existence or non-impairment, of contracts.
60. The obligation of a contract defined.
61. Legislation as to remedies.
62. The term "contracts" defined.
63. State insolvent laws.
64. Judgments as contracts.
65. Municipal taxation.
66. History of the prohibition.
67. State grants.
68. Express contracts of exemption from taxation.
69. Express grants of peculiar privileges.
70. Contracts between a state and its political subdivisions.
71. Implied contracts in charters of incorporation.
72. Implied corporate exemption from taxation.
73. Implied grants of peculiar privileges.
74. Implied exemption from the operation of the police power.
75. Implied contracts as to matters of public concern.
76. The withdrawal by a state of its consent to be sued.
77. The force and effect of the prohibition as construed by the Supreme Court.

## CHAPTER VI.

### EX POST FACTO LAWS AND BILLS OF ATTAINDER.

78. The constitutional provisions.
79. The distinction between retrospective and *ex post facto* laws.
80. *Ex post facto* laws defined.
81. Illustrations of *ex post facto* laws.
82. Illustrations of laws which are not *ex post facto*.
83. Bills of attainder and bills of pains and penalties.

## CHAPTER VII.

### THE PROHIBITION OF STATE BILLS OF CREDIT.

84. Bills of credit defined.
85. What are, and what are not, bills of credit.

## CHAPTER VIII.

### STATE COMPACTS.

86. What compacts are permitted, and what are forbidden.

## CHAPTER IX.

### FUGITIVES FROM JUSTICE.

87. The constitutional provision.
88. The concurrent jurisdiction of the federal and state courts.

## CHAPTER X.

### THE JUDICIAL POWER.

89. The necessity for the existence of a judicial department of the United States.
90. The constitutional provisions.
91. The terms of the grant of federal jurisdiction.
92. The exclusive jurisdiction.
93. The original jurisdiction.
94. Removal of causes from state courts to the courts of the United States.
95. The appellate and supervisory jurisdiction.
96. The requisites of a judicial case.
97. Courts-martial.
98. Impeachment.
99. The judicial construction of the Constitution.
100. The XI Amendment.
101. Section 2 of Article III of the Constitution, and the IV Amendment.
102. The V Amendment.
103. The VI Amendment.
104. The VII Amendment.
105. The exemption of federal process from state control.
106. Limitation of federal process by the reserved rights of the states.
107. The limitations of state jurisdiction and process by the federal supremacy.
108. The rule as to conflict of jurisdiction.
109. The XIV Amendment as affecting state jurisdiction.
110. The effect of Section 1 of Article IV of the Constitution.

## CHAPTER XI.

### RIGHTS OF PERSON AND OF PROPERTY.

111. Citizenship of the United States.
112. Citizenship of a state.

113. The right of suffrage.
114. The right of serving on juries.
115. Congressional regulation of the election of senators and representatives.
116. Personal and property rights.
117. The rights within a state of citizens of other states.
118. Foreign corporations.
119. The XIII Amendment.
120. The XIV Amendment.
121. The police power.

## CHAPTER XII.

### THE FEDERAL SUPREMACY AND THE RESERVED RIGHTS OF THE STATES.

122. The constitutional declaration of the federal supremacy.
123. The supremacy of the Constitution.
124. The supremacy of the acts of Congress.
125. The supremacy of treaties.
126. The results of federal supremacy.
127. The constitutional reservation of the rights of the states.
128. The nature and extent of those reserved rights.
129. The importance of the preservation of the rights of the states.

# TABLE OF CASES CITED.

THE REFERENCES ARE TO THE PAGES.

| | PAGE | | PAGE |
|---|---|---|---|
| Abbott, Renaud v., 116 U. S. 277 | 245 | Amy, Bath County v., 13 Wall. 244 | 233 |
| Ableman v. Booth, 21 How. 506 | 11, 237 | v. Shelby County, 114 U. S. 387 | 179 |
| Achison v. Huddleson, 12 How. 293 | 123 | v. Supervisors, 11 Wall. 136 | 233 |
| Adams, County of, Osborne v., 106 U. S. 181, 109 id. 1 | 20 | Anderson v. Dunn, 6 Wheat. 204 | 11 |
| | | McMillen v., 95 U. S. 37 | 240 |
| Adams v. Nashville, 95 U. S. 19 | 31 | Terry v., 95 U. S. 628 | 150 |
| Ætna Co., Aldrich v., 8 Wall. 591 | 59 | Antoni v. Greenhow, 107 U. S. 769 | 152 |
| Aiken, O. P. Co. v., 121 U. S. 444 | 19, 106 | Arkansas, Curran v., 15 How. 304 | 172, 223 |
| Alabama v. Georgia, 23 How. 505 | 189, 198 | Beers v., 20 How. 527 | 180, 181 |
| Alabama, Bank of, v. Dalton, 9 How. 522 | 234, 244, 248 | Bank v., 20 How. 530 | 180 |
| Pace v., 106 U. S. 583 | 265 | Armstrong v. Lear, 8 Pet. 52 | 212 |
| R. R. v., 101 U. S. 832 | 180 | v. Carson, 2 Dall. 303 | 244 |
| Alderson, Freeman v., 119 U. S. 185 | 246 | Aronson v. Murphy, 109 U. S. 238 | 232 |
| | | Arrowsmith v. Harmoning, 118 U. S. 194 | 242 |
| Allen v. Louisiana, 103 U. S. 80 | 274 | Arredondo, U. S. v., 6 Pet. 691 | 275 |
| v. Newberry, 21 How. 244 | 47, 197 | Aspinwall v. Daviess County, 22 How. 364 | 154 |
| Almy v. California, 24 How. 169 | 36, 41, 72, 84 | Assessors, The, Van Allen v., 3 Wall. 573 | 29, 30 |
| Albany Bridge Case, The, 2 Wall. 403 | 97 | Asylum v. New Orleans, 105 U. S. 362 | 33, 167, 168 |
| Alling, Sherlock v., 93 U. S. 99 | 60 | Atlee, M. & St. P. R. R. v., 94 U. S. 179 | 178 |
| Allen, Crapo v., 1 Sprague, 184 | 60 | | |
| Alabama, Boyd v., 94 U. S. 645 | 178, 269 | Aurora City, West v., 6 Wall. 39 | 209 |
| Smith v., 124 U. S. 465 | 268 | Augusta, Bank of, v. Earle, 13 Pet. 519 | 40, 260 |
| Alexandria Council, Downham v., 10 Wall. 173 | 35, 81, 258 | Augusta, Home Ins. Co. v., 93 U. S. 116 | 34, 171 |
| Aldrich v. Ætna Co., 8 Wall. 491 | 59 | Austin, Low v., 13 Wall. 29 | 25, 83 |
| Alabama, Bank of, Darrington v., 13 How. 12 | 188 | Ayres, In re, 123 U. S. 524 | 180, 220 |
| A. Mfg. Co., Head v., 113 U. S. 9 | 240 | A. & G. R. R. v. Georgia, 98 U. S. 359 | 169 |
| Ames v. Kansas, 111 U. S. 449 | 196, 205, 209 | | |
| American Ins. Co., Grace v., 109 U. S. 278 | 199 | Bates v. Clark, 95 U. S. 204 | 224 |
| | | Bacon v. Howard, 20 How. 22 | 244 |
| Amedy, U. S. v., 11 Wheat. 392 | 243 | Bailey v. Magwire, Collr., 22 Wall. 215 | 177 |
| American Steamboat Co. v. Chase, 16 Wall. 522 | 60 | Ballard, Caperton v., 14 Wall. 238 | 243 |
| American Bridge Co., Cardwell v., 113 U. S. 205 | 98 | Bank of Alabama v. Dalton, 9 How. 522 | 234, 244, 248 |

xi

## TABLE OF CASES CITED.

Bank of Columbia v. Okely, 4 Wheat. 235    231
Bank of U. S. v. Deveaux, 5 Cr. 61    259
Ball, The Daniel, 10 Wall. 557    46, 52, 75, 197
Baltimore, Barron v., 7 Pet. 243    224, 254
     Guy v., 100 U. S. 434    35, 97, 106, 258
Bank of U. S., Vorhees v., 10 Pet. 449    245
Barry, Gunn v, 15 Wall. 610    146, 153
Barbier v. Connelly, 113 U. S. 27    269
Barbour, Barton v., 104 U. S. 126    230
Bartemeyer v. Iowa, 18 Wall. 129    267
Barron v. Baltimore, 7 Pet. 243    224, 254
Barton v. Barbour, 104 U. S. 126    230
Barrett v. Holmes, 102 U. S. 651    241
Barnard, Clark v., 108 U. S. 436    219
Bank of Kentucky, Briscoe v , 11 Pet. 317    2, 187, 188, 215, 223
Banks, The, v. The Mayor, 7 Wall. 16    26
Bank v. Supervisors, 7 Wall. 26    26
Banks, Carneal v., 10 Wheat. 181    275
Bank of Georgia, Breithaupt v., 1 Pet. 238    199
Bank of Washington v. Arkansas, 20 How. 530    180
Bain, Ex parte, 121 U. S. 1    226
Bank of Hamilton v. Dudley's Lessee, 2 Pet. 492    193
Baldwin v. Franks, 120 U. S. 678    274, 275
     v. Hale, 1 Wall. 223    154, 157, 158
Barron v. Burnside, 121 U. S. 186    262
Barings v. Dabney, 19 Wall. 1    172
Barber v. Barber, 21 How. 582    197
Barney v. Keokuk, 94 U. S. 324    46, 48, 105
Barry, Gunn v., 15 Wall. 610    146, 153
Bank Tax Cases, The, 2 Wall. 200    26
Baker v. Boulton, 1 Camp. 493    60
Batty, McNulty v., 10 How. 72    209
Bank of U. S. v. Halstead, 10 Wheat. 51    231
Bath County v. Amy, 13 Wall. 244    233
Beer Co. v. Mass., 97 U. S. 25    67, 81, 267, 269
Beers v. Arkansas, 20 How. 527    180, 181
Beasley, Burlington v., 94 U. S. 310    20

Bedford, Parsons v., 3 Pet. 433    200, 230
Bevans, United States v., 3 Wheat. 337    50, 200
Berry, Williamson v., 8 How. 495    245
Beebe, Doe v., 13 How. 25    255
Benedict v. Williams, 8 How. 107    234, 238
Betsy, Sloop, Glass v., 3 Dall 7    245
Belfast, The, 7 Wall. 624    47, 59, 197, 236
Bigler v. Waller, 14 Wall. 297    13
Binghamton Bridge, The, 3 Wall. 51    171, 177
Billings, Providence Bank v., 4 Pet. 514    23, 33, 176
Bischoff v. Wethered, 9 Wall. 812    245
Bingham v. Cabot, 3 Dall. 382    199
Biddle, Green v., 8 Wheat 1    149, 166, 172
Blackbird Creek Marsh Co., Willson v., 2 Pet. 250    93, 98, 111
Blair v. Cuning County, 111 U. S. 363    20
Blake, Loughborough v., 5 Wheat. 317    11, 20
W. & St. P. R. R. v., 94 U. S. 180    178
Blount v. Windley, 95 U. S. 173    151, 154, 158
Blyew v. U. S., 13 Wall. 581    196
Board of Liquidation, Guarantee Co. v., 1.5 U. S. 622    151
Board of Public Works v. College, 17 Wall. 521    244, 245
Borden, Luther v., 7 How. 1    211, 212
Boswell v. Otis, 9 How. 336    239, 245
Bollman and Swartwout, Ex parte, 4 Cr. 75    228
Borer v. Chapman, 119 U. S. 587    231
Bonaparte v. Tax Court, 104 U. S. 592    18, 24
Bors v. Preston, 111 U. S. 252    205
Booth, Ableman v., 21 How. 506    11, 237
Boulton, Baker v., 1 Camp. 493    60
Bond, Nugent v., 3 How. 426    235
Boyd v. Alabama, 94 U. S. 645    178, 269
Boyer v. Boyer, 113 U. S 689    31
Boom Co. v. Patterson, 98 U. S. 403    197
Boyle v. Zacharie, 6 Pet. 635    154, 156
Boyce v. Tabb, 18 Wall. 546    :64
Boyd, Ex parte, 105 U. S. 647    197
     v. United States, 116 U. S. 616    226
Bridge Co. v. United States, 105 U. S. 470    99

## TABLE OF CASES CITED. xiii

Branch, Tomlinson v., 15 Wall. 460    34, 171
Briscoe v. Bank of Kentucky, 11 Pet. 257    2, 188, 215, 223
Brown v. Houston, 114 U. S. 622    35, 74, 85
   v. Maryland, 12 Wheat. 419    25, 40, 82, 216, 269
Brant, Landes v., 10 How. 348    244
Brown, Parkersburg v., 106 U. S. 487    20
   v. Huger, 21 How. 305    224
Broadnax, Suydam v., 14 Pet. 67    154, 156, 238
Brown, Mills v., 16 Pet. 525    199
Bruffy, Williams v., 96 U. S. 176    189
Breithaupt v. Bank, 1 Pet. 238    199
Brown v. Keene, 8 Pet, 115    199
Bronson v. Kenzie, 1 How. 311    153
Bradwell v. The State, 16 Wall 130    257, 265
Bridge Case, The Albany, 2 Wall. 403    97
Bridge Proprietors v. Hoboken Co., 1 Wall. 116    149, 171, 172
Bridges, The Passaic, 3 Wall. (App.) 782    97
Bronson v. Kimpton, 8 Wall. 44    12
   v. Rodes, 7 Wall. 229    12
Bradley v. The People, 4 Wall. 459    30
Britton, Evansville v., 105 U. S. 322    32
Brewster, Chittenden v., 2 Wall. 191    133
Bull, Fretz v., 12 How. 466    197
Buckner v. Finley, 2 Pet. 586    2
Butler v. Penna., 10 How. 402    154, 179
Bull, Calder v., 3 Dall. 386    182, 183, 184
Buck v. Coldbath, 3 Wall. 334    238
Burgess, Turpin v., 117 U. S. 504    82
Burlington, Rogers v., 3 Wall. 654    20
Burnside, Barron v., 121 U. S. 186    262
Burton. Koskonong v., 104 U. S. 668    150, 153
Burgess, Pace v., 92 U. S. 372    81
Bush v. Kentucky, 107 U. S. 110    200, 241, 242
Bugbee, Howard v., 24 How. 461    153
Butchers' Union v. C. C. Co., 111 U. S. 760    178, 269
Burlington v. Beasley, 94 U. S. 310    20
Buckley, Withers v., 20 How. 84    226, 254
Butter v. Horwitz, 7 Wall. 258    12
Bucher, Higgins v., Yelv. 89    60

Byrne v. Missouri, 8 Pet. 40    187
B. & O. R. R., U. S. v., 17 Wall. 322    23
   v. Maryland, 21 Wall. 456    19, 36, 124
   Maryland v., 3 How. 534    173
   Marshall v., 16 How. 314    259
   v. Koontz, 104 U. S. 5    261
B. & S. R. R. v. Nesbit, 10 How. 395    182, 183
Carpenter v. Pennsylvania, 17 How. 456    23, 34, 182, 183
Caldwell v. Carrington, 9 Pet. 86    244
Caperton v. Ballard, 14 Wall. 238    243
Calder v. Bull, 3 Dall. 386    182, 183, 184
California, Hurtado v., 110 U. S. 517    241
Cannon v. N. O., 20 Wall. 577    25, 67, 121
Carskadon, Pierce v., 16 Wall. 234    153, 185, 186
Carson, Armstrong v., 2 Dall. 305    244
Cardwell v. A. Bridge Co., 113 U. S. 205    98
Case of the State tax on foreign held bonds, 15 Wall. 300    23, 24, 154
Case of the State freight tax, 15 Wall. 232    18, 36, 125, 135
Campbell v. Holt, 115 U. S., 620    241
Carrington, Caldwell v., 9 Pet. 86    244
Cabot, Bingham v., 3 Dall. 382    199
Catlettsburg, Packet Co. v., 105 U. S. 559    19, 106
Capron v. Van Noorden, 2 Cr. 126    199
Caleb, Hawthorne v., 2 Wall. 10    153
Carey, Ottawa v., 108 U. S. 110    20
Carneal v. Banks, 10 Wheat. 181    275
California, Almy v., 24 How. 169    36, 41, 72, 84
Campbell, Robinson v., 3 Wheat. 212    200
Carryl, Taylor v., 20 How. 583    238
Card, Maguire v., 21 How. 248    47, 197
Case, Perriman's, 103 U. S. 714    149
Carroll v. Safford, 3 How. 441    27
Carpenter, Haines v., 91 U. S. 254    233
C., B. & Q. R. R. v. Iowa, 94 U. S. 155    126, 178, 268, 269
C. C. Co., Butchers' Union v., 111 U. S. 760    178, 269
Perrine v., 9 How. 192    177
C. D. Co. v. Shepherd, 20 How. 232    259
Cease, Robertson v., 97 U. S. 646    199
C. Gas Co., Louisiana Gas Co. v., 115 U. S. 683    172

## TABLE OF CASES CITED.

Chase, Steamboat Co. v., 16 Wall. 522 — 60
Chapman, Borer v., 119 U. S. 587 — 231
Charleston, Murray v., 96 U. S. 432 — 34, 172
Weston v., 2 Pet. 449, — 26
Church v. Kelsey, 121 U. S. 282 — 179, 241
Chemung Canal Bank v. Lowery, 93 U. S. 72 — 258
Chicago, Escanaba Co. v., 107 U. S. 678, — 98, 268
Chisholm v. Georgia, 2 Dall. 419 — 199, 217
Chicago v. Sheldon, 9 Wall. 50 — 33, 147, 167
Ducat v., 10 Wall. 410 — 40, 260, 261, 262
Chy Lung v. Freeman, 92 U. S. 275 — 36, 71
Cherokee Nation v. Georgia, 5 Pet. 1 — 143, 198, 212
Chambers, Kennett v., 14 How. 38 — 213
Christ Church v. Philadelphia, 24 How. 300 — 168
Christmas v. Russell, 5 Wall. 290 — 244
Chicago Life Ins. Co. v. Needles, 113 U. S. 574 — 177
Church v. Hubbart, 2 Cr. 187 — 212
Chirac v. Chirac, 2 Wheat. 259 — 111, 251, 275
Cherokee Tobacco, The, 11 Wall. 616 — 274
Charles River Bridge v. Warren Bridge, 11 Pet. 420 — 177
Cheever v. Wilson, 9 Wall. 108 — 244
China, The, 7 Wall. 53 — 115, 116
Challen, Holland v., 110 U. S. 15 — 200
Chittenden v. Brewster, 2 Wall. 191 — 233
City, The, v. Lawson, 9 Wall. 477 — 147
Civil Rights Cases, 109 U. S. 3 — 266
Clarke, Ex parte, 100 U. S. 399 — 254
Clark, Bates v., 95 U. S. 204 — 224
Clark v. Barnard, 108 U. S. 436 — 219, 225
Clark, Mitchell v., 110 U. S. 333 — 232
Claflin v. Houseman, 93 U. S. 130 — 235, 236
Clark, Keith v., 97 U. S. 454 — 146, 172
Clarke, Waring v., 5 How. 441 — 46, 197, 200
Close v. Glenwood Cemetery, 107 U. S. 400 — 169
Clinton Bridge, The, 10 Wall. 454 — 99
C. M. I. Co., Goodwin v., 110 U. S. 1 — 263
C. M. L. Ins. Co. v. Cushman, 108 U. S. 51 — 150

Coe v. Errol, 116 U. S. 517 — 18, 24, 35, 74, 75, 82
Cole v. La Grange, 113 U. S. 1 — 20
Collet v. Collet, 2 Dall. 294 — 254
Columbia College, Board, etc., v., 17 Wall. 521 — 244, 245
Compagnie G. T., People v., 107 U. S. 59 — 36, 87
Commissioners, Newton v., 100 U. S. 548 — 179
Connolly, Barbier v., 113 U. S. 27 — 269
Cook v. Penna., 97 U. S. 566 — 25, 40, 83
Cooper Mfg. Co. v. Ferguson, 113 U. S. 727 — 215, 263
Cooper v. Reynolds, 10 Wall. 306 — 245, 246
County of Ralls v. Douglass, 105 U. S. 728 — 147
County of Mobile v. Kimball, 102 U. S. 691 — 40, 90
Coster, Runyan v., 14 Pet. 122 — 260
Cohen, McElmoyle v., 13 Pet. 312 — 244
Connelly, Robb v., 111 U. S. 624 — 191, 237
Coupon Cases, Virginia, 114 U. S. 270 — 172, 188, 224, 274
Cook v. Moffat, 5 How. 295 — 154, 157
Collector, Hornthall v., 9 Wall. 560 — 199
Commissioners, The, The People v., 2 Bl. 620 — 26
People v., 104 U. S. 466 — 35, 62
People v., 4 Wall 244 — 29, 30
Dobbins v., 16 Pet. 435 — 26
Cooley v. The Board of Wardens. 12 How. 299 — 111, 116, 134
Commissioners of Taxes, etc., People v., 94 U. S. 415 — 32, 33, 155
of Tippecanoe v. Lucas, 93 U. S. 108 — 241
Cowles v. Mercer County, 7 Wall. 118 — 260
Commonwealth, Nat. Bank v., 9 Wall. 353 — 28, 30, 33
Coombs, U. S v., 12 Pet. 72 — 46
Conway v. Taylor, 1 Bl. 603 — 101, 268
Coudry, Smith v., 1 How. 28 — 243
Continental Ins. Co., Doyle v., 94 U. S. 535 — 262
Cox, St. Clair v., 106 U. S. 350 — 245, 247, 261
Commonwealth. Pervear v., 5 Wall. 475 — 20, 254, 269
Commissioners, The, Mitchell v., 91 U. S. 206 — 126
Coite, Society for Savings v., 6 Wall. 594 — 26
Commonwealth, The, McGuire v., 3 Wall. 387 — 29, 269

## TABLE OF CASES CITED.

Corson v. Maryland, 120 U. S. 502    35, 77, 258
Commissioners of Immigration v. North German Lloyd, 92 U. S. 269    36, 71
Cohens v. Virginia, 6 Wheat. 264    193, 194, 195, 196, 197, 199, 201, 209, 211, 215, 216, 222
Cooper, The Mayor v., 6 Wall. 253    193, 196, 209
Collidge, U. S. v., 1 Wheat. 415    200
Covell v. Heyman, 111 U. S. 176    237, 238
Coldbath, Buck v., 3 Wall. 334    238
Corfield v. Coryell, 4 Wash. C. C. 371    256
Coryell, Corfield v., 4 Wash. C.C. 371    256
Conner v. Elliot, 18 How. 593    257
Craig v. Missouri, 4 Pet. 411    187
Crandall v. State of Nevada, 6 Wall. 35    28, 73, 84, 87, 125, 134, 258
Creighton, Green v., 23 How. 90    238
Crowninshield, Sturges v., 4 Wheat. 122    2, 4, 16, 40, 111, 146, 149, 153, 154, 155, 157, 164, 201, 215
Crowley, Soon Hing v., 113 U. S. 703    269
Crow Dog Ex parte, 109 U. S. 556    144
Cruikshank, U. S. v., 92 U. S. 542    201, 251, 253, 254
Crapo v. Allen, 1 Sprague, 184    60
C. S. Ry. v. Gebhard, 109 U. S. 527    262
Cummings v. Nat. Bank, 101 U. S. 677    32
Curran v. Arkansas, 15 How. 304    172, 223
Cunningham v. M. & B. R. R. 109 U. S. 446    220
Cushman, C. M. L. Ins. Co. v., 108 U. S. 51    150
Culver, Queensbury v., 19 Wall. 83    20
Cutting v. Seabury, 1 Sprague, 522    60
Cummings v. Missouri, 4 Wall. 277    184, 185, 186
Cuming County, Blair v., 111 U. S. 363    20
Curtis, Ex parte, 106 U. S 371    12
Curtis v. Whitney, 13 Wall. 68    150
C. & A. R. R. v. W. F. Co., 119 U. S. 615    212, 213, 243
C. & B. Co. v. N. O., 99 U. S. 97    26
C. & A. R. R. v. W. F. Co., 108 U. S. 18    244
C. & F. R. R. v. Hecht, 95 U. S. 168    149

C. & N. W. R. R. v. Fuller, 17 Wall. 560    126, 268
v. Whitton, 13 Wall. 270    60, 200, 232
C. & N. W. Ry., Peck v., 94 U. S. 164    127, 178, 268
D'Arbel, Urtetiqui v., 9 Pet 692    248
Darlington, County of Livingston v., 101 U. S. 407    20
Dabney, Barings v., 19 Wall.    172
Daviess County, Aspinwall v., 22 How. 364    154
Davenport, Sinnot v., 22 How. 227    53, 68, 122, 270
Foster v., 22 How. 244    53, 68, 122, 270
Daniel Ball, The, 10 Wall. 557    46, 52, 75, 197
Dartmouth College Case, 4 Wheat. 518    154, 173, 174, 178
D'Arcy v. Ketchum, 11 How 165    245
Dalton, Bank of Alabama v., 9 How. 522    234, 244, 248
Davidson v. N. O., 96 U. S. 97    226, 240, 254
Davis v. Gray, 16 Wall. 203    166, 218
Daggs, Ewell v., 108 U. S. 143    150
Davis, Tennessee v., 100 U. S. 257    200, 209
Darlington v. The Bank of Alabama, 13 How. 12    188
Davis v. Packard, 7 Pet. 276    236
Day v. Gallop, 2 Wall. 97    238
Day, The Collector v., 11 Wall. 113    23
Darst, Duncan v., 1 How. 301    237
De Cuir, Hall v., 95 U. S. 485    54, 270
Delmas v. Ins. Co., 14 Wall. 661    148, 149, 152
Delaware, Neal v., 103 U. S. 370    253
R R. Tax, The, 18 Wall. 206    34, 35, 133, 177
De Treville v. Smalls, 98 U. S. 517    22
Deveaux, The Bank v., 5 Cr. 61    259
De Young, League v., 11 How. 185    146, 150
Dea v. Jersey Co., 15 How. 426    47
De Bolt, Ohio L., 1. & T. Co. v., 16 How. 416    147, 149, 177
Dennick v. R. R. Co., 103 U. S. 11    197
Demire, Harris v., 3 Pet. 292    236
Dewitt, U. S. v., 9 Wall. 41    200, 267
Dial v. Reynolds, 96 U. S. 340    233
Dietzsel v. Huidekoper, 103 U. S. 494    233
Dillin, Hamilton v., 21 Wall. 73    11

## TABLE OF CASES CITED.

| | PAGE |
|---|---|
| Diggs v. Wulcot, 4 Cr. 179 | 233 |
| Donoghue, Hanley v., 116 U. S. 1 | 213, 245 |
| Doe v. Beebe, 13 How. 25 | 255 |
| Dorrance, Van Horne v., 2 Dall. 304 | 193 |
| Downham v. Alexandria Council, 10 Wall. 173 | 35, 81, 258 |
| Dodge v. Woolsey, 18 How. 331 | 193 |
| Dobbins v. The Commissioners, 16 Pet. 435 | 26 |
| Dooley v. Smith, 18 Wall. 604 | 13 |
| Douglass v. County of Pike, 101 U. S. 677 | 147 |
| County of Rall v., 105 U. S. 728 | 147 |
| Dowley, Waite v., 94 U. S. 527 | 33 |
| Doyle v. Continental Ins. Co., 94 U. S. 535 | 262 |
| Dred Scott v. Sandford, 19 How. 393 | 199, 251 |
| Drehman v. Stifle, 8 Wall. 595 | 151 |
| Drew, Paut v., 10 How. 218 | 172 |
| Trigg v., 10 How. 224 | 174 |
| Drogan, Hobart v., 10 Pet. 108 | 111, 116, 197, 232 |
| Duncan, Witherspoon v., 4 Wall. 210 | 23 |
| v. Darst, 1 How. 301 | 237 |
| Ducat v. Chicago, 10 Wall. 410 | 40, 260, 261, 262 |
| Dudley's Lessee, Bank v., 2 Pet. 492 | 193 |
| Dunn, Anderson v., 6 Wheat. 204 | 11 |
| Duryee, Mills v., 7 Cr. 481 | 244 |
| Duluth, Wisconsin v., 96 U. S. 379 | 89 |
| Dupasseur v. Rochereau, 21 Wall. 130 | 249 |
| Durant, The Supervisors v., 9 Wall. 415 | 233 |
| Dynes v. Hoover, 20 How. 65 | 213 |
| D. & R. C. Co., Rundle v., 14 How. 30 | 47 |
| East Saginaw, Salt Co v., 13 Wall. 373 | 168 |
| East Hartford v. Hartford Bridge Co., 10 How. 511 | 173 |
| Earle, Bank of Augusta v., 13 Pet. 519 | 40, 260 |
| Easton, Lehigh Water Co. v., 121 U. S. 88 | 147, 148 |
| Eagle, The, 8 Wall. 15 | 197 |
| East St. Louis, Wiggins Ferry Co. v., 107 U. S. 365 | 34, 35, 41, 43, 66, 102, 170 |
| Edwards v. Kearzey, 96 U. S. 595 | 146 |
| v. Elliott, 21 Wall. 532 | 59, 200, 230, 233, 236, 254 |

| | PAGE |
|---|---|
| Edwards, Hughes v., 9 Wheat. 496 | 275 |
| Effinger v. Kenney, 115 U. S. 566 | 152 |
| Elmendorf v. Taylor, 10 Wheat. 152 | 243 |
| Elliott, Edwards v., 21 Wall. 532 | 59, 200, 230, 233, 236, 254 |
| v. Piersol, 1 Pet. 328 | 245 |
| Ellis, Parrish v., 16 Pet. 451 | 200 |
| Ellerman, R. R. v., 105 U. S. 166 | 173 |
| Elizabeth Oil Cloth Co., Herdritter v., 112 U. S. 294 | 238 |
| Elliott, Conner v., 18 How. 593 | 257 |
| Embry v. Palmer, 107 U. S. 3 | 11, 248 |
| Ennis v. Smith, 14 How. 40 | 212, 245 |
| Errol, Coe v., 16 U. S. 517 | 18, 24, 35, 74, 75, 82 |
| E. Ry. v. Penna., 21 Wall. 492 | 34, 36, 177 |
| Erie Railway Co. v. Penna., 15 Wall. 282 | 136 |
| Erwin v. Lowry, 7 How. 181 | 234, 238 |
| Escanaba Co. v. Chicago, 107 U. S. 678 | 98, 268 |
| Evansville Bank v. Britton, 105 U. S. 322 | 32 |
| Ewell v. Daggs, 108 U. S. 143 | 150 |
| Ewing, Gastler v., 3 How. 767 | 153 |
| Express Co. v. Kountze, 8 Wall. 342 | 259 |
| Exchange Bank, Knox v., 12 Wall. 379 | 148 |
| Hill v., 108 U. S. 319 | 32 |
| Ex parte Garland, 4 Wall. 333 | 184, 186 |
| Pennsylvania, 107 U. S. 174 | 116 |
| Madrazzo, 7 Pet. 627 | 220 |
| Bollman & Swartwout, 4 Cr. 75 | 200, 228 |
| Boyd, 105 U. S. 647 | 197 |
| Curtis, 106 U. S. 371 | 12 |
| Clark, 100 U. S. 399 | 254 |
| Fonda, 117 U S. 516 | 210 |
| Jackson, 96 U. S. 727 | 11 |
| Lange, 18 Wall. 163 | 228, 229 |
| Royall, 117 U. S. 241 | 210 |
| Wall, 107 U. S. 265 | 226 |
| Wilson, 114 U. S. 417 | 226 |
| Yarborough, 110 U. S. 651 | 252, 254 |
| Bain, 121 U. S. 1 | 226 |
| Crow Dog, 109 U. S. 556 | 144 |
| Hagar, 104 U. S. 520 | 116 |
| Reggel, 114 U. S. 642 | 190, 191 |
| Siebold, 100 U. S. 371 | 254 |
| Milligan. 4 Wall. 2 | 213, 225, 228 |
| Mason, 105 U. S. 696 | 213 |
| Virginia, 100 U. S. 339 | 242, 246, 253 |
| Christie, 3 How. 318 | 235 |

# TABLE OF CASES CITED. xvii

*Ex parte* McNiel, 13 Wall. 236
        115, 116
 Gordon, 104 U. S. 515 60, 200
 Ferry Co., 104 U. S. 519 60, 200
 Eyster *v.* Gaff, 91 U. S. 521 235

Fanning *v.* Gregoire, 16 How.
 524    101, 177, 268
Fargo *v.* Michigan, 121 U. S. 230
      36, 84, 132, 137
Falconer, R. R. Co. *v.*, 103 U. S.
 821       159
Farrington *v.* Tennessee, 95 U. S.
 679       167
Fenno, Veazie Bank *v.*, 8 Wall.
 533     10, 22, 23
Ferguson, Cooper Mfg. Co. *v.*,
 113 U. S. 727   215, 263
 Tucker *v.*, 22 Wall. 527
     27, 33, 34, 170, 177
Ferrera, U. S. *v.*, 13 How. 40 209
Felton, Teal *v.*, 12 How. 284 235
Ferguson *v.* Harwood, 7 Cr. 408 243
Fertilizing Co. *v.* Hyde Park, 97
 U. S. 659    178, 269
Feusier, Lammon *v.*, 111 U. S. 17 239
Finley, Buckner *v*, 2 Pet. 586 2
Fisher, U. S. *v*, 2 Cr. 358 10
Fitzhugh, Genessee Chief *v.*, 12
 How. 443   46, 47, 197
Fisk *v.* Jefferson Police Jury, 116
 U. S. 131 146, 154, 159, 179
First Municipality, Permoli *v.*, 3
 How. 589     255
F. L. R. R. *v.* Lowe, 114 U. S.
 525       27
Fletcher *v.* Peck, 6 Cr. 87
    153, 164, 182, 183, 274
Fleeger, Poole *v.*, 11 Pet 185 189
Fleming, McLean *v.*, 96 U. S.
 248       61
Florida *v.* Georgia, 17 How. 478
        189, 198
F. L. & T. Co., Stone *v.*, 116 U.
 S. 307     128, 178
Forbes *v.* Gracey, 94 U. S. 762 28
Foster *v.* Neilson, 2 Pet. 253 274
Fonda, *Ex parte*, 117 U. S. 516 210
Foreign held bonds, State tax
 on, 15 Wall. 300 23, 24, 154
Ford *v.* Surget, 97 U. S. 594 147, 189
Foster *v.* Kansas, 112 U. S. 201 267
 *v.* Davenport, 22 How. 244
      53, 68, 122, 270
 *v.* Master and Wardens of
  the Port of New Orleans,
  94 U. S. 246    120
Fouvergne *v.* New Orleans, 18
 How. 470     197
Fowler *v.* Lindsay, 3 Dall. 411 222

Fox *v.* Ohio, 5 How. 432 235, 254
 U. S. *v.*, 95 U. S. 670 185, 200, 201
 U. S. *v.*, 94 U. S. 315 255
Frazer, The John, The Jas. Gray
 *v.*, 21 How. 184  121, 268
Freeborn *v.* Smith, 2 Wall. 160 183
French, Ins. Co. *v.*, 18 How. 404
      245, 246, 261
Freeman, Chy Lung *v.*, 92 U. S.
 275      36, 71
Freight Co., Greenwood *v.*, 105
 U. S. 13     169
Freeman *v.* Alderson, 119 U. S.
 185       246
Frederickson *v.* Louisiana, 23
 How. 445     275
Franks, Baldwin *v.*, 120 U. S. 678
        274, 275
Fretz *v.* Bull, 12 How. 466 197
Fremont *v.* U. S., 17 How. 542 213
French *v.* Hay, 22 Wall. 250 233
Freeman *v.* Howe, 24 How. 450
        237, 238
Furman *v.* Nichol, 8 Wall. 44 172
Fuentes, Gaines *v.*, 92 U. S. 18 197
Fuller, C. & N. W. R. R. *v.*, 17
 Wall. 560    126, 268
F. and M. Nat'l Bank *v.* Smith,
 6 Wheat. 131  154, 156, 157

Garland, *Ex parte*, 4 Wall. 333
        184, 186
Gage, Machine Co. *v.*, 100 U. S.
 676     35, 78, 258
Gaines. R. R. Cos. *v.*, 97 U. S.
 697   33, 34, 155, 168, 171
Gantly *v.* Ewing, 3 How. 107 153
Garrett, Merriwether *v*, 102 U. S.
 472    19, 154, 159
Gaines *v.* Fuentes, 92 U. S. 18 197
Gaff, Eyster *v.*, 91 U. S. 521 235
Galceran, Leon *v.*, 11 Wall. 185 236
Gallup, Day *v.*, 2 Wall. 97 238
Gebhard, C. S. Ry. *v.*, 109 U. S.
 527       263
Georgia, A & G. R. R. *v.*, 98 U.
 S. 359      169
 Cherokee Nation *v.*, 5 Pet. 1
       143, 198, 212
 Governor of, *v.* Madrazzo, 1
  Pet. 110    219, 220
 Chisholm *v.*, 2 Dall. 419 199, 217
 *v.* Stanton, 6 Wall. 71 212
 South Carolina *v.*, 93 U. S. 4
        87, 122
 Worcester *v.*, 6 Pet. 515
      143, 144, 209
 Alabama *v.*, 23 How. 505 189, 198
 Florida *v.*, 17 How. 478 189, 198
 *v.* Brailsford, 2 Dall. 402 219

TABLE OF CASES CITED.

Gelston, Hoyt v., 3 Wheat. 324 201, 212, 237
Genesee Chief v. Fitzhugh, 12 How. 443 46, 47, 197
G. Ferry Co. v. Pennsylvania, 114 U. S. 196 36, 41, 65, 100, 103
Gilman v. Sheboygan, 2 Bl. 510 19, 159
— v. Philada., 3 Wall. 713 4. 95, 97, 134, 201
Gibbons v. Ogden, 9 Wheat. 1 8, 16, 34, 40, 41, 42, 44, 50, 86, 100, 108, 117, 123, 215, 216
Gilfillan v. Union Canal Co., 109 U. S. 401 150
Glass v. Sloop Betsy, 3 Dall 7 245
Glenwood Cemetery, Close v., 107 U. S. 466 169
Glover, Huse v., 119 U. S. 543 19, 91, 98
G. N. & P. S. S. Co., Lord v., 102 U. S. 541 57
Goodwin v. C. M. I Co., 110 U. S. 1 263
Gordon v. U. S., 2 Wall. 561 209
Goodtitle v. Kibbie, 9 How. 471 255
Godfrey v. Terry, 97 U. S. 171 199
Gray, The Jas., v. The John Fraser, 21 How. 184 121, 268
Grace v. American Ins. Co., 109 U. S. 278 199
Gray, Davis v. 16 Wall. 203 166, 218
Grisar v. McDowell, 6 Wall. 363 224
Greenhow, Antoni v., 107 U. S. 769 152
Greenman, Juilliard v., 110 U. S. 421 3, 12, 13, 215
Greenhow, Hartman v., 102 U. S. 672 172
Greenwood v. Freight Co., 105 U. S. 13 169
Greneaux, Prevost v., 19 How. 1 275
Gregoire, Fanning v., 16 How. 524 101, 177, 268
Grima, Mager v., 8 How. 490 18, 24
Griffith, Stevens v., 111 U. S. 48 147
Gross v. U. S. Mtge. Co., 108 U. S. 477 149, 265
Groves v. Slaughter, 15 Pet. 449 83, 252, 255
Greenhow, Moore v., 114 U. S. 338 152
Graham, Strader v., 10 How. 93 252
Griswold, Hepburn v., 8 Wall. 603 13
Gracey, Forbes v., 94 U. S. 762 28
Green v. Biddle, 18 Wheat. 1 149, 166, 172
— v. Creighton, 23 How. 90 238

Guarantee Co. v. Board of Liquidation, 105 U. S. 622 151
Gut v. The State, 9 Wall 35 185
Guy v. Baltimore, 100 U. S. 434 35, 77, 106, 254
Gunn v. Barry, 15 Wall. 610 146, 153
G. & C. Co., Knowles v., 19 Wall. 58 247

Hagar, Ex parte, 104 U. S. 520 116
Hager, Brown v., 21 How. 305 224
Hagar v. Reclamation District, 111 U. S. 701 12, 240
Harris v. Dennie, 3 Pet. 292 236
Harwood, Ferguson v., 7 Cr. 408 243
Hagood v. Southern, 117 U. S. 52 219
Halstead, Bank of U. S. v, 10 Wheat. 51 231
Haile, Mason v., 12 Wheat. 327 149
Hall v. Wisconsin, 103 U. S. 5 172
Hamilton v. Dillin, 21 Wall. 73 11
U. S. v., 3 Dall. 17 28
Hamersley, N. H. & N. Co. v., 104 U. S. 1 178, 269
Hauenstein v. Lynham, 100 U. S. 483 275
Hanley v. Donoghue, 116 U. S. 1 213, 245
Hampton v. McConnell, 3 Wheat. 234 244
Happersett, Minor v., 21 Wall. 163 252, 265
Harmony, Mitchell v., 13 How. 114 224
Harris v. Hardman, 14 How. 334 239, 245
Hardman, Harris v., 14 How. 334 239, 245
Harmoning, Arrowsmith v., 118 U. S. 194 242
Hart, White v., 13 Wall. 646 146, 152, 264
Hall v. De Cuir, 95 U. S. 485 54, 270
Hale, Baldwin v., 1 Wall. 223 154, 157, 158
Haas, U. S. v., 3 Wall. 407 144
Hagan, Pollard v., 3 How. 212 2, 48, 255
— v. Lucas, 10 Pet. 400 233, 238
Hackett v. Ottawa, 99 U. S. 86 20
Hamilton, Bank of, v. Dudley's Lessee, 2 Pet. 492 193
Haines v. Carpenter, 91 U. S. 254 233
Hartford Bridge Co., East Hartford v., 10 How. 511 172
Harris, U. S. v., 106 U. S. 629 2, 264, 266, 274
Hamilton v. V. S. & P. R. R., 119 U. S. 280 98

## TABLE OF CASES CITED. xix

| | PAGE |
|---|---|
| Hayburn's Case, 2 Dall. 409 | 209 |
| Hawthorne v. Calef, 2 Wall. 10 | 153 |
| Harbor Comm'rs, Weber v., 18 Wall. 57 | 47, 48, 255 |
| Hayward, McCracken v., 2 How. 608 | 153 |
| Haver v. Yaker, 9 Wall. 32 | 275 |
| Hartman v. Greenhow, 102 U. S. 672 | 172 |
| Havemeyer v. Iowa Co., 3 Wall. 294 | 147 |
| Hamilton Co. v. Massachusetts, 6 Wall. 632 | 26 |
| Hays v. P. M S. S. Co., 17 How. 596 | 36, 64 |
| Hay, French v., 22 Wall 250 | 233 |
| Head v. A. Mfg. Co., 113 U. S. 9 | 40 |
| v. The University, 19 Wall. 526 | 179 |
| Hecht, R. R. v., 95 U S. 168 | 149 |
| Henderson v. The Mayor of N. Y., 92 U. S. 259 | 36, 69, 70 |
| Hepburn v. School Directors, 23 Wall. 480 | 31, 32 |
| v. Griswold, 8 Wall. 603 | 13 |
| Herdritter v. Elizabeth Oilcloth Co., 112 U. S 294 | 238 |
| Heyman, Covell v., 111 U. S. 176 | 237, 238 |
| Hinson v. Lott, 8 Wall. 148 | 35, 78, 258 |
| Hickey's Lessee v. Stewart, 3 How. 750 | 245 |
| Hill v Exchange Bank, 105 U. S. 319 | 32 |
| Hine, The, v. Trevor, 4 Wall. 556 | 59, 197, 235 |
| Higgins v. Bucher, Yelv. 89 | 60 |
| Himely, Rose v., 4 Cr. 272 | 212, 245 |
| Howard, Peyroux v., 7 Pet. 324 | 46 |
| Hogeland, Wurts v., 114 U. S. 606 | 240 |
| Holliday. U. S. v., 3 Wall. 407 | 144 |
| Howard v. Bugbee, 24 How. 461 | 53 |
| Holkee, Phelps v., 1 Dall. 261 | 246 |
| Holyoke Co. v. Lyman, 15 Wall. 500 | 170 |
| Hollingsworth v.Virginia, 3 Dall. 378 | 217 |
| Holmes, Barrett v. 102 U. S. 651 | 241 |
| Hornthall v. Collector, 9 Wall. 560 | 199 |
| Holt, Campbell v., 115 U. S. 620 | 241 |
| Home Insurance Co. v. Morse, 20 Wall. 445 | 262 |
| Hopkins, Wo Lee v., 118 U. S. 356 | 265, 269 |
| Yick Wo v., 118 U. S. 356 | 265, 269 |
| Houpt v. Utah, 110 U. S. 574 | 185 |
| Howard, Bacon v., 20 How. 22 | 244 |

| | PAGE |
|---|---|
| Hoyt v. Gelston, 3 Wheat. 324 | 201, 212, 237 |
| Houston, Brown v., 114 U. S. 622 | 35, 74, 85 |
| Hotchkiss, Kirtland v., 100 U. S. 491 | 18 23, 24 |
| Houston v. Moore, 5 Wheat. 49 | 4, 111, 201, 213, 235 |
| Howe, Freeman v., 24 How. 250 | 237, 238 |
| Holmes, Barrett v., 102 U. S. 651 | 150 |
| Home Ins. Co. v. Augusta, 93 U. S. 116 | 34, 177 |
| Holmes v. Jennison, 14 Pet. 540 | 188, 252, 255 |
| Hoover v. Dynes, 20 How. 65 | 213 |
| Horwitz, Butler v., 7 Wall. 258 | 12 |
| Hoboken Co., Bridge Proprietors v., 1 Wall. 116 | 149, 171, 172 |
| Hobart v. Drogan, 10 Pet. 108 | 111, 116, 179, 232 |
| Houseman, Claflin v., 93 U. S. 130 | 235, 236 |
| Hook, Payne v., 7 Wall. 425 | 197 |
| Holland v. Challen, 110 U. S. 15 | 200 |
| Hoboken L. & I. Co., Murray's Lessee v., 18 How. 272 | 226, 229 |
| Hoyt v. Sprague, 103 U. S. 613 | 255 |
| Hubbart, Church v., 2 Cr. 187 | 12 |
| Humes, N. P. Ry. v., 115 U. S. 512 | 268 |
| Hughes v. Edwards, 9 Wheat. 489 | 275 |
| Humphrey v. Pegues, 16 Wall. 244 | 167, 168, 171 |
| Huidekoper, Dietzsch v., 103 U. S. 494 | 233 |
| Hunter's Lessee, Martin v., 1 Wheat. 304 | 1, 2, 6, 8, 11, 193-5, 202, 204, 206, 215, 232 |
| Huse v. Glover, 119 U. S. 543 | 19, 91, 98 |
| Huddleson, Achison v., 12 How. 293 | 123 |
| Hudson, U. S. v., 7 Cr 32 | 200, 205 |
| Hunt v. Pallas, 4 How. 589 | 209 |
| Hull. Owings v., 9 Pet. 607 | 213, 243 |
| Hudson, Lenox v., 109 U. S. 468 | 233 |
| Hurtado v. California, 110 U. S. 517 | 241 |
| Husen, R. R. v., 95 U. S. 465 | 119, 127, 270 |
| Hyde Park, Fertilizer Co. v, 97 U. S. 659 | 178, 269 |
| Hyde, Crippendorf v., 110 U. S. 276 | 239 |
| Hylton v. U. S., 3 Dall. 171 | 22 |
| Hyde v. Stone, 20 How. 170 | 197, 238 |
| H. & St. J. R. R. v. Husen, 95 U. S. 465 | 119, 127, 270 |

# TABLE OF CASES CITED.

I. C. R. R., Stone v., 116 U. S.
  347                    128, 178
Illinois, Moore v., 14 How. 13   235
  Munn v., 94 U. S. 113   126, 268
  Presser v., 116 U. S. 252
                         254, 269
  Ruggles v., 108 U. S. 526
                         178, 269
  W. St. L. & P. Ry. v., 118
    U. S. 557       128, 268, 271
  Spies v., 123 U. S. 131
                    209, 240, 254
Indseth, Pierce v., 106 U. S. 546  212
Inman S. S. Co. v. Tinker, 94 U.
  S. 23                   25, 67
Insurance Co., Delmas v., 14.
  Wall. 661         148, 149, 152
Iowa, Bartemeyer v, 18 Wall.
  129                        267
  C., B. & Q. R. R. v., 94 U. S.
    155         123, 178, 263, 269
  County, Havemeyer v., 3
    Wall. 294                 47
  Missouri v., 7 How. 660  189, 198
I. R. C. Co., Ochiltree v., 21 Wall.
  249                        151

Jackson, Ex parte, 96 U. S. 727   11
  Wilcox v., 13 Pet. 498   224, 245
  v. Lamphire, 3 Pet. 280     150
  R. R. v., 7 Wall. 262        24
J. B. Bank v. Skelly, 1 Bl. 436
                   33, 149, 167, 177
Jennison, Holmes v., 14 Pet. 450
                    189, 252, 255
Jefferson Police Jury, Fisk v., 116
  U. S. 131    146, 154, 159, 179
Jefferson, The Thomas, 10 Wheat.
  423                     46, 47
Jenners, Peck v., 7 How. 612  234, 238
Jersey Co., Den v., 15 How. 426   47
Jersey City, Provident Institu-
  tion v., 113 U. S. 506      240
Jessup, Tomlinson v, 15 Wall. 454 169
Jones v. Soulard, 24 How. 41   47
  Scott v., 5 How. 343        146
Johnson, R. R. v., 15 Wall. 195  13
  Mississippi v., 4 Wall. 498  212
  Nations v., 24 How. 195  240, 246
Joliffe, Steamship Co. v., 2 Wall.
  450                    115, 116
Johnston, Rosenblatt v., 104 U. S.
  462                         29
Jones, Watson v., 13 Wall. 697  233
Johnson County, Riggs v., 6 Wall.
  166                        233
Juilliard v. Greenman, 110 U. S.
  421                   3, 12, 13
Jumel, Louisiana v., 107 U. S.
  711                        220

Justices, The, v. Murray, 9 Wall.
  274                    231, 254

Kansas, Ames v., 111 U. S 449
                    196, 205, 209
  Foster v., 112 U. S. 201    267
  Indians, The, 5 Wall. 737    27
  Mugler v., 123 U. S. 623    267
Kearzey, Edwards v., 96 U. S. 595  146
Keith v. Clark, 97 U. S. 454  146, 172
Keisey, Church v., 121 U. S. 282
                         179, 241
Kenney, Effinger v., 115 U. S.
  566                        152
Kennett, v. Chambers, 14 How.
  38                         212
Kelly v. Pittsburgh, 104 U. S. 78
                    20, 226, 240, 254
Keene, Brown v., 8 Pet. 115    190
Kentucky Ry. Tax Cases, 115 U.
  S 321                      240
  Patterson v., 97 U. S. 501  269
  Bush v., 107 U. S. 110
                         200, 241, 242
  Bank of, Briscoe v., 11 Pet.
    257         2, 188, 215, 223
  v. Ohio, 24 How. 66
                190, 191, 193, 198, 219
  Bank of, v. Wisler, 2 Pet. 318  223
Keehler, U. S. v., 9 Wall. 83  189
Keokuk, Barney v., 94 U. S. 324
                      46, 48, 105
  Packet Co. v., 95 U. S. 80
                     19, 105, 274
Ketchum, D'Arcy v., 11 How. 165  245
Kendall, Postmaster General, v.
  Stockton, 12 Pet. 527       212
Keyes v. U. S., 109 U. S. 336  213
Kearney, Ex parte, 7 Wall. 38  228
Kilbourn v. Thompson, 103 U. S.
  168                         11
King, W. & W. R. R. v., 91 U. S. 3  152
Kimball, County of Mobile v., 102
  U. S. 691                40, 90
Kibbie, Goodtitle v., 9 How. 471  255
Kinzie, Bronson v., 1 How. 311  153
Kimpton, Bronson v., 8 Wall. 444  12
Kirtland v. Hotchkiss, 100 U. S.
  491                  18, 23, 24
Knowles v. The G. & C. Co., 19
  Wall. 58                   247
Knox v. Exchange Bank, 12
  Wall. 379                  148
Knopp, State Bank v., 16 How.
  369                        149
Koontz, B. & O. R. R. v., 104 U.
  S. 5                       261
Kohl v. U. S., 91 U. S. 367    11
Koshkonong v. Burton, 104 U. S.
  668                    150, 153

## TABLE OF CASES CITED. xxi

Kountze, Express Co. v., 8 Wall. 342 — 259
Kring v. Missouri, 107 U. S. 221 — 184
Kreiger, Randall v., 23 Wall. 137 — 149
Krippendorf v. Hyde, 110 U. S. 276 — 239

Lafayette Insurance Co. v. French, 18 How. 404 — 245, 246
Lange, Ex parte, 18 Wall. 163 — 228, 229
Langford v U. S., 101 U. S. 34 — 2
Landes v. Brant, 10 How. 348 — 244
Lamphire, Jackson v, 3 Pet. 280 — 150
Laird, Stuart v., 1 Cr. 299 — 215
La Grange, Cole v., 113 U. S. 1 — 20
Lane County v. Oregon, 7 Wall. 71 — 12
Lammon v. Feusier, 111 U. S. 17 — 259
Lawler v. Walker, 14 How. 149 — 199
L. C. & C. R. R. v. Letson, 2 How. 497 — 223, 259
League v. DeYoung, 11 How. 185 — 146, 150
Le Bois, U. S v., 121 U. S. 278 — 144
Lear, Armstrong v., 8 Pet. 52 — 212
Leon v. Galceran, 11 Wall. 185 — 235
Legal Tender Cases, 12 Wall. 457 — 12, 13, 274
Lewis, Siebert v., 122 U. S. 284 — 160
Lee, U. S. v. 106 U. S. 196 — 224
Le oux v. Hudson, 109 U. S. 468 — 233
Letson, L. C. & C. R. R. v., 2 How. 497 — 223, 259
Lewis, Missouri v., 101 U. S. 22 — 241
Lehigh Water Co. v. Easton, 121 U. S. 388 — 147, 148
License Cases, 5 How. 504 — 108, 109, 267
License Tax Cases, 5 Wall. 462 — 34, 177
Lionberger v. Rouse, 9 Wall. 468 — 30
Liquidation, Board of, v. McComb, 92 U. S. 541 — 223, 224
Livingston, County of, v. Darlington, 101 U. S. 407 — 20
v. Story, 9 Pet. 632 — 200
Lindsay, Fowler v, 3 Dall. 411 — 222
L. Ins. Co. v. French, 18 How. 404 — 261
Liverpool Ins Co. v. Mass, 10 Wall. 566 — 40, 259, 260, 261, 262
Livingston v. M. Ins. Co., 6 Cr. 274 — 212
v. Moore, 7 Pet. 469 — 182, 183, 254
Loan Association v. Topeka, 20 Wall. 655 — 20
Lott, Hinson v., 8 Wall. 148 — 35, 78, 258
Lottawanna, The, 21 Wall. 558 — 59, 200, 233

Louisiana, Frederickson v., 23 How. 445 — 275
Nathan v., 8 How. 73 — 35, 40, 62
Low v. Austin, 13 Wall. 29 — 25, 83
Lord v. S. S. Co., 102 U. S. 541 — 57
Lord, The Mayor v., 9 Wall. 409 — 233
Lowery, Chemung Canal Bank v., 93 U. S. 72 — 258
Louisiana, Allen v., 103 U. S. 80 — 274
Morgan v., 93 U. S. 217 — 33, 118, 155, 168
v. Jumel, 107 U. S. 711 — 220
v. Mayor of New Orleans 109 U. S. 285 — 153, 159, 241
New York v., 108 U. S. 76 — 220
New Hampshire v, 108 U. S. 76 — 198, 220
v. Pilsbury, 105 U. S. 278 — 154, 158, 160
v. New Orleans, 102 U. S. 203 — 150, 154, 180
Loughborough v. Blake, 5 Wheat. 317 — 11, 20
Louisiana Board of Health, Morgan S. S. Co. v., 118 U.S. 455 — 19
Lowry, Erwin v., 7 How. 181 — 234, 238
Louisiana Gas Co. v. C. Gas Co., 115 U. S. 683 — 172
Louisiana Light Co., New Orleans Gas Co. v., 115 U. S. 650 — 146, 172
Williams v, 103 U. S. 637 — 149
Lowe, F. L. R. R. v., 114 U. S. 525 — 27
L. R. R., R. R. R. v., 13 How. 81 — 177
Lucas, Strother v., 6 Pet. 763 — 212
Commissioners v., 93 U. S. 108 — 241
Hagan v., 10 Pet. 400 — 233, 238
Lull, Nash v., 102 Mass. 60 — 236
Luther v. Borden, 7 How. 1 — 211, 212
Lynn, Schiver's Lessee v., 2 How. 43 — 245
Lynham, Hauenstein v, 100 U. S. 483 — 275
Lyman, Holyoke Co. v., 15 Wall. 500 — 170
L. & N. R. R. v. Palmes, 109 U. S. 244 — 149

Machine Co. v. Gage, 100 U. S. 676 — 35, 78, 258
Mackin v. U. S, 117 U. S. 248 — 226
Madison, Marbury v., 1 Cr. 137 — 2, 193, 205, 212, 274
Magwire, Col'r., Bailey v., 22 Wall. 215 — 177
Maguire, Trask v., 18 Wall. 391 — 33, 155, 168

## TABLE OF CASES CITED.

Maguire, N. M. R. R. v., 20 Wall.
46     176
P. R. R. v., 20 Wall. 36    33, 167
Madrazzo, Governor, etc, v.. 1
Pet. 110      219. 220
Marshall v. B. & O. R. R., 16
How. 314      259
Maryland, Ward v., 12 Wall. 418
35, 75. 79, 258
Martin v. Mott, 12 Wheat. 19    213
v. Hunter's Lessee, 1 Wheat.
304     1, 2, 6. 5, 11, 193, 195,
202, 204 206, 215, 232
Marbury v. Madison 1 Cr. 137
2, 193, 205, 212, 274
Maryland, Brown v., 12 Wheat.
419     25, 40 82, 216, 269
McCulloch v., 4 Wheat. 316
1, 3. 8, 9, 10, 14, 18, 29, 217
Turner v., 107 U. S. 38
25, 86, 87
Mason v. Haile, 12 Wheat. 327    149
Massachusetts, L. Ins. Co. v. 10
Wall. 566 40, 259, 260, 261, 262
Ins. Co., Livingston v., 6 Cr.
274      212
Madrazzo, *Ex parte*, 7 Pet. 627    220
Maryland, B. & O. R. R. v., 21
Wall. 456     19. 36, 124
Marigold, U. S. v., 9 How. 560
11, 235
Martin v. Waddell, 16 Pet. 367    47
Matthewson, Satterlee v., 2 Pet.
380      182, 183
Mager v. Grima, 8 How. 490   18, 24
Maguire v. Card, 21 How. 248
47, 197
Mayor, The, Waring v., 8 Wall.
110      85
Massachusetts, Rhode Island v.,
12 Pet. 657 2, 189, 198, 215, 216
Maxwell v. Stewart, 22 Wall. 77
244, 245, 246
Maryland, Smith v., 18 How. 71
47, 48, 254, 255, 268
Mayor of New Orleans, Louisiana
v., 109 U.S. 285     153, 241
of New York, Miller v., 109
U. S. 385      99
of New York, Henderson v.,
92 U. S. 259     36, 69, 70
Mayhew v. Thatcher, 6 Wheat.
129      245
Massachusetts, Beer Co. v., 97 U.
S. 25     178, 267, 269
Maryland v. B. & O. R. R., 3 How.
534      173
Mayor, The, The Banks v., 7
Wall. 16     26
v. Lord, 9 Wall. 409    233

Massachusetts, Provident Institution v., 6 Wall. 611    26
Hamilton Co. v., 6 Wall. 632    26
Maryland, Corson v., 120 U S.
502     35, 77, 253
Mayor, The, v. Cooper, 6 Wall.
253     193, 196, 209
Maybury, Slocum v., 2 Wheat. 9
201, 236, 238
Master and Wardens of the Port
of New Orleans, Foster v.,
94 U. S. 246.     120
McBratney, U. S. v., 104 U. S. 621   274
McClurg's Lessee, Meigs v., 9 Cr.
11      224
McClure, O. & M R. R. v., 10
Wall. 511     146, 148
McCready v. Virginia, 94 U. S.
391     49, 255, 257, 258, 268
McCulloch v. Maryland. 4 Wheat
316 1, 3, 8, 9, 10, 14, 18, 29, 217
McDowell. Grisar v., 6 Wall. 363   224
McElmoyle v. Cohen, 13 Pet. 312   244
McElrath v. U. S., 102 U. S. 426
197, 230
McConnell, Hampton v., 3 Wheat.
234      244
McMillen v. Anderson, 95 U. S.
37      240
McComb, Liquidation v., 92 U.
S. 541     223, 224
McShane, U. P. Ry. v., 22 Wall.
444      27
McCracken v. Hayward, 2 How.
608      153
McNamee, Wilson v., 102 U. S.
572     115, 116
McNeal, *Ex parte*, 13 Wall. 236
115, 116, 232
McConnell, Wallace v., 13 Pet
136     237, 238
McGuire v. The Commonwealth,
3 Wall. 387     29, 269
McLean v. Flemming, 96 U. S.
248      61
McClurg v. Silliman, 6 Wheat.
598      236
McMillan v. McNeil, 4 Wheat.
209     154, 155, 157
McNeil, McMillan v., 4 Wheat.
209     154, 155, 157
McNulty v. Batty, 10 How. 72   209
McKim v. Voorhees, 7 Cr. 279   237
McIver, Smith v., 9 Wheat. 532   238
Meigs v. McClurg's Lessee. 9 Cr.
11      224
Mercer County, Cowles v., 7 Wall.
118      260
Memphis Gas Light Co. v. Shelby
County, 109 U. S. 398   23, 33, 176

## TABLE OF CASES CITED. xxiii

Merriwether v. Garrett, 102 U. S. 472   19, 154, 159
Merchants' Bank, N. J. Navigation Co. v., 6 How. 314   197
Memphis v. U. S., 97 U. S. 293   154, 158, 160
  U. S. v., 97 U. S. 284   179
Mercantile Bank v. New York, 121 U. S. 138   31
Mercer, Watson v., 8 Pet. 88   182, 183
Miller v. Mayor of New York, 109 U. S. 385   99
Minor v. Happersett, 21 Wall. 163   252, 265
Michigan, Fargo v., 121 U. S 230   36, 84, 132, 137
Missouri, Craig v, 4 Pet. 411   187
  Cummings v., 4 Wall. 277   184, 185, 186
  Kring v., 107 U. S. 221   184
  v. Lewis, 101 U. S. 22   241
  Welton v., 91 U. S. 275   35, 76, 258
Mitchell v. Clark, 110 U. S. 333   232
  v. Harmony, 13 How. 114   224
Mills v. Duryee, 7 Cr. 481   244
  v. Brown, 16 Pet. 525   199
  v. St. Clair County, 8 How. 581   177
Michigan, Walling v., 116 U. S. 446   258
Middleton v. Mullica Township, 112 U. S. 433   20
Miln, City of New York v., 11 Pet. 103   54, 68, 111, 121, 267
Michigan, Walling v., 116 U. S. 446   35, 77
Mississippi, Stone v., 101 U. S. 814   178, 269
Mitchell v. The Commissioners, 91 U. S. 206   26
Missouri, Byrne v., 8 Pet. 40   187
  v. Iowa 7 How. 660   189, 198
Mississippi v. Johnson, 4 Wall. 475   212
Mixter, Pacific Nat'l Bank v., 124 U. S. 721   236
M. N. Bank, Tappan v., 19 Wall. 490   32
Mobile, Osborn v, 16 Wall. 479   35, 132
  v. Watson, 116 U. S. 289   154, 158, 159
Moore v Greenhow, 114 U. S. 338   152
Mobile County v. Kimball, 102 U. S. 691   40, 90
Moran v. New Orleans, 112 U. S. 69   36, 66
Morgan v. Parham, 16 Wall. 471   36, 64

Morgan S. S. Co. v. La. Board of Health, 118 U. S. 455   19
Peete v., 19 Wall. 581   25, 67, 118, 121
  v. Louisiana, 93 U. S. 217   33, 118 155, 168
Morse, Ins. Co. v., 20 Wall. 445   262
Mott, Martin v., 12 Wheat. 19   213
Moore, Livingston v., 7 Pet. 469   182, 183, 254
  v. Illinois, 14 How. 13   235
  Houston v., 5 Wheat. 49   4, 111, 201, 213, 235
Moor, Veazie v, 14 How. 568   55, 92
Morris, N. O. v., 105 U. S. 600   179
Moffat, Cook v., 5 How. 295   154, 157
Moses Taylor, The, 4 Wall. 411   55, 197, 201, 203, 204, 235
Montello, The, 20 Wall. 430   46, 197
Moultrie, County of, v. R. I. C. S. Bank, 92 U. S. 631   154, 159
M. R. Improvement Co., Sands v., 123 U. S. 288   19 92, 98
Mumma v. Potomac Co., 8 Pet. 281   197
Munn v. Illinois, 94 U. S. 113   126, 268
Murphy v. Ramsey, 114 U. S. 15   185
  Aronson v, 100 U. S. 238   232
Murray v. Charleston, 96 U. S. 432   34, 172
  The Justices v., 9 Wall. 274   231, 254
Mullica Township, Middleton v., 112 U. S. 433   20
Murray's Lessee v. Hoboken L. & I. Co., 18 How. 272   226, 229
Mugler v. Kansas, 123 U. S. 623   267
M. & B. R. R., Cunningham v., 109 U. S. 446   220
M. & C. R. R. v. Tennessee, 101 U. S. 337   180, 181
M. & M. R. R. v. Rock, 4 Wall. 177   148, 199
  v. Ward 2 Bl. 485   96
M. & N. W. R. R., Rice v., 1 Bl. 358   177
M. & St. P. R. R. v. Atlee, 94 U. S. 179   178

Nagle, Wright v., 101 U. S. 791   149, 177
Nathan v. Louisiana, 8 How. 73   35, 40, 62
Nations v. Johnson, 24 How. 195   240, 245
National Bank, Ottawa v., 105 U. S. 343   20
  Pelton v., 101 U. S. 143   32
  Cummings v., 101 U. S. 077   32

## TABLE OF CASES CITED.

National Bank v. Commonw'th, 9 Wall. 353    28, 30, 33
v. U. S., 101 U. S. 1    22
Nashville, Adams v., 95 U. S. 191    31
Nash v. Lull, 102 Mass. 60    236
Neal v. Delaware, 103 U. S. 370    253
Newberry, Allen v., 21 How. 244    47, 197
Neff, Pennoyer v., 95 U. S. 714    227, 239, 44, 245, 246
Nelson v. St. Martin's Parish, 111 U. S. 716    154, 158, 160
New Orleans, U. S. v., 98 U. S. 381    19
   Cannon v., 20 Wall. 577    25, 67, 121
   C. & B. Co. v. 99 U. S. 97    26
   Water Works, St. T. W. W. v., 120 U. S. 64    172
Nesbit, B. & S. R. R. v., 10 How. 395    182, 183
Nevada Bank v. Sedgwick, 104 U. S. 111    18
New York, Mercantile Bank v., 121 U. S. 138    31
   v. Louisiana, 108 U. S. 76    220
   City of, v. Miln, 11 Pet. 103    54, 68, 111, 121, 267
New Hampshire v. Louisiana, 108 U. S. 76    198, 220
Newton v. Commissioners, 100 U. S. 548    179
Neil v. Ohio, 3 How. 720    123
New Orleans, Davidson v., 96 U. S. 97    226. 240, 254
   Louisiana v., 102 U. S. 203    150, 154, 180
   Moran v., 112 U. S. 69    36, 66
   Wolff v., 103 U. S. 358    154, 158, 160
   Gas Co. v. Louisiana Light Co., 115 U. S. 650    146, 172
   Water Works v. Rivers, 115 U. S. 674    172
   Fouvergne v., 18 How. 470    197
   Asylum v., 105 U. S. 362    33, 167, 168
New York Indians, The, 5 Wall. 761    27
   P. F. Association v., 119 U. S. 110    40, 259, 260, 262, 265
   Miller v., 109 U. S. 385    99
Nevada, State of, Crandall v., 6 Wall. 35    28, 73, 84. 87, 125, 134, 258
Needles, Chicago Life Ins. Co. v., 113 U. S. 574    177
Neilson, Foster v., 2 Pet. 253    274
New Jersey v. Yard, 95 U.S. 104    33, 167, 169

New Jersey v. Wilson, 7 Cr. 64    33, 166
N. H. & N. Co. v. Hamersley, 104 U. S. 1    178, 269
Nicholson. Osborn v., 13 Wall. 654    164, 264
Nichol, Furman v., 8 Wall. 44    172
N. J. Navigation Co. v. M'ch'ts Bank, 6 How. 344    197
N. M. R. R. v. Maguire, 20 Wall. 46    176
N. O. v. Morris, 105 U. S. 600    179
Norton v. Shelby County, 118 U. S. 425    193, 274
North German Lloyd, Commissioners of Immigration v., 92 U. S. 260    36, 71
Norwich Co. v. Wright, 13 Wall. 104    57
   City of, 118 U. S. 468    57
Northrop v. Vaughan, 15 Pet. 1    234, 238
Nugent v. Bond, 3 How. 426    235
N. & W. R. R. v. Johnson, 15 Wall. 195    13

Ochiltree v. I. R. C. Co., 21 Wall. 249    151
Ogden, Gibbons v., 9 Wheat. 1    8, 16, 34, 40, 41, 42. 44, 50, 86, 100, 108, 117, 123, 215, 216
   v. Saunders, 12 Wheat. 213    154, 156, 158, 176, 182
Ohio, Neil v., 3 How. 720    123
   Shields v., 95 U. S. 319    33, 155, 169
   Kentucky v., 24 How. 66    190, 191, 193, 198, 219
   L. I. & T. Co. v. DeBolt, 16 How. 416    147, 149, 177
   Fox v., 5 How. 432    235, 254
Okely, Bank of Columbia v., 4 Wheat. 235    231
Olcott v. The Supervisors, 16 Wall. 678    20, 147
O. Packet Co., Aiken v., 121 U.S. 444    19
Oregon, Lane County v., 7 Wall. 71    112
Orleans v. Phœbus, 11 Pet. 175    46
Ortega, U. S. v., 11 Wheat. 467    196, 205
Osborne v. County of Adams, 106 U. S. 181; 109 id. 1    20
   v. Mobile, 16 Wall. 479    35, 132
   Pulliam v., 17 How. 471    238
Osborn v. The Bank of the U. S., 9 Wheat. 738    10, 29, 186, 199. 211, 218, 224
   v. Nicholson, 13 Wall. 654    146, 264

## TABLE OF CASES CITED. XXV

| | PAGE |
|---|---|
| Otoe, County of, R. R. v., 16 Wall. 667 | 20 |
| Otis, Boswell v., 9 How. 336 | 239, 245 |
| Ottawa, Hackett v., 99 U. S. 86 | 20 |
| v. National Bank, 105 U. S. 343 | 20 |
| v. Carey. 108 U. S. 110 | 20 |
| Ouachita Packet Co. v. Aiken, 121 U. S. 444 | 106 |
| Owings v. Speed, 5 Wheat. 420 | 88, 146 |
| v. Hull, 9 Pet. 607 | 213, 243 |
| O. & M. R. R v. McClure, 10 Wall. 511 | 146, 148 |
| v. Wheeler, 1 Bl. 286 | 259, 260 |
| Pace v. Burgess, 92 U. S. 372 | 81 |
| v. Alabama, 106 U. S. 583 | 265 |
| Packet Co. v. Catlettsburg, 105 U. S. 559 | 19, 106 |
| v. St. Louis, 100 U. S. 423 | 19, 23, 106 |
| v Keokuk, 95 U. S. 80 | 19, 105, 274 |
| Parkersburg, Transportation Co. v., 107 U. S. 691 | 19, 106 |
| Palmer, Embry v., 107 U. S. 3 | 11, 248 |
| Palmes, L. & N. R. R. v., 109 U. S. 244 | 149 |
| Patterson v. Kentucky, 97 U. S. 501 | 269 |
| Parham, Morgan v., 16 Wall. 471 | 36, 64 |
| Parrish v. Ellis, 16 Pet. 451 | 200 |
| Paul v. Virginia, 8 Wall. 168 | 40, 41, 256, 259, 260, 261, 262 |
| Parsons v. Bedford, 3 Pet. 433 | 200, 230 |
| Parkinson v. U. S., 121 U. S. 281 | 226 |
| Payson, Turnbull v., 95 U. S. 418 | 248 |
| Paut v. Drew, 10 How 218 | 172 |
| Parham, Woodruff v., 8 Wall. 123 | 35, 41, 73, 79, 84, 85, 134 |
| Pacific R. R., Thomson v., 9 Wall. 579 | 28 |
| Insurance Co. v. Soule, 7 Wall. 433 | 22 |
| Passaic Bridge Case, The, 3 Wall. [App.] 752 | 97 |
| Passenger Cases, The, 7 How. 283 | 34, 36, 42, 68, 70, 134 |
| Patterson, Boom Co. v., 98 U. S. 403 | 197 |
| Payne v. Hook, 7 Wall. 425 | 197 |
| Pallas, Hunt v., 4 How. 589 | 209 |
| Parks, Ex parte, 93 U. S 18 | 228 |
| Packard, Davis v, 7 Pet. 276 | 236 |
| Pacific Nat'l Bank v. Mixter, 124 U. S. 721 | 236 |

| | PAGE |
|---|---|
| Pervear v. The Comm'th, 5 Wall. 475 | 29, 254, 269 |
| Pennsylvania, Carpenter v., 17 How. 456 | 23, 24, 182, 183 |
| Pearson v. Yewdall, 95 U. S. 294 | 230, 240, 254 |
| Penna. College Cases, 13 Wall. 190 | 170 |
| Peck, Fletcher v., 6 Cr. 87 | 153, 164, 182, 183, 274 |
| Peete v. Morgan, 19 Wall. 581 | 25, 67, 118, 121 |
| Pegues, Humphrey v., 16 Wall. 244 | 167, 168, 171 |
| Peik v. C. & N. W. Ry., 94 U. S. 164 | 127, 178, 268 |
| Peniston, U. P. R. R. v., 18 Wall. 5 | 23 |
| Pennoyer v. Neff, 95 U. S. 714 | 227, 239, 244, 245, 246 |
| Penniman's Case, 103 U. S. 714 | 149 |
| Pennsylvania, G. Ferry Co. v., 114 U. S. 196 | 30, 41, 65, 100, 103 |
| Cook v., 97 U. S. 566 | 25, 40, 83 |
| E. Ry. v., 21 Wall.492 | 34, 36, 171 |
| Prigg v., 16 Pet. 539 | 12, 193, 252, 255 |
| People v. Compagnie G. T., 107 U. S. 59 | 36, 71, 87 |
| v. Commissioners, 104 U. S. 466 | 35, 62 |
| Peters, U. S. v., 5 Cr. 115 | 223, 232 |
| Perot. U. S. v., 98 U. S. 430 | 213 |
| People v. Comm'srs of Taxes, etc., 94 U. S. 415 | 32, 33, 155 |
| Perrine v. C. C. Co., 9 How. 192 | 177 |
| People, The, v. The Commissioners, 2 Bl. 620 | 26 |
| Pensacola Tel. Co. v. W. U. Tel. Co., 96 U. S. 1 | 40, 41, 141, 142, 260 |
| Pennsylvania, Erie Ry. v., 15 Wall. 282 | 136 |
| Butler v. 10 How. 402 | 154, 170 |
| v. Wheeling & Belmont Bridge Co., 18 How. 421 | 94, 123 |
| Ex parte, 109 U. S. 174 | 116 |
| Peale v. Phipps, 14 How. 368 | 234, 238 |
| People v. Weaver, 100 U. S. 539 | 32 |
| Permoli v. First Municipality, 3 How. 589 | 255 |
| People v. Commissioners, 4 Wall. 244 | 29, 30 |
| People, Bradley v., 4 Wall. 459 | 30 |
| Pelton v. National Bank, 101 U. S. 143 | 32 |
| People, University v., 99 U. S. 309 | 33, 148, 167, 168 |

## TABLE OF CASES CITED.

Pennsylvania P & S. S. S. Co. v.,
122 U. S. 326
36, 42, 54, 72, 84, 105, 132, 138
Peters, Wheaton v., 8 Pet. 591   200
Pennsylvania, Twitchell v., 7
Wall. 321   209, 230, 254
Peck v. Jenness, 7 How. 612   234, 238
Pendleton, W. U. T. Co. v., 122
U. S. 347   143
Peyroux v. Howard, 7 Pet. 324   46
P. F. Association v. New York,
119 U. S. 110
40, 259, 260, 262, 265
Phelps v. Holker, 1 Dall. 261   246
Ph len v Virginia, 8 How. 163   178
Philada., Christ Church v., 24
How. 300   168
Gilman v., 3 Wall. 713
4, 95, 97, 131, 201
U. P. Ry. v., 101 U. S. 528
34, 170
Phœbus, The Orleans v., 11 Pet.
175   46
Philadelphia v. The Collector, 5
Wall. 720   209
Phipps, Peale v., 14 How. 368
234, 238
Pickard v. P. S. C. Co., 117 U. S.
34   36, 136
Pierce v. Indseth, 106 U. S. 546   212
  v. Carskadon, 16 Wall. 234   153
185, 186
Piersol, Elliott v . 1 Pet. 328   245
Pike, County of, Douglass v., 101
U. S. 677   147
Pilsbury, Louisiana v., 105 U S.
278   153, 158, 160
Pittsburgh, Kelly v., 104 U. S.
78   20, 226, 240, 254
Bank, Bank of the U. S. v., 9
Wheat. 904   223
Bank v. Sharp, 6 How. 301   172
P. M. S. S. Co., Hays v., 17 How.
596   36, 64
Poole v. Fleeger, 11 Pet. 185   189
Pound v. Turck, 95 U. S. 459   198
Portwardens, Steamship Co. v,
6 Wall. 31   36, 66, 67, 120
Pollard v. Hagan, 3 How. 212
2, 48, 255
Potomac Co , Mumma v., 8 Pet.
281   177
Preston, Bors v., 111 U. S. 252   205
Presser v. Illinois, 116 U. S. 252
254, 269
Prevost v. Greneaux, 19 How. 1   272
Providence Bank v. Billings, 4
Pet. 514   23, 33, 176
Prigg v. Pennsylvania, 16 Pet.
539   12, 193, 252, 255

Provident Institution v. Jersey
City, 113 U. S. 506   240
Institution v. Massachusetts,
6 Wall. 611   26
Prescott, R. R. v , 16 Wall. 603   27
P. R. R. v. Maguire, 20 Wall. 36
33, 167
Thompson v., 9 Wall. 579   28
P. S. C. Co., Pickard v., 117 U.
S. 34   36, 136
Tennessee v., 117 U. S. 51
36, 137
P. Telegraph Co. v. W. U. Telegraph Co., 96 U S. 1
40, 41, 141, 142, 260
Pulliam v. Osborne, 17 How. 471   238
P. & S. S. S. Co. v. Pennsylvania,
122 U. S. 326
36, 42, 54, 72, 84, 105, 132, 133

Queen v. Mil is, 10 Cl. & Fin. 534, 97
Queensbury v. Culver, 19 Wall. 83   20
Quincey, Van Hoffman v., 4 Wall.
552   152

Railroad Companies v. Gaines,
97 U. S 697   33, 34, 155, 168, 171
Railway Gross Receipts, State
Tax on, 15 Wall. 284   36
Ramsey, Murphy v., 114 U. S.
15   185
Randall v. Kreiger, 23 Wall. 137   149
R. R., Dennick v., 103 U. S. 11   197
  v Jackson, 7 Wall. 262   24
  v. Elleman, 105 U. S. 166   173
Railway Co. v. Whiton, 13 Wall.
270   197, 259
Railroad Co. v. Richmond, 96
U. S. 521   268
R. R. v. Prescott, 16 Wall. 603   27
Reclamation District Hagar v.,
111 U. S. 701   12, 240
Reid, U. S. v., 12 How. 361   232
Reese, U. S. v., 92 U. S. 214   201, 253
Renaud v. Abbott, 116 U. S. 277   245
Reid, W. R. R. v., 13 Wall. 264
33, 167
Relfe v. Rundle, 103 U. S. 222   263
Reid. Webster v., 11 How. 437   246
R. & G. R. R. v., 13 Wall.
269   33, 167
Scholey v., 23 Wall. 331   22
Removal Cases, The, 100 U. S.
457   209
Reynolds v. U. S., 98 U. S. 145   230
Cooper v., 10 Wall. 308   245, 246
Dinl v , 96 U. S. 340   233
Rhode Island v. Massachusetts, 12
Pet. 657   2, 189, 198, 215

## TABLE OF CASES CITED. xxvii

Richmond, Railroad Co. v., 96 U.
S. 521    268
Rice v. M. & N. W. R. R., 1 Bl.
358    177
Rinker, Tiernan v., 102 U. S. 123
   35, 80, 258
Riggs v. Johnson County, 6 Wall.
166    233
Rives, Virginia v., 100 U. S. 313
   242, 253
Rivers, New Orleans Waterworks
v., 115 U. S. 674    172
Robbins, Shaw v., 12 Wheat. 369
   156, 158
Robinson v. Campbell, 3 Wheat.
212    200
Rochereau, Dupasseur v., 21 Wall.
130    249
Rock, M. & M. R. R. v., 4 Wall.
177    148, 199
Rose v. Himely, 4 Cr. 272   212, 245
R bertson v. Ce se, 97 U. S. 616   199
Rogers v. Burlington, 3 Wall. 654   20
R les. Bronson v., 7 Wall. 229   12
Rolls County Court v. U. S., 105
U. S 733   154, 158, 160
Royall v. Virginia, 121 U. S. 105   172
Rouse. Lionberger v., 9 Wall. 468   30
Robb v. Connolly 111 U. S. 624
   191, 237
Rosenblatt v. Johnston. 104 U. S.
462    29
Robbins v. Shelby County, 120
U. S. 489    35, 79, 258
R. R. v. Rock, 4 Wall. 177   148, 199
R. R. R. v. L. R. R., 13 How. 81   177
R. T. C. S. Bank, Moultrie, Co. of,
v., 92 U. S. 631    154, 159
Russell, Christmas v., 5 Wall. 290   244
Ruggles v. Illinois, 108 U. S. 526
   178, 269
Runyan v. Coster, 14 Pet. 122   260
Rundle, Relfe v., 103 U. S. 222   263
D. & R. C. Co. v., 14 How. 807   47
R. & Y. R. R. v. Reid, 13 Wall.
269    33, 167

Sands v. M. R. Improvement Co,
123 U. S. 288    19, 92, 98
Santa Clara County v. S. P. R. R.,
118 U. S. 394    259, 265
Sandford, Dred Scott v., 19 How.
393    199, 256
Sauvinet, Walker v., 92 U. S. 90
   230, 241, 254
Sampson, Wiswall v., 14 How. 52
   234, 238
Satterlee v. Matthewson, 2 Pet.
380    182, 183
Safford, Carroll v., 3 How. 441   27

Saunders, Ogden v., 12 Wheat.
213   154, 156, 158, 176, 182
Schottler, S. V. Waterworks v.,
110 U. S. 317    175, 269
School Directors, Hepburn v., 23
Wall. 4-0    31, 52
Schurmeier St. P. & P. R. v, 7
Wall. 272    47
Scholery v. Rew, 23 Wall. 331   22
Scott v. Jones, 5 How. 343   146
Seabury, Cutting v., Sprague 522   60
Searight v. Stokes, 3 How, 151   123
Sedgwick, Nevada Bank v., 104
U. S. 111    18
Seeman, Talbot v., 1 Cr. 1   212
Shaw v. Robbins, 12 Wheat. 369
   156, 158
Sheboygan, Gilman v., 2 Bl. 510
   19, 159
Shelby County, Robbins v., 1 0
U. S. 489    35, 79, 258
Norton v., 118 U. S. 425
   193, 274
Memphis Gas Light Co. v.,
109 U. S. 398   23, 33, 176
Amy v., 114 U. S. 387   179
Shepherd, C. D. Co. v, 20 How.
232    259
Sharp, Planters' Bank v., 6 How.
301    172
Sherlock v. Alling, 93 U. S. 99   60
Shields v. Ohio, 95 U. S. 319
   33, 155, 169
Shriver's Lessee v. Lynn, 2 How.
43    245
Shelden, Chicago v., 9 Wall. 50
   33, 147, 167
Siebert v. Lewis, 122 U. S. 284   160
Siebold Ex parte, 100 U. S. 371   254
Silliman, McClurg v., 6 Wheat.
598    236
Sinnot v. Davenport, 22 How. 227
   53, 68, 122, 270
Singer, U. S. v., 15 Wall. 111   22
Skelly, J. B. Bank v., 1 Bl. 436
   33, 149, 167, 177
Slaughter House Cases, 16 Wall.
36   250, 251, 256, 264, 265, 269
Slaughter, Groves v., 15 Pet. 449
   83, 252, 255
Sloop Betsy, Glass v., 3 Dall. 7   245
Slocum v. Mayberry, 2 Wheat. 9
   201, 236, 238
Smales, De Treville v., 98 U. S.
517    122
Smith v. Condry, 1 How. 28   243
Ennes v., 14 How. 400   212, 245
Freeborn v. 2 Wall. 160   183
F. & M. Bank v., 6 Wheat.
131    154, 156, 157

## TABLE OF CASES CITED.

Smith v. Maryland, 18 How. 71
  47, 48, 254, 255, 268
White's Bank v., 7 Wall.
 446    57
Dooly v., 18 Wall. 604   13
 v. McIver, 9 Wheat. 532   238
 v. Alabama, 124 U. S. 465   268
Sneed, Tennessee v., 96 U. S. 69   151
Society for Savings v. Coite, 6
 Wall. 594    26
Soulard, Jones v., 24 How. 41   47
Soulé, Pacific Insurance Co. v., 7
 Wall. 433    22
Soon Hing v. Crowley, 113 U. S.
 703    269
Southard. Wayman v., 10 Wheat. 1   231
South Carolina v. Georgia, 93 U.
 S. 4    87, 122
Southern, Hagood v., 117 U. S. 52   219
Speed, Owings v., 5 Wheat. 420
   88, 146
Sprague, Hoyt v., 103 U. S. 613   255
Sprott v. U. S., 20 Wall. 459   189
S. P. R. R., Santa Clara County v.,
 118 U. S. 314    259, 265
Springer v. U. S., 102 U. S. 586
   22, 228
Spies v. Illinois, 123 U. S. 137
   209, 240, 254
Spraige v. Thompson, 118 U. S.
 90    115, 274
State, Bradwell v., 16 Wall. 130
   257, 265
 Bank v. Knopp, 16 How.
  369    149
 Turnpike Co. v., 3 Wall. 210   177
 Freight Tax, Case of, 15
  Wall. 232    18, 36, 125, 135
 Miller v., 15 Wall. 478   170
 Tax on Ry. Gross Receipts, 15
  Wall. 281   72, 84, 131, 138, 139
 Tonnage Tax Cases, 12 Wall.
  204    25, 66
Stewart, Maxwell v., 22 Wall. 77
   244, 245, 246
St. Martin's Parish, Nelson v.,
 111 U. S. 716   154, 158, 160
Stone v. Wisconsin. 94 U. S. 181   178
 v. Mississippi, 101 U. S. 814
   178, 269
 v. F. L. & T. Co., 116 U. S.
  307    128, 178
 v. I. C. R. R., 116 U. S. 347
   128, 178
Stockdale v. The Ins. Cos, 20
 Wall. 323    183
St. Clair v. Cox, 106 U. S. 350
   245, 247, 261
Strauder v. West. Va., 100 U. S.
 303    241, 253

Stacy v. Thrasher, 6 How. 44   247
Stanton, Georgia v., 6 Wall. 71   212
Strother v. Lucas, 6 Pet. 763   212
Stifle, Drehman v., 8 Wall. 595   151
Sturges v. Crowninshield, 4
 Wheat. 122    2, 4, 16, 40,
 111, 146, 149, 153, 154, 155,
   157, 164, 201, 215
St. Tammany Water Works v. N.
 O. W. Works, 120 U. S. 64   172
St Clair Co., Mills v., 8 How. 581   177
St. P. & P. R. R. v. Schurmeier,
 7 Wall. 272    47
Stevens v. Griffith, 111 U. S. 48   147
Strader v. Graham, 10 How. 93   252
St. Louis, Packet Co. v., 100 U.
 S. 423    19, 23, 106
Stanley v. Supervisors, 121 U. S.
 535    32
Steamship Co. v. Joliffe, 2 Wall.
 450    115, 116
 v. Port Wardens. 6 Wall. 31
   25, 36, 66, 67, 120
Stuart v. Laird, 1 Cr. 299   215
Stone, Hyde v., 20 How. 170   197, 238
St. Lawrence, The, 1 Bl. 522   197
Stuart, Lessee of Hickey v., 3
 How. 750    245
Stockton, Postmaster Gen. Kendall
 v., 12 Pet. 527   212
Story, Livingston v., 9 Pet 632   200
Stokes. Searight v., 3 How. 151   123
Supervisors, Amy v., 11 Wall. 136   233
 v. Durant, 9 Wall. 415   233
 Bank v., 7 Wall. 26    26
 Wadsworth v., 102 U. S. 534   154
 Olcott v., 16 Wall. 678   20, 147
 Stanley v., 121 U. S. 535   32
Surget, Ford v., 97 U. S. 594   147, 189
Suydam v. Broadnax, 14 Pet. 67
   154, 156, 238
 Williamson v., 6 Wall. 723   150
S. V. Waterworks v. Schottler,
 110 U. S. 347    178, 269
S. & N. A. R. R. v. Alabama, 101
 U. S. 832    180

Tabb, Boyce v., 18 Wall. 546   264
Taylor v. Ypsilanti, 105 U. S. 60   20
 Conway v., 1 Bl. 603   101, 268
 Terrett v., 9 Cr. 43    166
 v. Carryl, 20 How. 583   238
Talbot v. Seeman, 1 Cr. 1   212
Tappan v. M. N. Bank, 19 Wall.
 490    32
Tarble's Case, 13 Wall. 397   237
Taylor, Elmendorf v., 10 Wheat.
 152    243
Tax Court, Bonaparte v., 104 U.
 S. 592    18, 24

## TABLE OF CASES CITED.

Telegraph Co. v. Texas, 105 U.
S. 460    26, 33, 142, 143
   v. W. U. Telegraph Co.,
   96 U. S. 1    40, 41, 141, 142
Tennessee v. Davis, 100 U. S. 257
   200, 209
   v. P. S. C. Co., 117 U. S. 51   36, 137
   v. Sneed, 96 U. S. 69    151
Van Brocklin v., 117 U. S.
   151    27
M. & C. R. R. v., 101 U. S.
   337    180, 181
   Farrington v., 95 U. S 679    167
Teal v. Felton, 12 How. 284    235
Terrett v. Taylor, 9 Cr. 43    166
Terry v. Anderson, 95 U. S. 628    150
   Godfrey v., 95 U. S. 171    199
Texas v. White, 7 Wall. 701
   1, 2, 199. 212, 277
   Telegraph Co. v., 105 U. S.
   460    26, 36, 142, 143
Thatcher, Mayhew v., 6 Wheat.
   129    245
Thrasher, Stacy v., 6 How. 44    247
Thomas v. The City of Richmond,
   12 Wall. 349
Thompson, Spraigue v., 118 U S.
   90    115, 274
   Kilbourne v., 103 U. S. 163    11
   v. Whitman, 18 Wall. 457
   245, 247
Thomson v. P R. R., 9 Wall. 579    28
Tiernan v. Rinker, 102 U. S.
   123    35, 80, 258
Tinker, Inman S. S. Co. v., 94 U.
   S. 238    25, 67
Tobin, Vicksburg v., 100 U. S. 430
   19, 106
Tomlinson v. Branch, 15 Wall.
   460    34, 171
   v. Jessup, 15 Wall. 454    169
Topeka, Loan Ass'n v., 20 Wall.
   655    20
Trade-Mark Cases, 100 U. S. 82
   41, 61, 274
Transportation Co. v. Parkersburg. 107 U. S. 691    19, 106
   v. Wheeling, 99 U. S. 273
   34, 35, 43, 65, 103
Trask v. Maguire, 18 Wall. 391
   33, 155, 168
Trapnall, Woodruff v., 10 How.
   190    172
Trigg v. Drew, 10 How. 224    172
Trevor, The Hine v., 4 Wall. 556
   59, 197, 235
Turnpike Co. v. State, 3 Wall.
   210    177
Tucker v. Ferguson, 22 Wall. 527
   27, 33, 34, 170, 177

Turek, Pound v., 95 U. S. 459    98
Turner v. Maryland, 107 U. S. 38
   25, 86, 87
Turnbull v. Payson, 95 U. S. 418   248
Turpin v. Burgess, 117 U. S. 504   82
Twitchell v. Pennsylvania, 7
   Wall. 321    209, 230, 254

United States v. Bevans, 3 Wheat.
   337    50, 200
   Boyd v., 116 U. S. 616    226
   v. Arrendondo, 6 Pet. 691    275
   v. B. & O. R. R., 17 Wall.
   322    23
   v. Cruickshank, 92 U. S. 542
   201, 251, 253, 254
   v. 43 Gallons of Whiskey, 93
   U. S. 188    144, 275
   v. Fisher, 2 Cr. 358    10
   v. Fox, 94 U. S. 315    255
   v. Hall, 98 U. S. 343    10
   v. Hamilton, 3 Dall. 17    228
   v. Perot, 98 U. S. 430    213
   v. Harris, 106 U. S 629
   2, 264, 266, 274
   Hylton v., 3 Dall. 171    22
   Kohl v., 91 U. S. 367    11
   Langford v., 101 U. S. 341    2
   v. Amedy, 11 Wheat. 392    243
   Mackin v., 117 U. S. 348    226
   McElrath v., 102 U. S. 426
   197, 230
   v. McBratney, 104 U. S. 621   274
   v. Marigold, 9 How. 560   11, 235
   Memphis v., 97 U. S. 293
   154, 158, 160
   v. Memphis, 97 U. S. 284    179
   National Bank v., 101 U. S.
   1    22
   v. Peters, 5 Cr. 115    223, 232
   v. Ortega, 11 Wheat. 467
   196, 205
   Rolls County Court v., 105 U.
   S. 733    154, 158, 160
   Reynolds v., 98 U. S. 145    230
   v. Reese, 92 U. S. 214    201, 253
   Springer v., 102 U. S. 586
   22, 228
   Sprott v., 20 Wall. 459    189
   v. Waddell, 112 U. S. 76   12, 228
   v. Le Bris, 121 U. S. 278    144
   Parkinson v., 121 U. S. 281    226
   v. Singer, 15 Wall. 111    22
   v. Coombs, 12 Pet. 72    46
   Mtge. Co., Gross v., 108 U.
   S. 477    149, 265
   Fremont v., 17 How. 542    213
   v N. O., 98 U. S. 381    19
   v. Haas, 3 Wall. 407    144
   v. Hudson, 7 Cr. 32    200, 205

xxx TABLE OF CASES CITED.

United States v. Coolidge, 1
  Wheat. 415 200
  v. Holliday, 3 Wall. 407 144
  Gordon v., 2 Wall. 561 209
  v. Reid, 12 How. 361 232
  v Ferrera, 13 How. 40 209
  Bleyew v, 13 Wall. 581 196
  Bridge Co. v., 105 U. S. 470 99
  v. Fox, 95 U. S. 670 185, 200, 201
  v. Keehler, 9 Wall. 83 189
  v. De Witt, 9 Wall. 41 2 0, 267
University, Head v., 19 Wall.
  523 179
  v. People 99 U. S. 309
    33, 148, 167, 168
Union Canal Co , Gilfillan v , 109
  U. S. 401 150
U. P. R. R. v. Peniston, 18 Wall.
  5 28
U. P. Ry. v. McShane, 22 Wall.
  444 27
  v. Philadelphia, 101 U. S.
  528 34, 170
Urtetiqui v. D'Arbel. 9 Pet. 692 248
Utah, Hopt v., 110 U. S. 574 185

Vance v. Vance, 108 U. S. 514 150
Van Brocklin v. Tennessee, 117
  U. S. 151 27
Van Horne v. Dorrance, 2 Dall.
  304 193
Van Noorden, Capron v , 2 Cr.
  126 199
Van Hoffman v. Quincy, 4 Wall.
  552 152
Vaughan v. Northrop, 15 Pet. 1
  234, 238
Van Allen v. The Assessors, 3
  Wall. 513 29, 30
Veazie v Moor, 14 How. 568 55, 92
  Bank v. Fenno, 8 Wall. 533
    10, 22, 23
Vicksburg v. Tobin, 100 U. S. 430
  19, 106
Virginia, Phalen v , 8 How. 163 178
  Paul v , 8 Wall. 168
    40, 41, 256, 259, 260, 261, 262
  Royall v., 121 U. S. 105 172
  Ex parte, 100 U. S. 339 242 253
  Coupon Cases, 114 U. S. 270
    172, 188, 224, 274
  Cohens v., 6 Wheat 264 193,
    194, 195, 196, 197, 199, 201,
    215, 216, 222, 209
  v Rives, 100 U. S. 313 242, 253
  Hollingsworth v., 3 Dall. 378 217
  McCready v , 94 U. S. 391
    48, 255, 257, 258, 268
  v. West Virginia 11 Wall. 39
    189, 198

Virginia, Webber v., 103 U. S.
  344 29, 35, 76, 258
Vorhees v. Bank of U. S., 10 Pet.
  449 245
  McKim v., 7 Cr. 279 237
V. S. & P. R. R., Hamilton v.,
  119 U. S. 280 98

Walling v. Michigan, 116 U. S.
  446 35, 77, 258
Ward, M. & M. R. R v., 2 Bl 485 96
  v. Maryland, 12 Wall. 418
    35, 75, 79, 258
Wadsworth v Supervisors, 102 U.
  S. 534 154
Waddell, Martin v., 16 Pet. 367 47
  U. S. v., 112 U. S. 76 12, 228
Watson v. Jones, 13 Wall. 679 233
Warren Bridge, Charles River
  Bridge v , 11 Pet. 420 177
Waite v. Dowley, 94 U. S. 527 33
Wall, Ex parte, 107 U. S. 265 226
Wallace v McConnell, 13 Pet. 136
  237, 238
Walcot v Diggs. 4 Cr 179 233
Walker v. Sauvinet, 92 U. S. 90
  230, 241, 254
  Lawler v.. 14 How. 149 199
  v. Whitehead, 16 Wall. 314 153
Waller, Bigler v., 14 Wall. 297 13
Waring v. The Mayor, 8 Wall.
  110 85
  v. Clarke, 5 How. 441 86, 197, 201
Watson v. Mercer, 8 Pet. 88 182, 183
  Mobile v., 116 U. S. 289
    154, 158, 159
Wardens, etc., Board of, Cooley v.,
  12 How 299 111, 116, 134
Board of, Steamship Co. v., 6
  Wall. 31 25
Wales v. Whitney, 114 U S. 564 213
Wayman v. Southard, 10 Wheat.
  1 231
Webber v. Va., 103 U. S. 344
  29, 35, 76, 258
Webster v. Reid, 11 How. 437 245
Weber v. Harbor Commissioners,
  18 Wall. 57 47, 48, 255
Welton v. Missouri, 91 U. S. 275
  35, 76, 258
Weston v. Charleston, 2 Pet. 449 26
Western Union Tel. Co., P. Tel.
  Co. v., 96 U. S. 1
    40, 41, 141, 142, 260
West v. Aurora City, 6 Wall. 139 209
Wells, Ex parte, 18 How. 307 228
West Virginia, Strauder v., 100
  U. S. 303 241, 253
  Virginia v., 11 Wall. 39 189, 198
Wethered, Bischoff v., 9 Wall. 812 245

# TABLE OF CASES CITED. xxxi

Weaver, People v., 100 U. S. 539 32
W. F. Co., C. & A. R. R. v., 119
  U. S 615    212, 213, 243
  C. & A. R. R. v., 108 U. S.
  18   244
  St. Louis v., 11 Wall. 423 36, 103
Wheeling, Transportation Co. v.,
  99 U. S. 273 34, 35, 43, 65, 103
  & B. Bridge Co., Penna. v.,
  18 How. 421   94, 123
Wheeler, R. R. v., 1 Bl. 286 259, 260
Whitehead, Walker v., 16 Wall.
  314   153
Whiskey, 43 gallons, U. S. v., 93
  U. S. 188   144, 275
Whitman, Thompson v., 18 Wall.
  457   245, 247
White v. Hart, 13 Wall. 646
  146, 152, 264
Whitten, Ry. v., 13 Wall. 270
  60, 197, 200, 232. 259
Whitney. Curtis v., 13 Wall. 68 150
  Texas v., 7 Wall. 701
  1, 2, 199, 212, 277
White's Bank v. Smith, 7 Wall.
  446   57
Wheaton v. Peters, 8 Pet. 591 200
Whitney, Wales v., 114 U. S. 564 213
Williamson v. Suydam, 6 Wall.
  723   150
Wiggins Ferry Co. v. East St.
  Louis, 107 U S. 365
  34, 35, 41, 43, 66, 102, 170
Williams v. Louisiana, 103 U. S.
  637   149
  v. Bruffy, 96 U. S. 176   189
Williamson v. Berry, 8 How. 495 245
Wilson, Ex parte, 114 U. S. 417 226
Wilcox v. Jackson, 13 Pet. 498 245
  v. Jackson, 13 Pet. 498   224
Wilson. Cheever v., 9 Wall. 108 244
  v. McNamee, 102 U. S. 572
  115, 116
  New Jersey v., 7 Cr. 64 33, 166
  v. B. C. Marsh Co., 2 Pet. 250
  93, 98, 111
Wisconsin, Hall v., 103 U. S. 5 172
Wister, Bank of Kentucky v., 2
  Pet. 318   223
Withers v. Buckley, 20 How 84
  92, 226, 254

Wisconsin, Stone v., 94 U. S. 181 178
  v. Duluth, 96 U. S. 379   89
Windley, Blount v., 95 U. S. 173
  151, 154, 158
Witherspoon v. Duncan, 4 Wall.
  210   23
Wise v. Withers, 3 Cr. 331   213
Withers, Wise v., 3 Cr 331   213
Williams v. Benedict, 8 How. 107
  234, 238
Wiswall v. Sampson, 14 How. 52
  234, 238
Wo Lee v. Hopkins, 118 U. S.
  356   265, 269
Wolff v. New Orleans, 103 U. S
  358   154, 158, 160
Woodruff v. Trapnall, 10 How.190 172
Woolsey, Dodge v., 18 How. 341 193
Worcester v. Georgia, 6 Pet. 515
  134, 144, 209
Woodruff v. Parham, 8 Wall. 128
  35, 41, 73. 79. 84, 85, 134
W. R. R. v. Reid, 13 Wall. 264
  33, 167
Wright v. Nagle, 101 U. S. 791
  149, 177
  Norwich Co. v, 13 Wall. 104 57
W. St. L. & P. Ry. v. Illinois,
  118 U. S. 557   125, 268, 271
Wurts v. Hogeland. 114 U S. 606 240
W. U. T. Co. v. Pendleton, 122
  U. S. 347   143
W. & B. Bridge Co., Penna. v, 18
  How. 421   99, 123, 200
W. & St. P. R. R. v. Blake, 94 U.
  S. 180   178
W. & W. R. R. v. King, 91 U.
  S. 3   152

Yarborough, Ex parte, 110 U. S
  651   11, 12, 228
Yard, New Jersey v., 95 U. S. 104
  33, 167, 169
Yaker, Haver v., 9 Wall. 321   275
Yewdall, Pearson v., 95 U. S. 294
  230, 240, 254
Yick Wo v. Hopkins, 118 U. S.
  356   265, 269
Ypsilanti, Taylor v., 105 U. S. 60 20

Zacharie, Boyle v., 6 Pet. 635 154, 156

# CHAPTER I.

## THE RELATION OF THE STATES TO THE UNITED STATES AND TO EACH OTHER.

1. The sanction of the Constitution.
2. The indissolubility of the Union.
3. The autonomy of the states.
4. The delegated character and limited powers of the government of the United States.
5. The federal supremacy.
6. The restraints upon the states.
7. The force and effect of the preamble to the Constitution.

1. The Constitution, though framed by a convention, whose members were elected by the legislature of the states, was ratified in the several states by conventions whose members were elected by the people of their respective states. It derives its whole authority from that ratification, and when thus adopted, it was of complete obligation and it thenceforth bound the states, and the citizens of each state.[1]

2. The union of the states under the Constitution was, from and after the ratification of that instrument, indissoluble, and, until an amendment be adopted, authorizing a dissolution of the union, or a withdrawal of a state from the union, it is not possible for a state, without violating the constitutional compact, to withdraw from the union, or to deprive itself of its rights as one of the United States, or to emancipate itself from the restraints imposed by the Constitution on freedom of state action.[2]

---

[1] Martin v. Hunter's Lessee, 1 Wheat. 304, 324; McCulloch v. Maryland, 4 Wheat. 316, 404.

[2] Texas v. White, 7 Wall. 700; White v. Hart, 13 Wall. 646; Keith v. Clark, 97 U. S. 454.

3. The thirteen original states were existing governments when the Constitution was ratified; and, states admitted to the union under the Constitution have as regards the United States and the other states, in all respects in which the effect of that instrument has not been changed by amendment, the same rights, powers, and obligations as the thirteen original states.[1] Therefore, in so far as the states are not controlled by the expressed, or implied, restrictions, contained in the Constitution of the United States, they may severally exercise all the powers of independent governments.[2] The states, though united under the sovereign authority of the Constitution, are, so far as their freedom of action is not controlled by that instrument, foreign to, and independent of each other.[3]

4. The government of the United States, in its relation to the several states and to the citizens of those states, is one of delegated and limited powers, which are, expressly or by necessary implication, granted by its written Constitution.[4] The Constitution has created a government, divided into three departments, legislative, executive, and judicial. As the chief function of the executive department, apart from its participation in legislation by the exercise of a qualified veto, is that of administering the laws of Congress, and as the primary duty of the judicial department is that of expounding the Constitution and the laws in their application to subject-matters of judicial cognizance, either civil or

---

[1] Pollard *v.* Hagan, 3 How. 212; Texas *v.* White, 7 Wall. 700.

[2] Amendments to the Constitution, articles ix and x; Martin *v.* Hunter's Lessee, 1 Wheat. 304, 325; Sturges *v.* Crowninshield, 4 Wheat. 193; Texas *v.* White, 7 Wall. 700, 721.

[3] Buckner *v.* Findley, 2 Pet. 586, 590; Rhode Island *v.* Massachusetts, 12 Pet. 722.

[4] Martin *v.* Hunter's Lessee, 1 Wheat. 304, 326; Marbury *v.* Madison, 1 Cr. 137, 176; Briscoe *v.* Bank of Kentucky, 11 Pet. 317; U. S. *v.* Harris, 106 U. S. 627; Langford *v.* U. S., 101 U. S. 34.

criminal, it is obvious, that the powers conferred by the Constitution upon the government of the United States are, in the main, powers of legislation. The powers granted by the Constitution to the government of the United States are either expressed or implied. The expressed powers are those which are specifically stated in the Constitution. The implied powers are those which authorize the use of appropriate means, which are consistent with the letter and spirit of the Constitution, for the accomplishment of legitimate ends, which are not prohibited, and which are within the scope of the Constitution.[1] The powers granted by the Constitution to the United States are subject to certain expressed exceptions, which are contained in the 9th section of article I of the Constitution, and in the first eleven of its amendments.

5. Article VI of the Constitution declares, that "this Constitution and the laws of the United States, which shall be made in pursuance thereof, and all treaties made, or which shall be made, under the authority of the United States, shall be the supreme law of the land; and the judges in every state shall be bound thereby, anything in the Constitution or laws of any state to the contrary notwithstanding." By force of this constitutional provision, the government of the United States, as Marshall, C. J., said in McCulloch v. Maryland,[2] "though limited in its powers, is supreme within its sphere of action," and, to the extent, and in the exercise, of the powers delegated to it, it is a sovereignty.[3]

6. The restraints imposed by the Constitution upon

---

[1] *Infra*, chapter II; Constitution, art. I, sec. 8; McCulloch v. Maryland, 4 Wheat. 421.

[2] 4 Wheat. 316, 405.

[3] Alexander Hamilton's argument of 23 February, 1791, as to the constitutionality of a national bank. 3 Lodge's Hamilton's Work, 181; Julliard v. Greenman, 110 U. S. 421.

the states are either expressed or implied. The expressed restraints are those which are specifically stated in the Constitution. The implied restraints are those which result from the express grant by the Constitution of certain powers, whose nature, or the terms of whose grant, require that they should be exclusively exercised by the United States.[1] The expressed restraints, are, *first*, those which affect the relations of the several states to other states, foreign and domestic; and, *second*, those which have reference to the relations between the states and their citizens, and which limit the exercise by the states of their powers of legislation. The expressed restraints of the first class include the prohibition of treaties, alliances, confederations, agreements, or compacts with another state or with a foreign power; the obligation not to issue letters of *marque* and reprisal, or to maintain troops or ships of war in times of peace, or to engage in war unless actually invaded or in such imminent danger as will not admit of delay; the requirements that full faith and credit shall be given in each state to the public acts, records, and judicial proceedings of every other state, and that the citizens of each state shall be entitled to all the privileges and immunities of citizens of the several states, and that fugitives from justice shall be surrendered from one state to another. The expressed restraints of the second class include the prohibition of the grant of titles of nobility, of the coinage of money, of the emission of bills of credit, of the establishment of any legal tender other than gold and silver coin, of the imposition of duties of tonnage and duties on imports or exports, excepting such as may absolutely be necessary for the execution of inspection laws; of

---

[1] Sturges *v.* Crowninshield, 4 Wheat. 122, 193; Houston *v.* Moore, 5 id. 49; Gilman *v.* Philadelphia, 3 Wall. 730.

the rehabilitation of slavery or involuntary servitude, except as a punishment for crime; of the deprivation of any person of life, liberty, or property without due process of law; of the denial to any person of the equal protection of the law; of disfranchisement on account of race, colour, or previous condition of servitude, or for any cause, except for participation in rebellion or other crime, of any of the male inhabitants of a state who are twenty-one years of age and citizens of the United States; of "the election or the appointment to office under a state of any person, who, having previously taken an oath as a member of Congress, or as a member of any state legislature, or as an executive or judicial officer of any state, to support the Constitution of the United States, shall have engaged in insurrection or rebellion against the same, or given aid or comfort to the enemies thereof," and whose disabilities shall not have been removed by a vote of two-thirds of each house of Congress, of the assumption or payment of any debt or obligation incurred in aid of insurrection or rebellion against the United States, or of any claim for the loss or emancipation of any slave; and of the enactment of bills of attainder, *ex post facto* laws, or laws impairing the obligation of contracts.

The implied restraints limit the action of the states with regard to taxation, the regulation of commerce, and the personal and property rights of their citizens, and of the citizens of other states.

Many of the restraints are so clear in their terms, and so little require judicial construction, that no question has ever been raised as to their legal effect, but others of those restraints have been frequently subjects of litigation. For the purposes of this treatise it is unnecessary to make further reference to the restraints with regard to the issue of letters of *marque* or reprisal, the maintenance of troops or ships of war in time of peace, the engagement in war unless actually invaded or in such imminent danger as will not admit of delay, the grant of titles of nobility, or the coinage of money. As, happily for the peace and prosperity of the country, slavery is of past, and not of present, interest, it is not deemed necessary to refer to that subject further than to note that the XIII Amendment has abolished it in every form, and forbidden its re-establishment.

7. The preamble to the Constitution declares that "We, the people of the United States, in order to form a more perfect union, establish justice, insure domestic tranquillity, provide for the common defense, promote the general welfare, and secure the blessings of liberty to ourselves and our posterity, do ordain and establish this Constitution for the United States of America." That the true significance of that declaration may be understood, it must be remembered that the people, whose ratification of the instrument gave it its legal validity were citizens of independent states, which had been theretofore bound together in a confederation, and which were thenceforth to be united under a government which, though limited in its action by the reservation to the several states of all powers not delegated to the United States, should yet be supreme within its defined bounds.[1]

Therefore, the government created by the Constitution is, to the extent of the powers vested in that government, national in its character, and, by force of the rights reserved to the states, it is, also, a league of sovereign and independent states; and every citizen of each state, while owing allegiance to his state in all matters not controlled by the powers granted to the

[1] Martin *v.* Hunter's Lessee, 1 Wheat. 304, 325.

United States, owes also a paramount allegiance to the United States in all that is made by the Constitution of federal obligation. In view of this dual, and yet undivided, allegiance due by those who are citizens of the United States and also citizens of a state, it was, in the hour of its formation, and it has ever since been, essential to the right administration of the government of the United States under the Constitution that there should be a clear appreciation of the complex character of that government, and a careful maintenance of the balance of power as between the government of the United States and the governments of the several states.

# CHAPTER II.

### THE IMPLIED POWERS.

8. The necessity of their existence.
9. Their constitutional recognition.
10. The test of the relation of the means to the ends.
11. Illustrations of the exercise of the implied powers.
12. The legal tender question.
13. The possible scope of the legal tender cases as authorities.

8. The Constitution was not framed to meet only the exigencies of the period of its formation, nor does it purport to be a code, which with minute detail prescribes all that may be done and all that may not be done by Congress in the execution of the powers specifically granted.[1] As Mr. Webster said in his argument in Gibbons v. Ogden,[2] and as Marshall, C. J., repeated in his judgment in that cause,[3] the Constitution enumerates, but does not define, the powers which it grants, nor does it prescribe the means which may rightfully be used in executing those powers, and without whose use, the grant of the powers would be nugatory.[4] Therefore, if the Constitution contained no clause recognizing the existence of powers which are subsidiary or incidental to the powers expressly granted, it would be impossible to avoid the conclusion that there is an implied grant of such incidental powers, for otherwise the powers expressly granted would be practically inoperative. Nor

---

[1] McCulloch v. Maryland, 4 Wheat. 406; Martin v. Hunter's Lessee, 1 id. 326.
[2] 6 Webster's Works 9.
[3] 9 Wheat. 189.
[4] McCulloch v. Maryland, 4 Wheat. 407.

is the force of this conclusion at all affected by the X Amendment, for while that amendment in terms forbids the exercise by Congress of any undelegated power, it does not forbid the exercise of powers which are delegated by implication.[1]

9. Section 8 of article I of the Constitution declares that "the Congress shall have power . . . . . to make all laws which shall be necessary and proper for carrying into execution the foregoing powers, and all other powers vested by this Constitution in the government of the United States or in any department or officer thereof." But it may be said, who is to conclusively determine whether or not any statute is, within the terms of the Constitution, "necessary and proper for carrying into execution" a power granted by the Constitution to Congress? If Congress can so determine, obviously any and every act of Congress must be regarded as constitutional. If in the exercise of judicial jurisdiction the final determination of that question is to be made by the court, what principles are to guide the judges in coming to a conclusion, and by what test are they to determine the relation between the means and the end, and the degree of the necessity and the propriety of the use of the particular means?

10. The result of the authorities, so far as they afford an answer to this question, can be best stated by the quotation of a famous *dictum* originated by Mr. Hamilton[2] and paraphrased by Chief Justice Marshall in the judgment in McCulloch v. Maryland,[3] and which, in its final perfected form, is as follows: "let the end be legitimate, let it be within the scope of the Constitution, and all means which are appropriate, which are plainly

---

[1] Mr. Hamilton's argument as to a national bank. 3 Lodge's Hamilton's Works 183; McCulloch v. Maryland, 4 Wheat. 406.

[2] Argument as to a national bank. 3 Lodge's Hamilton's Works 190.

[3] 4 Wheat. 421.

adapted to the end, which are not prohibited, but consist with the letter and spirit of the Constitution, are constitutional."[1] This dictum means that Congress may, in the execution of a power expressly granted, adopt any means which (1) are not expressly prohibited by the Constitution, nor (2) inconsistent with the letter and spirit of the Constitution, and which are (3) not the only possible means, nor an absolutely or indispensably necessary means, but an appropriate and plainly adapted means, to the attainment of an end authorized by the Constitution. From this it follows, that if the relation of the means to the end be shown to exist, and if the use of the particular means be not expressly or impliedly forbidden by the Constitution, the question of the degree of its appropriateness, of its greater or less adaptation, and of its relative or absolute necessity is purely political, and the determination of Congress with regard thereto is binding upon the courts.

11. Under the doctrine of the implied powers, it has been held that Congress may enact statutes creating banking corporations as fiscal aids to the government;[2] imposing upon national and state banks a tax upon the amount of the notes of state banks paid out by them;[3] giving priority to the United States as a creditor in the distribution of the assets of a bankrupt;[4] declaring that the embezzlement by a guardian of his ward's pension granted by the United States is a crime against the United States;[5] taxing lands in the District of Colum-

---

[1] The opposing view, sustaining the strict construction of the Constitution, is, perhaps, most strongly put by Mr. Jefferson. Memoirs, vol. IV, pp. 197, 207, 526; 4 Elliot's Debates 609.

[2] McCulloch v. Maryland, 4 Wheat. 316; Osborn v. The Bank of the United States, 9 id. 738.

[3] Veazie Bank v. Fenno, 8 Wall. 533.

[4] U. S. v. Fisher, 2 Cr. 358.

[5] U. S. v. Hall, 98 U. S. 343.

bia;[1] declaring it to be a crime to bring into the United States from a foreign place, counterfeit coins forged in the similtude of coins of the United State;[2] constituting a judicial system to carry into execution the judicial powers vested by the Constitution in the United States;[3] regulating the carriage of the mails and determining what may be transported and what must be excluded from the mails;[4] punishing for contempt others than members of Congress;[5] protecting citizens of the United States in the exercise of the rights of suffrage at elections for members of Congress;[6] authorizing a limited intercourse on prescribed conditions with the enemy in time of war;[7] prescribing the effect to be given in state courts to judgments and decrees rendered in courts of the United States;[8] authorizing the issue by courts of the United States of writs of *habeas corpus ad subjiciendum* in cases of restraint of personal liberty under the process of state courts issued in violation of rights claimed under the Constitution or laws of the United States;[9] authorizing the removal to the courts of the United States of causes depending in state courts and involving questions of Federal cognizance;[10] exercising the right of eminent domain with regard to land within the bounds of a state and held in private ownership;[11] in order to protect purchasers under the homestead laws

---

[1] Loughborough v. Blake, 5 Wheat. 317.
[2] The United States v. Marigold, 9 How. 560.
[3] Ableman v. Booth, 21 How. 506, 521.
[4] *Ex parte* Jackson, 96 U. S. 727.
[5] Anderson v. Dunn, 6 Wheat. 204; *sed. cf.* Kilbourn v. Thompson, 103 U. S. 168.
[6] *Ex parte* Yarbrough, 110 U. S. 651.
[7] Hamilton v. Dillin, 21 Wall. 73.
[8] Embry v. Palmer, 107 U. S. 3.
[9] *Ex parte* Royall, 117 U. S. 241; *Ex parte* Fonda, *ibid.* 516.
[10] Martin v. Hunter's Lessee, 1 Wheat. 304, 349.
[11] Kohl v. The United States, 91 U. S. 367.

of lands belonging to the United States but situated within the limits of a state, punishing those who conspire to intimidate such purchasers and drive them away from the land so purchased,[1] and prohibiting, under penalties, officers of the United States from requesting, giving to, or receiving from any other officer money or property, or other things of value, for political purposes.[2]

12. It has also been held that Congress may issue a paper currency and declare that that currency shall be a legal tender in payment of debts. Until in 1862 the financial needs of the government in carrying on a war for the suppression of the rebellion rendered it, in the opinion of Congress, necessary that the treasury notes of the United States should be made a legal tender in the payment of debts, neither statesmen nor jurists had asserted that Congress had, under the Constitution, the power of making anything but gold or silver coin a legal tender. The acts of Congress of 25 February, 1862; 11 July, 1862, and 3 March, 1863,[3] declared that the notes issued thereunder should be "lawful money and a legal tender in payment of all debts, public and private, within the United States, except duties on imports, etc." Under these acts it has been decided that neither taxes imposed by state authority,[4] nor private obligations payable by their terms in gold or silver coin,[5] are

---

[1] United States v. Waddell, 112 U. S. 76.

[2] *Ex parte* Curtis, 106 U. S. 371; Stat. 15 Aug., 1876, c. 287, sec. 6.

For further illustrations of the implied powers of legislation which Congress may exercise, see the judgments of Story, J., in Prigg v. Penna., 16 Pet. 619; of Strong, J., in The Legal Tender Cases, 12 Wall. 457, 535; of Gray, J., in Juilliard v. Greeman, 110 U. S. 421, 444, and of Miller, J., in *Ex parte* Yarbrough, 110 U. S. 658.

[3] 12 Stat. 345, 532, 709.

[4] Lane County v. Oregon, 7 Wall. 71; Hagar v. Reclamation District, 111 U. S. 701.

[5] Bronson v. Rhodes, 7 Wall. 229; Butler v. Horwitz, *ibid.* 258; Bronson v. Kimpton, 8 *id.* 444.

debts within the terms of the acts of Congress dischargeable by payment in legal tender notes. In Hepburn *v.* Griswold,[1] the court held that the Legal Tender Acts applied to debts contracted before as well as to debts contracted after the enactment of those statutes, and that, so far as they applied to debts contracted before their passage, the statutes were unconstitutional, but in the Legal Tender Cases[2] Hepburn *v.* Griswold was overruled, so far as regards the second branch of the proposition laid down in it, and the constitutionality of the Legal Tender Acts was sustained, the ground of decision being that the power to impress the notes of the government with the quality of legal tender, though not expressed in the Constitution, was "necessary and proper for carrying into execution" the express powers to "coin money," "to regulate the value thereof," "to pay the debts," "to borrow money," "to raise and support armies," and "to provide and maintain a navy;" that the Constitution does not expressly prohibit the issue of legal tender notes by the United States; that their issue is not inconsistent with the letter or the spirit of the Constitution, and that the end being constitutional and the means being appropriate, the degree of its appropriateness is subject to legislative, and not judicial, determination. The Legal Tender Cases are followed and supported by Dooley *v.* Smith,[3] Bigler *v.* Waller,[4] N. & W. R. R. *v.* Johnson,[5] and Juilliard *v.* Greeman,[6] in the last of which cases it was held, that the power to make treasury notes a legal tender exists in time of peace as well as in time of war, and that legal tender notes when redeemed by the Treasury and reissued under the Act of 31 May, 1878, retain their legal tender quality.

[1] 8 Wall. 603.
[2] 12 Wall. 457.
[3] 18 Wall. 604.
[4] 14 *id.* 297.
[5] 15 *id.* 195.
[6] 110 U. S. 421.

If the question were not concluded by authority, and if it were open to examination on principle, it would be difficult of solution, and those who have studied it the most thoroughly would most hesitate to dogmatically state a conclusion either for or against the constitutionality of the Legal Tender Acts. The Constitution does not expressly authorize, nor prohibit, the enactment of such statutes by Congress; it does expressly forbid the states to coin money, emit bills of credit, or make anything but gold and silver coin a legal tender; it makes the government of the United States a sovereignty, whose powers are, it is true, enumerated, but which is none the less, within the limits of those powers, a sovereignty, to whose control are intrusted "the sword and the purse, all the external relations, and no inconsiderable portion of the industry of the nation,"[1] and which in the execution of its great powers is entitled to use the appropriate means; it forbids the states, but it does not forbid the United States, to impair the obligation of contracts; and it expressly empowers the United States "to coin money," and "to regulate the value thereof." It seems to me, as Mr. Justice Holmes has said,[2] that the controversy really turns on the construction of the last clause quoted. The government's promissory note, payable on demand, is, if it be not a legal tender, nothing more than an evidence of indebtedness on the part of the government, and as such assignable by the original creditor to other persons, and its issue is as plainly authorized by the power to borrow money as is the issue of government bonds; but when the government undertakes to impress on that promissory note the quality of a legal tender in satisfaction of the antecedently contracted

---

[1] Per Marshall, C. J., McCulloch v. Maryland, 4 Wheat. 407.
[2] 4 Am. Law Rev. 768: 1 Kent's Com. 254, Ed. 1873.

debts of those who are not parties to the transaction of borrowing between the government and its original creditor, the note is made to be something more than an evidence of indebtedness, and it then becomes "money," for it not only circulates in fact, but it performs those offices which "money" only can perform; that is, it not only serves as a medium of exchange and a measure of values, but it also is the efficient means of a compulsory legal discharge of a debt. Various things that are not "money" may perform one or more of these offices, but it is "money" alone which can discharge all of them. Now, if the government, when it borrows, or pays its debts, or makes its purchases, can give to its creditor that which has no intrinsic value, but which that creditor can compel his creditor to receive in satisfaction of an antecedent debt, it is somewhat difficult to see how or why the delivery of that thing of no intrinsic value as the equivalent for materials purchased by the government, or money loaned to the government, or as the legal discharge of a debt due by the government, will not greatly facilitate borrowing, purchases, and payments by the government. From this it would seem to follow that the issue of legal tender notes, however unwise in statesmanship, is a plainly adapted means to the end of raising and supporting armies, providing and maintaining a navy, borrowing money, and paying the debts of the United States. The use of that means is not prohibited expressly.

It is not prohibited impliedly, unless the implication of a prohibition can be deduced from the specific grant of power to "coin money." If that grant means that Congress may issue a metallic currency and make that a legal tender, certainly the force of the maxim, *expressio unius est exclusio alterius*, converts that limited grant of power over the currency into an implied prohibition of the impression of the legal tender quality on notes. If, on the other hand, the word "money," in the constitutional sense of the term, means only, as Professor Thayer has argued,[1] a medium of exchange which does not involve the idea of a legal tender, the power to coin money does not expressly authorize the issue of a metallic legal tender, nor does it impliedly forbid the issue of a paper legal tender. Of course, the same conclusion must be reached, if the word "coin" does not mean to stamp metal discs, but means only to issue a currency of any material. In support of that view, Mr. McMurtrie has said,[2] that the Constitution was framed by men who were versed in the technical terms of English law, and that in English law the phrase "to coin money" meant to issue a currency of any material and to give to that currency all the qualities of a circulating medium. But it is settled that the Constitution is to be judicially construed as the act, not of the convention which framed it, but of the people who ratified it, and that in construing it, its words are to be read in their natural sense,[3] departing from and varying by construction the natural meaning of the words only where different clauses of the instrument bear upon each other and would conflict, unless the words were construed otherwise than by their natural and common import.[4] Applying to the Constitution these principles of construction, there is certainly some force in the view that the power to " coin money," whatever it may have been intended to accomplish, expressly authorizes the issue of metallic " money," and therefore impliedly forbids the issue of paper "money." In view of these

[1] 1 Harvard Law Rev. 83.
[2] Observations on Mr. George Bancroft's Plea for the Constitution, pp. 20 et seq.
[3] Gibbons v. Ogden, 9 Wheat. 1.
[4] Sturges v. Crowninshield, 4 Wheat. 122.

conflicting arguments, it may well be said that, on principle and apart from authority, the legal tender question is one of difficulty, on which there may well be an honest difference of opinion, without liability, on the one side or the other, to a just imputation of either ignorance of constitutional law or moral perversity. The power of Congress to create a national bank was quite as bitterly controverted in the early days of the Republic, yet few, if any, now doubt that the power exists.

13. If Congress have an implied power to issue a legal tender currency as a means to the end of borrowing money for and paying the debts of the United States, and if the express power to "coin money" is to be construed as an authorization of the issue of a metallic legal tender currency and an implied prohibition of the issue of a paper legal tender currency, it inevitably follows that the Legal Tender cases are an authority for the proposition, of possibly wide application, that no express grant of power to the United States to accomplish any end in any definite way can avail to prevent the attainment of that end in any other way, if permission to use that other way be implied in and deducible from any other express grant of powers.

# CHAPTER III.

### TAXATION.

14. Taxation defined and limited.
15. Taxation by the United States.
16. Direct taxation.
17. The requirement of uniformity.
18. Exemption of state agencies from taxation by the United States.
19. Charges which are not taxes exempt from constitutional restraints.
20. Taxation by the states.
21. The expressed restraints upon state taxation.
22. The implied restraint upon state taxation resulting from the federal supremacy.
23. Taxation of national banks.
24. State taxation as affected by the prohibition of the impairment of the obligation of contracts.
25. State taxation as affected by the grant to Congress of the power of regulating commerce.

14. Taxation is the compulsory exaction by a government, in the exercise of its sovereignty, of a payment of money or surrender of property by any person, natural or corporate, who, or whose property so taxed, is subject to the sovereign power of that government.[1] Taxation operates upon real property and upon tangible personal property by reason of its *situs* or presence within the territory of the taxing power.[2] It operates upon choses in action by reason of the subjection of the owner thereof to the jurisdiction of the government imposing the tax.[3] Every possible exaction of money or property by a government from

[1] The State Freight Tax, 15 Wall. 277; McCulloch *v.* Maryland, 4 Wheat. 420.

[2] Mager *v.* Grima, 8 How. 490; Coe *v.* Errol, 116 U. S. 557.

[3] Bonaparte *v.* Tax Court, 104 U. S. 592; Kirtland *v.* Hotchkiss, 100 U. S. 491; Nevada Bank *v.* Sedgwick, 104 U. S. 111.

those who are subject to its jurisdiction is not a tax; thus, a duty of so much *per* passenger, imposed by the United States in the exercise of the power to regulate commerce on owners of vessels bringing passengers from foreign ports into ports of the United States, in order to raise a fund to mitigate the evils incident to immigration, is " not a tax or duty within the meaning of the Constitution ;"[1] for, as Miller, J., said in the judgment in that cause,[2] "the money thus raised, though paid into the treasury, is appropriated in advance to the uses of the statute, and does not go to the general support of the government. It constitutes a fund raised from those who are engaged in the transportation of those passengers, and who make profit out of it, for the temporary care of the passengers whom they bring among us and for the protection of the citizens among whom they are landed." On the same principle a charge made by a state for facilities furnished by it, directly or indirectly, for the movement of commerce, in the form of improved water ways,[3] or wharves,[4] or railways,[5] or a charge for quarantine examination, cannot be said to be a tax.[6] The power of taxation is vested in the legislative department of the government,[7] but it may be delegated by states to political subdivisions, such as counties and municipalities,[8] and a state

[1] The Head Money Cases, 112 U. S. 580.
[2] p. 595.
[3] Huse *v.* Glover, 119 U. S. 543 ; Sands *v.* M. R. Improvement Co., 123 *id.* 238.
[4] Packet Co. *v.* Keokuk, 95 U. S. 80; Packet Co. *v.* St. Louis, 100 *id.* 423 ; Vicksburg *v.* Tobin, *id.* 430; Packet Co. *v.* Cattlesburg, 105 *id.* 559 ; Transportation Co. *v.* Parkersburg, 107 *id.* 69; O. Packet Co. *v.* Aitken, 121 *id.* 444.
[5] B. & O. R. R. *v.* Maryland, 21 Wall. 456.
[6] Morgan *v.* Louisiana, 118 U. S. 455.
[7] Merriwether *v.* Garret, 102 U. S. 472.
[8] Gilman *v.* Sheboygan, 2 Bl. 510 ; United States *v.* New Orleans, 98 U. S. 381.

may determine the bounds of a municipality and prescribe its rate of taxation.[1] By whomsoever exercised, or to whomsoever delegated, the power can only be exercised for public purposes. Taxes, therefore, cannot be imposed in aid of enterprises strictly private, such as the establishment of manufactories[2] or of private grist mills;[3] but when the purpose is public, though not directly connected with the administration of government, taxes may rightfully be laid to aid in its accomplishment, as in the cases of state reform schools;[4] grist mills, required by statute to grind for all customers on payment of certain tolls;[5] the improvements of water powers of rivers for general purposes;[6] the payment of bounties to volunteer soldiers in time of war;[7] the establishment of railways.[8] When bonds, though issued in aid of private purposes, on their face appear to have been issued for public purposes, they are valid and enforcible in the hands of *bona fide* holders for value and without notice.[9]

15. The power of taxation vested in the United States is coextensive with the territory of the United States, and it is operative in the District of Columbia,[10] in the territories, and, to the extent of the constitutional grant, in all of the states.

---

[1] Kelly *v.* Pittsburgh, 104 U. S. 78.

[2] Loan Association *v.* Topeka, 20 Wall. 655; Parkersburg *v.* Brown, 106 U. S. 487; Cole *v.* La Grange, 113 *id.* 1.

[3] Osborne *v.* County of Adams, 106 U. S. 181, 109 *id.* 1.

[4] County of Livingston *v.* Darlington, 101 U. S. 407.

[5] Burlington *v.* Beasley, 94 U. S 310.

[6] Blair *v.* Cuming County, 111 U. S. 363.

[7] Middleton *v.* Mullica Township, 112 U. S. 433.

[8] Rogers *v.* Burlington, 3 Wall. 654; Queensbury *v.* Culver, 19 *id.* 83; Taylor *v.* Ypsilanti, 105 U. S. 60; Olcott *v.* The Supervisors, 16 Wall. 678; R. R. *v.* Otoe, *ibid.* 667.

[9] Hackett *v.* Ottawa, 99 U. S. 86; Ottawa *v.* National Bank, 105 *id.* 343; Ottawa *v.* Carey, 108 *id.* 110, 118.

[10] Loughborough *v.* Blake, 5 Wheat. 317.

Section 8 of article I of the Constitution declares that "the Congress shall have power to lay and collect taxes, duties, imposts, and excises, to pay the debts and provide for the common defense and general welfare of the United States; but all duties, imposts, and excises shall be uniform throughout the United States." At one period in the history of the country political parties were at issue as to the construction to be given to this section of the Constitution, the Federalists contending that the section granted in express terms three substantive and independent powers, namely, (1) to lay and collect taxes, duties, imposts, and excises, (2) to pay the debts, and (3) to provide for the common defense and general welfare of the United States; and the Democrats asserting that the section granted but one substantive power, that to lay and collect taxes, duties, imposts, and excises, and limited the exercise of that power to the purpose of paying the debts and providing for the common defense and general welfare of the United States. The Federalist view was open to the objection that a power to legislate for the common defense and general welfare of the United States would authorize Congress to do anything and everything, and would render superfluous the delegation of other express powers of legislation in the same section; but the Democratic view, however sound in theory, could never be judicially affirmed, for as Congress has admittedly some power of taxation, a court, looking, as it is bound to look, not at the question of expediency but solely at the question of power, could never determine an act of Congress imposing a tax to be unconstitutional because it was intended for some purpose other than that of paying the debts and providing for the common defense and general welfare of the United States. That restraint, therefore, upon the congressional power of taxation, if it be a restraint, is of moral, and not of legal, sanction.

16. Section 9 of article I of the Constitution declares that, "no capitation, or other direct tax, shall be laid, unless in proportion to the census or enumeration hereinbefore directed to be taken." "Direct" taxes are capitation taxes, and taxes on real property, as, for instance, the tax imposed on land by the Act of 6 February, 1863.[1] Neither taxes laid on "carriages for the conveyance of persons,"[2] nor on personal incomes,[3] nor on distilled spirits,[4] nor succession duties on the "devolution of title to real estate,"[5] nor taxes on the notes of state banks paid out by national banking associations,[6] nor taxes on the receipts of insurance companies from premiums and assessments,[7] are direct taxes, but all such taxes are imposts or excises. The requirement that direct taxes must be laid "in proportion to the census or enumeration" is not violated by the statutory imposition of a penalty for non-payment of the tax.[8]

17. The only constitutional requirement with regard to imposts and excises is, that they "shall be uniform throughout the United States," and that requirement is satisfied, when the tax operates with the same effect in all places where the subject of taxation is found, though that subject be not equally distributed in all parts of the United States.[9]

18. The United States cannot, however, tax the

[1] 12. Stat. 640.
[2] Hylton v. U. S., 3 Dall. 171.
[3] Springer v. U. S., 102 U.S. 586.
[4] U. S. v. Singer, 15 Wall. 111.
[5] Scholey v. Reed, 23 Wall. 331.
[6] Veazie Bank v. Fenno, 8 Wall. 533; National Bank v. U. S., 101 U. S. 1.
[7] Pacific Insurance Company v. Soule, 7 Wall. 433.
[8] De Treville v. Smalls, 98 U. S 517.
[9] The Head Money Cases, 112 U. S. 580.

agencies of a state, as, for instance, the salary of a judicial officer of a state[1] nor the revenue of a municipal corporation derived from its loan of capital to a railway.[2]

19. The duty on the transportation of passengers by sea from foreign countries imposed by the United States in the exercise of the power of regulating commerce, not being in its nature a tax, is not subject to the constitutional restrictions on the exercise of the power of taxation,[3] and the same view has been taken of the tax imposed by the United States on the circulating notes of state banks for the purpose of preventing the circulation of any other than national bank notes.[4]

20. A state may, so far as it is not restrained by the Constitution, tax all persons, natural or corporate, and all property, real or personal, within its territory and subject to its sovereignty, and may regulate, in the exercise of legislative discretion, the manner of levying and collecting its taxes,[5] and the United States cannot, either by legislative or judicial action, afford any relief against " state taxation, however unjust, oppressive, or onerous," so long as that taxation " does not entrench upon the legitimate authority of the Union, or violate any right recognized or secured by the Constitution of the United States."[6]

Under the general rule which permits a government to tax all persons and property within its jurisdiction, the states may impose a succession duty on the devolu-

[1] The Collector *v.* Day, 11 Wall. 113.
[2] U. S. *v.* B. & O. R. R., 17 Wall. 322.
[3] The Head Money Cases, 112 U. S. 580.
[4] Veazie Bank *v.* Fenno, 8 Wall. 533.
[5] Witherspoon *v.* Duncan, 4 Wall. 210.
[6] Providence Bank *v.* Billings, 4 Pet. 563; St. Louis *v.* Ferry Co., 11 Wall. 423; The State Tax on Foreign Held Bonds, 15 *id.* 300; Kirtland *v.* Hotchkiss 100 U. S. 491, 498; Memphis Gas Co. *v.* Shelby County, 109 *id.* 398; Carpenter *v.* Pennsylvania, 17 How. 456.

tion of title to real estate from their citizens to alien non-residents;[1] they may tax goods and chattels which are actually within the state, when assessed for taxation, though owned by a non-resident;[2] and, for purposes of taxation, the *situs* of a debt being the residence of the creditor, the state may include in the taxable property of a resident so much of the registered public debt of another state as such resident may hold, although the debtor state may either exempt it from taxation or actually tax it.[3] On the same principle a state may tax her resident citizens for debts due to them by a non-resident and secured by his bond and also by his deed of trust or mortgage of real estate situated in another state.[4] As until the period of distribution arrives, the law of a decedent's domicile attaches to his personal property, that property is subject to a state collateral inheritance tax, though bequeathed by his will to non-resident legatees.[5] But the laws of a state can have no extra territorial effect, and, therefore, a state cannot, as a means of taxing corporate bonds held by non-residents, authorize the corporation to retain from the interest due on its bonds the amount of the tax.[6] Nor can a state tax in the hands of a non-resident holder corporate bonds issued under a mortgage of a railway formed by the consolidation of corporations, incorporated by the state, and other corporations incorporated by another state, and encumbering by a consolidated and non-severable lien property which is not within the jurisdiction of the taxing state.[7]

[1] Mager v. Grima, 8 How. 490.
[2] Coe v. Errol, 116 U. S. 517.
[3] Bonaparte v. Tax Court, 104 U. S. 592.
[4] Kirtland v. Hotchkiss, 100 U. S. 491.
[5] Carpenter v. Pennsylvania, 17 How. 456.
[6] Case of the State Tax on Foreign Held Bonds, 15 Wall. 301.
[7] R. R. v. Jackson, 7 Wall. 262.

21. Section 10 of article I of the Constitution declares, that "no state shall, without the consent of the Congress, lay any imposts or duties on imports or exports, except what may be absolutely necessary for executing its inspection laws; and the net produce of all duties and imposts, laid by any state on imports or exports, shall be for the use of the treasury of the United States; and all such laws shall be subject to the revision and control of the Congress. No state shall, without the consent of the Congress, lay any duty of tonnage." The nature and effect of the restrictions upon the taxing power of the states imposed by these constitutional provisions are more fully discussed in Chapter IV, and it is sufficient to say in this connection that a state cannot require importers of foreign goods by the bale or package and wholesale vendors of such goods to pay a license fee;[1] nor can a state impose an *ad valorem* tax on imported goods remaining in their original cases in the hands of the importer;[2] nor can a state tax an auctioneers' sales of imported goods for account of the importers;[3] but a state may prohibit the exportation of tobacco grown within its territory, save after inspection and on payment of a tax.[4] A state cannot tax ships upon their tonnage.[5]

22. The supremacy of the United States under the Constitution impliedly limits to some extent the exercise by the states of the power of taxation. Thus, a state can not tax the official salary of an officer of the United States, as, for instance, an officer in the revenue marine

---

[1] Brown *v.* Maryland, 12 Wheat. 419.
[2] Low *v.* Austin, 13 Wall 29.
[3] Cook *v.* Pennsylvania, 97 U. S. 566.
[4] Turner *v.* Maryland, 107 U. S. 38.
[5] State Tonnage Tax Cases, 12 Wall. 212; Steamship Co. *v.* Board of Wardens, 6 Wall. 31; Peeter. Morgan, 19 *id.* 581; Cannon *v.* New Orleans, 20 *id.* 577; I. S. S. Co. *v.* Tinker, 94 U. S. 238.

service;[1] nor can a state tax a telegraph company upon messages sent by officers of the United States on public business;[2] nor can a state authorize municipal taxation of the bonds issued by the government of the United States for money loaned to it;[3] nor can a state tax the notes of the United States;[4] nor can a state tax so much of the capital of a state bank as is invested in the bonds of the United States, that capital being assessed either at its actual value,[5] or at a valuation equal to the amount paid in, or secured to be paid in.[6] But a court will not aid, by the exercise of its equitable powers, a party who, for the purpose of evading state taxation of his money on deposit, makes a temporary investment of that money in the notes of the United States.[7] A corporation claiming an exemption from state taxation by reason of the investment of its surplus funds in the legal tender notes of the United States has, of course, the burden of proving the fact on which it rests its claim for exemption.[8] A state tax of a certain percentage of the total amount of the deposits on a given day,[9] or of the average amount of the deposits for a fixed period[10] of a saving fund society chartered by the state, and a state tax of a certain percentage upon the excess of the market value of the shares of the capital of a corporation chartered by a state over and above the value of its real estate and machinery[11]

---

[1] Dobbins v. The Commissioners of Erie Co., 16 Pet. 435.
[2] Telegraph Co. v. Texas, 105 U. S. 460.
[3] Weston v. Charleston, 2 Pet. 449; The Banks v. The Mayor, 7 Wall. 16.
[4] Bank v. Supervisors, 7 Wall. 26.
[5] The People v. The Commissioners of Taxes, 2 Black 620.
[6] The Bank Tax Case, 2 Wall. 200.
[7] Mitchell v. The Commissioners, 91 U. S. 206.
[8] C. & B. Co. v. New Orleans, 99 U. S. 97.
[9] Society for Savings v. Coite, 6 Wall. 594.
[10] Provident Institution v. Massachusetts, 6 Wall. 611.
[11] Hamilton Co. v. Massachusetts, 6 Wall. 632.

are in each case, a tax on the franchise and not on the property of the corporation, and the corporation cannot claim exemption from such taxation by reason of the investment, in the case of the saving funds, of their deposits, and in the case of the other corporations, of their capital and assets in the bonds of the United States. A state cannot tax lands held in severalty by members of an Indian tribe and protected by treaties between the United States and the tribe.[1] A state cannot tax public lands of the United States, though granted to a railway, but for which patents have not been issued, nor costs of survey paid, but from and after the vesting of an equitable title in any person the lands are subject to state taxation, though the costs of survey have not been paid.[2] Lands granted by act of Congress to a state, to be held by it to aid in the construction of a railway, though not taxable by the state when held by it as trustee, are taxable by it after their conveyance to the railway,[3] and, of course, in the case of lands ceded by a state to the United States for the construction of a railway, with an express reservation of the state's right of taxation, the state may lawfully exercise that right,[4] but land within a state, which, under laws of Congress for the collection of taxes due to the United States, has been sold for non-payment of such taxes, and at the sale thereof purchased by the United States and afterwards sold by the United States to a third party, or redeemed by the owner, is exempt from state taxation during the period of federal ownership thereof.[5] Although the title to land remain in

[1] The Kansas Indians, 5 Wall. 737; The New York Indians, *ibid.* 761.
[2] U. P. R. R. *v.* McShane, 22 Wall. 444; R. R. *v.* Prescott, 16 Wall. 603, Carroll *v.* Safford, 3 How. 441.
[3] Tucker *v.* Ferguson, 22 Wall. 527.
[4] F. L. R. R. *v.* Lowe, 114 U. S. 525.
[5] Van Brocklin *v.* Tennessee, 117 U. S. 151.

the United State, ore dug therefrom under a mineral claim is, as the personal property of the claimant, subject to state taxation.[1] The exemption of federal agencies from state taxation is dependent, not on the fact of the agency, nor on the character of the agents, nor on the mode of their appointment, but on the effect of state interference in depriving the agent of power to serve the government of the United States, or in hindering the agent in the efficient exercise of that power.[2] A state may, therefore, tax the property, real and personal, of a railroad, which has been chartered by act of Congress, is subject to a lien securing its debt to the United States, and is used as a federal agency for the transportation of mails, soldiers, government, supplies, and munitions of war;[3] and, it would seem, on the principle of that case, that a state may tax the property of any federal agency, wherever such taxation does not impair the efficiency of the agency in the performance of its duty to the government of the United States. The federal supremacy forbids a state to so tax the transit of passengers through the state by the ordinary modes of travel, as to impede their approach to the seat of government of the United States, the ports of entry through which commerce is conducted, and the various federal offices in the states.[4] The supremacy of the United States does not involve an exemption from state taxation of property which has been acquired by the exercise of an exclusive privilege granted by the United States, when there is no relation of agency between the United States and the grantee, thus letters patent, granted by the United

[1] Forbes *v.* Gracey, 94 U. S. 762.
[2] U. P. R. R. *v.* Peniston, 18 Wall. 5; National Bank *v.* The Commonwealth, 9 *id.* 353; Thompson *v.* P. R. R., *id.* 579.
[3] U. P. R. R. *v.* Peniston, 18 Wall. 5.
[4] Crandall *v.* State of Nevada, 6 Wall. 35.

States, do not exempt from state taxation the tangible property in which the invention or discovery is embodied.[1] Nor does a license granted, on payment of a license fee, by the United States under its Internal Revenue Statutes to a wholesale liquor dealer in a state exempt the dealer, or his business, or his goods from state control, regulation, or taxation.[2]

23. A state cannot tax the operations of banks incorporated by the government of the United States as fiscal agencies.[3] Nor can a state tax the assets of an insolvent national bank in the hands of a receiver appointed under the provisions of the national banking laws.[4] Of course, when Congress licenses state taxation of agencies of the government of the United States, such taxation is permissible within the limits imposed by the terms of the license;[5] thus in the case of national banks, state taxation is by the 41st section of the Act of 3 June, 1864,[6] permitted as to the shares in any bank, when "included in the valuation of the personal property of the owner or holder of such shares, in assessing taxes imposed by authority of the state within which the association is located," . . . . "subject only to the restrictions, that the taxation shall not be at a greater rate than is assessed upon other moneyed capital in the hands of individual citizens of such state, and that the shares of any national banking association owned by non-residents of any state shall be taxed in the city or town where the bank is located, and not

---

[1] Webber *v.* Virginia, 103 U. S. 344.
[2] McGuire *v.* The Commonwealth, 3 Wall. 387; Pervear *v.* The Commonwealth, 5 *id.* 475.
[3] McCulloch *v.* The State of Maryland, 4 Wheat. 316; Osborne *v.* The Bank of the U. S., 9 *id.* 738.
[4] Rosenblatt *v.* Johnston, 104 U. S. 462.
[5] Van Allen *v.* The Assessors, 3 Wall. 573; People *v.* The Commissioners, 4 *id.* 244.
[6] 15 Stat. 34, Rev. Stat. Sec. 5219.

elsewhere. The states may, therefore, tax shareholders in national banks within the limits of this license,[1] without regard to the investment of all or any part of the capital of the banks in United States securities. The National Bank Act of 3 June, 1864,[2] had imposed a further restriction on state taxation of national bank shares, declaring that such tax "shall not exceed the rate imposed upon the shares in any of the banks organized under the authority of the state," but in the re-enactment of this statute in 1868,[3] and in the Revised Statutes,[4] this condition was omitted. Under the Act of 1864 it was held that a state could not tax shares in national banks, when it taxed the capital of state banks, exempting so much thereof as was invested in the bonds of the United States, and failed to tax the shares of state banks.[5] It was also held that the limitation upon disparity of state taxation imposed by the Act of 1864 is not overstepped by a state which, having only two banks of issue and circulation, and having by contract bound itself not to tax these banks beyond a certain limit, but having numerous banks of deposit, which do not issue circulation, taxes generally and equally all shares of stock in banks and incorporated companies doing business in the state.[6] The terms of section 5219 of the Revised Statutes show clearly that Congress did not intend to curtail the taxing power of the states over national bank shares as entities distinct from the capital of the banks, and as the property of persons subject to state jurisdiction, but that it was in-

---

[1] National Bank *v.* The Commonwealth, 9 Wall. 353; People *v.* Commissioners, 4 *id.* 244; Van Allen *v.* The Assessors, 3 *id.* 573.
[2] 13 Stat. 111.
[3] 15 Stat. 34.
[4] Sec. 5219.
[5] Van Allen *v.* The Assessors, 3 Wall. 57; Bradley *v.* The People, 4 *id.* 459.
[6] Lionberger *v.* Rouse, 9 Wall. 468.

tended to guard the national banks against unfriendly discrimination by the states in the exercise of that taxing power.[1] The phrase "moneyed capital" includes capital employed in national banks and capital employed by individuals for the making of profit by its use, but it does not include capital in the hands of a corporation.[2] Therefore, the exemption from state taxation of some but not all of the moneyed capital in the state is not a discrimination against national bank shares within the terms of the license; as, for instance, in the case of exemption of "all mortgages, judgments, recognizances, and moneys owing upon articles of agreement for the sale of real estate;"[3] or of deposits in savings banks, shares in trust companies, and shares in other moneyed or stock corporations chartered by the state and deriving an income or profit from the use of their capital or otherwise.[4] Nor is there any inequality of taxation or unfriendly discrimination as against national bank shares, in the exemption by a state of that which it cannot lawfully tax, such as, shares owned by its residents in the capital stock of foreign corporations,[5] or in the exemption of that which is not a subject of taxation by the United States, such as the bonds of a municipal corporation created by the state;[6] but where a very material part of the other moneyed capital of a state in the hands of individual citizens within the state is exempted from state taxation, the state cannot tax the shares of national banks.[7]

[1] Adams v. Nashville, 95 U. S. 19; Mercantile Bank v. New York, 121 U. S. 138.
[2] Mercantile Bank v. New York, 121 U. S. 138.
[3] Hepburn v. The School Directors, 23 Wall. 480.
[4] Mercantile Bank v. New York, 121 U. S. 138.
[5] Mercantile Bank v. New York, 121 U. S. 138, 162.
[6] Mercantile Bank v. New York, 121 U. S. 138, 162.
[7] Boyer v. Boyer, 113 U. S. 689.

State statutes taxing personal property, including national bank shares, and permitting the party taxed to deduct his just debts from the valuation of his personal property other than national bank shares, tax such shares at a greater rate than other moneyed capital, and, therefore, are not effective under the terms of the license given by Congress;[1] but in the case of a national bank shareholder, who has no just debts to deduct, the taxing law is valid and operative.[2] A state may, under the act of Congress, tax the shares of a bank located within its jurisdiction without regard to the non-resident or resident ownership of such shares,[3] and the shares may be assessed for purpose of state taxation at their market value, though that exceed their par value.[4] But state taxation of national bank shares must be uniform and equal, and when a system of valuation for taxation purposes intended to operate unequally is adopted by the state authorities, whose duty it is to make the assessment, equity may properly interfere, on payment of the proper tax, to enjoin the collection of the illegal excess.[5] But where a state has provided a mode for the correction of error in the assessment of property for purposes of taxation, a party, aggrieved by an over-valuation of his property, cannot maintain an action at law to recover the alleged illegal excess of taxes paid by him, for the official action of the revising authority is judicial in character, and cannot be collaterally impeached.[6] A state may lawfully require a

[1] People v. Weaver, 100 U. S. 539; Supervisors v. Stanley, 105 id. 305; Hills v. Exchange Bank, id. 319; Evansville Bank v. Britton, id. 322.

[2] Supervisors v. Stanley, 105 U. S. 305.

[3] Tappan v. M. N. Bank, 19 Wall. 490.

[4] Hepburn v. The School Directors, 23 Wall. 480; People v. Commissioners of Taxes, 94 U. S. 415.

[5] Cummings v. M. National Bank of Toledo, 101 U. S. 153; Pelton v. National Bank, 101 U. S. 143; People v. Weaver, 100 U. S. 539.

[6] Stanley v. Supervisors, 121 U. S. 535.

national bank to act as the agent of the state in collecting from the shareholders of the bank the tax imposed by the state within the limits permitted by the act of Congress.[1] A state may also, under a penalty for his non-performance of the duty, require a cashier of a national bank to furnish to the state authorities a list of the names and respective holdings of the shareholders of his bank.[2]

24. The constitutional prohibition of the enactment by the states of laws impairing the obligation of contracts affects to some extent the exercise by the states of the power of taxation. While, as a general rule, the states may, in the exercise of legislative discretion, either tax property or exempt it from taxation, yet contracts of exemption from state taxation, not in terms contravening federal[3] or state[4] constitutional prohibitions, and contained in corporate charters[5] or stipulated by express agreement,[6] if supported by an adequate consideration, constitute contracts so binding upon the state, that their obligation is not to be permitted to be impaired by a subsequent legislative repeal of the charter, or by an imposition of a rate of taxation inconsistent with the state's contract.[7] But there cannot be implied from the grant of a charter an exemption of the corporate franchise or property from state taxation,[8] and the imposition in a charter of a specific form or rate of taxation is not, in the absence of an express

[1] National Bank v. The Commonwealth, 9 Wall. 353.
[2] Waite v Dowley, 94 U. S. 527.
[3] People v. Commissioners of Taxes, 94 U. S. 415.
[4] R. R. Co. v. Gaines, 97 U. S. 697; Trask v. Magwire, 18 Wall. 391; Morgan v. Louisiana, 93 U S. 217; Shields v. Ohio, 95 id. 319.
[5] J. B. Bank v. Skelly, 1 Bl. 436.
[6] New Jersey v. Wilson, 7 Cr. 64; New Jersey v. Yard, 95 U. S. 104.
[7] J. B. Bank v. Skelly, 1 Bl. 436; W. R. R. v. Reid, 18 Wall. 264; R. & G. R. v. Same, ibid. 269; Chicago v. Sheldon, 9 id. 50; P. R. R. v. Magwire, 20 id. 36; University v. People, 99 U. S. 309; Asylum v. New Orleans, 105 id. 362
[8] Providence Bank v. Billings, 4 Pet. 575; M. G. L. Co. v. Shelby County, 109 U. S. 398; Tucker v. Ferguson, 22 Wall. 527.

contract of exemption from other taxation, to be construed as an implied exemption from such other taxation,[1] and contracts of exemption from state taxation, when expressly made, are to be strictly construed.[2] A municipal corporation cannot, by the exercise of a statutory power of taxation, diminish the interest payable to the holder of a funded obligation of the municipality under the terms of the bond.[3] The subject of exemption by contract from state taxation is more fully discussed in Chapter V.

25. The constitutional grant to Congress of the power of regulating " commerce with foreign nations, and among the several states, and with the Indian tribes " also affects to some extent the exercise by the states of the power of taxation, but the states are not prohibited from taxing either the instrumentalities, or the subjects, of foreign or interstate commerce, provided that such taxation be imposed on those instrumentalities and subjects as component parts of the mass of property in the state, or by reason of the citizenship of their owners as subjects of the sovereignty of the state, and provided also, that that, which is in form taxation, be not in substance a regulation of, or a restraint upon, foreign or interstate commerce.[4] In accordance with this distinction, a state may tax ships and ferry boats as the personal property of their owners, where either the owner, by reason of his residence, or the property because of its *situs* is subject to the taxing power of

---

[1] The Delaware R. R. Tax, 18 Wall. 206; Erie Ry. v. Penna., 21 *id*. 492; The License Tax Cases, 5 *id*. 462; Home Insurance Company v. Augusta, 93 U. S. 116.

[2] Tucker v. Ferguson, 22 Wall. 527; W. F. Co. v. East St. Louis, 107 U. S. 365; U. P. Ry. v. Philadelphia, 101 U. S. 528; R. R. v. Gaines, 97 *id*. 697; Tomlinson v. Branch, 15 Wall. 460.

[3] Murray v. Charleston, 96 U. S. 432.

[4] Gibbons v. Ogden, 9 Wheat. 201; The Passenger Cases, 7 How. 479; Transportation Co. v. Wheeling, 99 U. S. 280; W. F. Co. v. East St. Louis, 107 *id*. 374.

the state;[1] and a state may tax goods brought from another state and mingled with the mass of property in the taxing state,[2] and goods within the state, intended for transportation to another state but not actually started on their voyage;[3] provided that the taxation is not so imposed as to discriminate against either the natural products of, or goods manufactured in, another state.[4] A state has the right to tax its own citizens for the prosecution of any particular business or profession within the state, even if that business be indirectly concerned with commerce; thus, a state may tax exchange brokers, and the fact that bills of exchange are instruments of foreign and interstate commerce will not relieve the broker from such taxation.[5] If property within a state and otherwise liable to taxation be in money at the date of its assessment for taxation, a subsequent investment thereof in a subject of commerce does not relieve that capital from liability to state taxation.[6] While a state cannot tax the interstate transportation of passengers or goods, it may require express companies doing business within its bounds by making contracts for interstate transportation to pay license fees;[7] it may tax its railway companies upon the cash value of their capital stock,[8] and it may by its charter of a railway charge a toll payable

---

[1] W. F. Co. v. East St. Louis 107 U. S. 365; Transportation Co. v. Wheeling, 99 id. 273.

[2] Woodruff v. Parham, 8 Wall. 173; Brown v. Houston, 114 U. S. 622.

[3] Coe v. Errol, 116 U. S. 517.

[4] Ward v. Maryland, 12 Wall. 418; Welton v. Missouri, 91 U. S. 275; Webber v. Virginia, 103 id. 344; Guy v. Baltimore, 100 id. 434; Corson v. Maryland, 120 id. 502; Walling v. Michigan, 116 id. 446; Robbins v. Shelby County, 120 id. 489; Sed. cf. Machine Co. v. Gage, 100 U. S. 676; Hinson v. Lott, 8 Wall. 148; Tiernan v. Rinker, 102 U. S. 123; Downham v. Alexandria Council, 10 Wall. 173.

[5] Nathan v. Louisiana, 8 How. 73.

[6] People v. The Commissioners, 104 U. S. 466.

[7] Osborne v. Mobile, 16 Wall. 479.

[8] The Delaware R. R. Tax, 18 Wall. 206.

to the state for the use of the improved facilities of travel furnished by the railway.[1] On the other hand, the states may not tax ships or ferry boats, when the owner is not by residence subject to the taxing power of the state, and when the ships or ferry boats only come within the jurisdiction of the state in the prosecution of foreign or interstate commerce.[2] Nor can a state tax the transportation of passengers coming by water into its ports from a foreign country or from another state;[3] nor can a state tax the interstate transportation of goods by water;[4] nor can a state impose port dues, that is, charges payable by all vessels, entering, remaining in, or leaving a port without regard to services rendered to, or received by, the vessel;[5] nor can a state tax a telegraph company upon messages transmitted by it to points outside of the state;[6] nor can a state tax the interstate transportation of passengers or goods. It, therefore, cannot tax interstate freight by the pound;[7] nor can it tax the operation of sleeping-cars, owned by a foreign corporation;[8] nor can it tax the gross receipts of corporations engaged in the business of running cars not their own property over a railway line within the state.[9]

[1] B. & O. R. R. v. Maryland, 21 Wall. 456.

[2] St. Louis v. W. F. Co., 11 Wall. 423; G. F. Co. v. Pennsylvania, 114 U. S. 196; P. & S. S. S. Co. v. Pennsylvania, 122 id. 326; Hays v. P. M. S. S. Co., 17 How. 596; Morgan v. Parham, 16 Wall. 471; Moran v. New Orleans, 112 U. S. 69.

[3] The Passenger Cases, 7 How. 283; Henderson v. The Mayor, 92 U. S. 259; Commissioners of Immigration v. North German Lloyd, ibid. 269; Chy-Lung v. Freeman, ibid. 275; People v. Compagnie Generale Transatlantique, 107 U. S. 59; P. & S. S. Co. v. Pennsylvania, 122 U. S. 326, overruling the case of the State Tax on Railway Gross Receipts, 15 Wall. 284.

[4] Almy v. California, 24 How. 169.

[5] Steamship Co. v. Port Wardens, 6 Wall. 31.

[6] W. U. T. Co. v. Texas, 105 U. S. 460.

[7] The State Freight Tax, 15 Wall. 232; Erie Ry. v. Pennsylvania, ibid. 282, note.

[8] Pickard v. P. S. C. Co., 117 U. S. 34; Tennessee v. P. S. C. Co., ibid. 51.

[9] Fargo v. Michigan, 121 U. S. 230.

# CHAPTER IV.

## THE REGULATION OF COMMERCE.

26. The constitutional provisions.
27. The history of the commercial clause.
28. Commerce defined.
29. The regulation of commerce defined.
30. The general distinction between the powers of the United States and of the states over commerce.
31. Navigable waters.
32. Title to the soil under navigable waters.
33. The regulation of navigation.
34. The regulation of subjects of commerce.
35. The taxation of ships.
36. Duties on tonnage.
37. The taxation of the water transportation of passengers.
38. The taxation of goods in interstate commerce.
39. Discriminating taxation against products and manufactures of other rates.
40. The taxation of exports by the United States.
41. State taxation of imports and exports, and inspection laws.
42. Improvements of navigation.
43. Dams and bridges.
44. Ferries.
45. Wharves and piers.
46. Pilotage.
47. Quarantine and sanitary regulations.
48. Port dues.
49. Port regulations.
50. Preferences of ports.
51. Interstate railway transportation.
52. Railway tolls.
53. The police regulation of railways.
54. State taxation of interstate transportation by railways.
55. Telegraphs.
56. Commerce with the Indian tribes.

26. The Constitution of the United States contains three clauses which directly bear upon the regulation of commerce. Section 8 of article I declares that " the

Congress shall have power . . . to regulate commerce with foreign nations, and among the several states, and with the Indian tribes." Section 9 of the same article enumerates among the exceptions from the powers granted to the United States, that " no tax or duty shall be laid on articles exported from any state. No preference shall be given, by any regulation of commerce or revenue, to the ports of one state over those of another ; nor shall vessels bound to or from one state be obliged to enter, clear, or pay duties in another." Section 10 of the same article, in its enumeration of the expressed restrictions upon the powers of the states, declares, that "no state shall, without the consent of the Congress, lay any imposts or duties on imports or exports, except what may be absolutely necessary for executing its inspection laws : and the net produce of all duties and imposts, laid by any state on imports or exports, shall be for the use of the treasury of the United States; and all such laws shall be subject to the revision and control of the Congress. No state shall, without the consent of the Congress, lay any duty of tonnage." There are also other clauses of the Constitution, which indirectly affect the regulation of commerce by the states. Thus, an act of a state legislature may be valid as a regulation of commerce in a matter of merely local concern, and yet the act, as affecting a particular person or corporation may be void as an impairment of the obligation of a legally enforcible contract, or the act may be void for repugnancy to those other clauses of the Constitution which, having regard to the rights of citizenship, forbid a state to discriminate in favour of its own citizens and against the rights of citizens of other states. These constitutional provisions are not only in full force and vigour to-day, but their application is wider and more far-reaching than the framers of the Constitution imagined to be within the bounds of possibility. In the century that has passed since the adoption of the Constitution the country has made great strides. Less than three millions of people have grown to be more than fifty millions in number. Discoveries in science and inventions in the arts have developed new subjects of trade, and have created new agencies of commerce. Steam and electricity have been made to do man's bidding. Sailing vessels have given way to steamships, and railways have superseded turnpike roads and Conestoga wagons. Telegraphs and telephones have annihilated distance. The growth of population, the creation of new subjects of trade, and the improvements in the movement of traffic have necessarily resulted in a vast enlargement in the volume of commerce. In view of these great changes in the conditions of the problem, it is more than ever important that the constitutional limits upon the regulation of commerce should be clearly comprehended, and that the line which separates the provinces of federal and of state authority over this subject of national interest should be, so far as is possible, accurately defined.

27. It is an historical fact that the Constitution was framed and adopted mainly because all of the states had suffered under the Confederation by reason of the selfish commercial policy of England in closing her markets to goods of American manufacture, and because some of the states had also suffered by reason of the no less selfish commercial policy of other states in the imposition of heavy duties on imported goods, and in the enforcement of vexatious restrictions upon trade. There were great differences of opinion as to other features of the Constitution, but, in the convention of 1787 and among the people, there was practical unanimity as to the expediency of vesting in the government of the

United States the power of so regulating commerce as to overcome the disintegrating forces which threatened the loss of all that had been gained by the success of the Revolution.[1]

28. The term "commerce," therefore, as the framers of the Constitution understood it, and as Marshall, C. J., construed it in Gibbons v. Ogden,[2] meant not only traffic, but also commercial intercourse in all its branches, including the purchase and sale of commodities, their transportation by sea and on land, their importation and exportation, and all that was necessarily incident to the transaction. As the Constitution is a frame of government intended to endure for all time, it follows that the term "commerce" must receive a construction sufficiently elastic to comprehend not only the subjects and instrumentalities of commerce known and used when the Constitution was framed, but also all present and future subjects of commerce and agencies of commercial intercourse.[3] Yet everything that is connected with commerce is not necessarily commerce. Bills of exchange may be given in payment for goods to be imported, and yet such bills are mere personal obligations, and are not in themselves subjects of commerce.[4] On the same principle, the issuing or negotiation of a policy of insurance against the loss by fire of any property, which is not made a subject of commerce, does not constitute a transaction of commerce.[5] So

---

[1] Gibbons v. Ogden, 9 Wheat. 11, 223; Brown v. Maryland, 12 id. 445; Cook v. Pennsylvania, 97 U. S. 574; County of Mobile v. Kimball, 102 id. 697; Chapters IV, V, VI, VII, and VIII of Mr. Bancroft's History of the Constitution.

[2] 9 Wheat. 1, 189.

[3] P. Telegraph Co. v. W. U. Telegraph Co., 96 U. S. 1.

[4] Bank of Augusta v. Earle, 13 Pet. 519, 531; Sturges v. Crowninshield, 4 Wheat. 147; Nathan v. Louisiana, 8 How. 73.

[5] Paul v. Virginia, 8 Wall. 168; Ducat v. Chicago, 10 Wall. 410; L. I. Co. v. Massachusetts, ibid. 566; P. F. Association v. New York, 119 U. S. 110.

also, a trade-mark, which identifies a particular article as one of a class which has as such acquired a special commercial value, is not in itself any part of commerce.[1] On the other hand, bills of lading of goods sold and transported in the course of interstate commerce are, by reason of their representative character, entitled to protection as commerce,[2] and the transmission of ideas by telegraph is commerce, for the reason that in the development of modern business methods the telegraph has become indispensable as a means of intercommunication in commercial intercourse.[3] Would not the same reasoning apply, in the case of goods admittedly subjects of commerce, to the trade-marks on such goods, the bills of exchange drawn for the price of the goods, and the policies of insurance against the loss of the goods by fire, or by the perils of navigation? Insurance, commercial paper, and trade-marks are as certainly nearly related to, and as truly incidents of commerce, as a telegraphic inquiry as to the state of the market, or a telegraphic order for the forwarding of the goods, though unlike the bill of lading, they do not represent the goods. Of course, if the subject-matter be in its nature commercial, it is immaterial whether the agency, by which commerce is carried on, be a natural person, or an association of natural persons, or a corporation.[4]

29. To regulate commerce is, as Marshall, C. J., said in Gibbons v. Ogden,[5] "to prescribe the rule by which commerce is to be governed." It is obvious that com-

---

[1] The Trade-Mark Cases, 100 U. S. 82, 95.
[2] Almy v. California, 24 How. 169; as explained by Miller, J., in Woodruff v. Parham, 8 Wall. 138.
[3] P. Telegraph Co. v. W. U. Telegraph Co, 96 U. S. 1, 9.
[4] Paul v. Virginia, 8 Wall. 168, 172; G. F. Co. v. Penna., 114 U. S. 196, 215, 217; W. F. Co. v. East St. Louis, 107 id. 374.
[5] 9 Wheat. 1, 196.

merce may be directly regulated by rules prescribing the manner in which its operations are to be conducted, or it may be indirectly regulated by the imposition of taxation upon its subjects or its instrumentalities. In Philadelphia and Southern Steamship Company v. Pennsylvania,[1] Bradley, J., said, "taxing is one of the forms of regulation. It is one of the principal forms." In Gibbons v. Ogden,[2] Marshall, C. J., clearly distinguishes between the power to regulate commerce and the power to tax, and it is a legitimate conclusion from that distinction, that Congress cannot, in the exercise of the power to regulate, tax commerce, and that the states are not prohibited from taxing either the instrumentalities or the subjects of foreign or interstate commerce, provided that such taxation be imposed on those instrumentalities and subjects of commerce as component parts of the mass of property in the country, and provided also that that which is in form taxation be not in substance a regulation, or, in other words, a restraint upon, or a prohibition of, foreign or interstate commerce. Taney, C. J., said in the Passenger Cases,[3] "it has always been held that the power to regulate commerce does not give to Congress the power to tax it, nor prohibit the states from taxing it in their own ports and within their own jurisdiction. The authority of Congress to lay taxes upon it is derived from the express grant of power in the eighth section of the first article to lay and collect taxes, duties, imposts, and excises, and the inability of the states to tax it arises from the express prohibition contained in the tenth section of the same article." In the same case,[4] McLean, J., said, "a state cannot regulate foreign commerce, but it may do many things which more

[1] 122 U. S. 336.
[2] 9 Wheat. 201.
[3] 7 How. 479.
[4] p. 402.

or less affect it. It may tax a ship or other vessel used in commerce the same as other property owned by its citizens. A state may tax the stages in which the mail is transported, but this does not regulate the conveyance of the mail any more than taxing a ship regulates commerce, and yet in both instances the tax on the property in some degree affects its use." The essential difference between taxation of commerce as property and regulation of commerce in the guise of taxation is elaborated in the judgments in Transportation Co. *v.* Wheeling[1] and in Wiggins Ferry Co. *v.* East St. Louis[2] and is illustrated by every case in which the Supreme Court of the United States has had to determine whether any particular tax imposed under state authority on a subject, or instrumentality, of foreign or interstate commerce be permitted, or forbidden, by the Constitution.

30. Recurring to the constitutional provisions affecting the regulations of commerce, as quoted in Sec. 27, and bearing in mind the general principles of constitutional construction, it will be observed that the constitutional provisions include: (1) an express grant to Congress of the power of regulating commerce "with foreign nations, and among the several states and with the Indian tribes;" with the expressed restriction that the United States shall not lay any tax or duty on articles exported from any state, nor give any preference, by any regulation of commerce, to the ports of one state over those of another, nor oblige vessels bound to or from one state to enter, clear, and pay duties in another; (2) an implied restraint upon state regulation of commerce, foreign, interstate, or with the Indian tribes; and (3) an expressed prohibition of state duties on imports, exports, and tonnage, save under certain defined restric-

[1] 99 U. S. 230.   [2] 107 U. S. 374.

tions, the most material of which restrictions is the consent of Congress. It is obvious that the power delegated to Congress is that of regulating, not all commerce, but commerce only of enumerated kinds, and under expressed restrictions. The result of the authorities, so far as they deal with the expressed grant of power to Congress, and the consequent implied restrictions upon the states, is that the internal commerce of a state, that is, that commerce which is begun, continued, and ended within a state, is exclusively a subject for the regulation of that state; and that foreign and interstate commerce, that is, that commerce, which, in its inception, or at any point of its progress, or at its conclusion, passes beyond the boundary of a state, is a subject of final regulation by Congress, but that, until Congress has regulated such commerce, the state may incidentally regulate it in points of merely local concern. The general distinction was clearly put by Marshall, C. J., when he said in Gibbons v. Ogden,[1] "the genius and character of the whole government seems to be, that its action is to be applied to all the external concerns of the nation, and to those internal concerns, which affect the states generally, but not to those which are completely within a particular state, which do not affect other states, and with which it is not necessary to interfere for the purpose of executing some of the general powers of the government. The completely internal commerce of a state, then, may be considered as reserved for the state itself." In the exercise of its power over commerce, Congress has regulated the registration and recording of the titles of ships,[2] the clearance and entry of ships and steamers,[3] the tonnage duties payable to the United States by vessels;[4] navi-

---

[1] 9 Wheat. 294
[2] Rev. Stat. Sec. 141, 31 et seq.
[3] Rev. Stat. 141, 97 et seq.
[4] Rev. Stat. 4219.

gation, including sailing rules, and the life-saving service,[1] the transportation of passengers and merchandise by sea,[2] the shipping of sailors,[3] and their pay and discharge;[4] the lighthouse service;[5] the coast survey;[6] the improvement of rivers and harbours;[7] and telegraphs.[8] It has authorized the transportation of government supplies, and mails, and troops by railway, and the connection of railways of different states so as to form a continuous line,[9] and by the Interstate Commerce Act[10] it has regulated the interstate transportation of passengers and freight by railways and it has constituted a commission to carry the statute into effect. The states have facilitated commerce by the improvement of navigation, the construction of railways, wharves, and bridges, and they have regulated it by the enactment of pilotage, quarantine, and police laws. The respective powers of the government of the United States and the governments of the states over commerce can best be illustrated by an analysis and classification of the cases in which the Supreme Court of the United States has been called upon to deal with the subject.

31. At the time of the adoption of the Constitution, commerce meant primarily the navigation of the sea and of the rivers flowing into it in the course of the transportation of goods from foreign countries, for the interstate transportation of goods, either by land or water, was then comparatively insignificant. It is natural, therefore, in considering the regulation of commerce under the Constitution to treat, first, of navigation, and, at the outset of the discussion, to determine what are, in law, navigable waters. In England navigable waters

[1] Sec. 4233.
[2] Sec. 4252.
[3] Sec. 4501 et seq.; Sec. 4509 et seq.
[4] Sec 4549.
[5] Sec. 4653.
[6] 4681.
[7] Sec. 5244.
[8] Sec. 5263.
[9] Sec. 5258.
[10] Act of Feb. 4, 1887.

in the legal sense of the term, and also in actual fact, are those only in which the tide ebbs and flows.[1] As the adoption of the English rule in this country would have necessarily taken the inland lakes and the rivers which are in fact navigable where there is no ebb or flow of the tide, out of the jurisdiction of admiralty and also out of the jurisdiction of Congress in the regulation of commerce, Congress by the 9th section of the Judiciary Act of 1789 constituted navigability in fact the test of navigability in law. Nevertheless, in certain of the earlier cases the English test of navigability in a legal sense was followed, although, as has been shown, the reason of the rule failed here,[2] but, in the later cases, it is laid down that waters in the United States which are navigable in fact are navigable in law, and, as such, subject to the regulating power of Congress in so far as they may be waterways of foreign and interstate commerce.[3]

In England the admiralty jurisdiction was further restricted by the requirement that the *locus in quo*, though within the ebb and flow of the tide, should not be *infra corpus comitatus*, nor at sea *infra fauces terræ*, but these restrictions are not applicable in the United States.[4] Before the court had abandoned the English test as to admiralty jurisdiction, it was questioned by

[1] Genessee Chief *v.* Fitzhugh, 12 How. 443, 454.
[2] The Thomas Jefferson, 10 Wheat. 428; The Orleans *v.* Phœbus, 11 Pet. 175; Peyroux *v.* Howard, 7 *id* 324; U. S. *v.* Coombs, 12 *id.* 72; Waring *v.* Clarke, 5 How. 441.
[3] The Genessee Chief *v.* Fitzhugh, 12 How. 443; The Daniel Ball, 10 Wall. 57; The Montello, 20 *id.* 430; Barney *v* Keoknk, 94 U. S. 324 As Davis, J., said in the Montello, 20 Wall. 441, "the capability of use by the public for purposes of transportation and commerce" affords the "true criterion of the navigability of a river, rather than the extent and manner of that use. If it be capable in its natural state of being used for purposes of commerce, no matter in what mode the commerce may be conducted, it is navigable in fact, and becomes in law a public river or highway."
[4] Waring *v.* Clarke, 5 How. 441.

Story, J., whether or not, the power to regulate commerce authorized an extension of the admiralty jurisdiction to the inland lakes,[1] but, in The Genessee Chief v. Fitzhugh,[2] Taney, C. J., showed clearly that the judicial power being defined by the Constitution could not be extended by legislation under the guise of a regulation of commerce, the legislative regulation of any subject-matter of jurisdiction being in its nature essentially distinct from the creation of a tribunal, and the vesting in that tribunal of jurisdiction over any particular subject-matter. The admiralty jurisdiction is, therefore, limited on inland waters to vessels engaged in and to maritime contracts and torts concerned with, or growing out of, interstate transportation.[3] Therefore, contracts of affreightment between ports of the same state on an inland lake,[4] and contracts for supplies furnished to vessels engaged in such trade[5] are matters of local jurisdiction, and not of admiralty jurisdiction in the courts of the United States.

32. Before the Revolution, the title to navigable waters and to the soil under them was vested in the crown, or in its grantees. After the Revolution, the people became sovereign, and thenceforth the title to navigable waters within the jurisdiction of a riparian state and to the soil under them became vested in that state for the public use of its citizens.[6] After the adoption of the Constitution, as before, the title to navi-

---

[1] The Thomas Jefferson, 10 Wheat. 428.
[2] 12 How. 443, 452.
[3] The Genessee Chief, 12 How. 443; Allen v. Newberry, 21 id. 244; Maguire v. Card, ibid. 248; The Belfast, 7 Wall. 624.
[4] Allen v. Newberry, 21 How. 244.
[5] McGuire v. Card, 21 How. 248.
[6] Martin v. Waddell, 16 Pet. 367; Den v. Jersey Co., 15 How. 426; Smith v. Maryland, 18 id. 71; Weber v. Harbor Commissioners, 18 Wall. 57; Rundle v. D. &. R. C. Co., 14 How. 807; Jones v. Soulard, 24 How. 41; St. P. & P. R. R. v. Schurmeier, 7 Wall. 272.

gable waters and to the soil under them and the right to fish therein remained in the riparian state, its proprietary title extending in the case of inland waters constituting its boundary[1] from ordinary high-water mark *ad medium filæ*, and in the case of the sea and its bays, to the distance that the international jurisdiction of the United States extended; and by force of the Constitution, the United States acquired only the right to exercise over navigable waters its power of regulating commerce, and states which were admitted to the Union subsequently to the adoption of the Constitution have, of course, in this respect the same rights of sovereignty and jurisdiction as the original thirteen states.[2] The distinction between rights of navigation over waters and the rights to the soil under them is illustrated by two cases. In Smith *v.* Maryland,[3] the facts were, that the state of Maryland, having enacted a statute prohibiting the taking of oysters in its waters in a certain manner under pain of forfeiting to the state the vessel employed for that purpose, the sloop Volant, owned by the plaintiff in error, and duly licensed as a coasting vessel under the statutes of the United States, was seized under the state statute and condemned to forfeiture in a regular proceeding in a state court. The Supreme Court of the United States affirmed the judgment of the state court, holding that the title to the soil under navigable waters within its jurisdiction being vested in the riparian state, that state could rightfully regulate the exercise of rights of fishing therein, and enforce by judicial proceedings a forfeiture of vessels whose navigators should fail to conform to

---

[1] Barney *v.* Keokuk, 94 U. S. 324.
[2] Pollard *v.* Hagan, 3 How. 212; Weber *v.* Harbor Commissioners, 18 Wall. 57.
[3] 18 How. 71.

the regulations so prescribed, and that a license to navigate granted by the United States confers "no immunity from the operation of valid laws of a state." The court, however, expressly declined to give any opinion as to the limits of the trust under which riparian states hold the soil under their navigable waters, or to decide whether rights of fishing in such waters could be enjoyed only by the citizens of the state, or by all citizens of the United States in common. The next case, McCready *v.* Virginia,[1] not only followed in the line of Smith *v.* Maryland, but also put at rest the question undetermined in that case. The facts were that, under a statute of Virginia similar in terms to the statute of Maryland, save that it also imposed a pecuniary fine upon the offender, McCready, a citizen of Maryland, was indicted, convicted, and fined in a state court, and the Supreme Court of the United States affirmed the conviction, holding that the riparian state is a trustee, not for all the citizens of the United States, but only for its own citizens as to the soil under its navigable waters, and the rights of fishing in such waters, and that, as Waite, C. J., said,[2] "the right which the people of the state thus acquire comes not from their citizenship alone, but from their citizenship and property combined," and " it is, in fact, a property right and not a mere privilege or immunity of citizenship," and, therefore, a right which does not, by force of the Constitution, vest in the citizens of other states. It has likewise been held, that the grant to the United States of jurisdiction in admiralty does not carry with it a cession of navigable waters, or of general jurisdiction over them, and, therefore, the case of a murder committed on board a vessel of the navy of the United States, while at anchor in navigable waters within the

[1] 94 U. S. 391.   [2] p. 395.

jurisdiction of a state, is not cognizable in a court of the United States.[1]

33. The controversy as to the respective provinces of the United States and of the states in the regulation of navigation was first brought to the attention of the court in the leading case of Gibbons v. Ogden,[2] wherein the facts were, that the state of New York had by statute granted to Livingston and Fulton the exclusive right, for a term of years not then expired, of navigating with boats moved by steam all the waters within the jurisdiction of New York, and that license had by *mesne* assignments become vested in Ogden, a citizen of New York. Gibbons, styled on the record a citizen of New Jersey, was then engaged in the business of transporting passengers on steamboats owned by him, licensed as coasting vessels by the United States, and plying between Elizabethtown in New Jersey and the city and port of New York. Ogden filed his bill in the Court of Chancery of New York, and obtained an injunction restraining Gibbons from running his steamboats in the waters of New York, and a final decree having been entered against Gibbons in the court of last resort of the state of New York, he removed the cause by appeal to the Supreme Court of the United States, which reversed the decree of the court below, and remanded the record with directions to dismiss the plaintiff's bill.[3] The

---

[1] U. S. v. Bevans, 3 Wheat. 336.  [2] 9 Wheat. 1.

[3] Mr. Justice Wayne, in his speech of 26th May, 1847, welcoming Mr. Webster to Savannah, referred to Gibbons v. Ogden as "a controversy begun by a Georgian in behalf of the constitutional rights of the citizen," and added, "when the late Mr. Thomas Gibbons determined to hazard a large part of his fortune in testing the constitutionality of the laws of New York limiting the navigation of the waters in that state to steamers belonging to a company, his own interest was not so much concerned as the right of every citizen to use a coasting license upon the waters of the United States, in whatever way their vessels were propelled. It was a sound view of the law

record, therefore, required the court to decide two questions, *first*, as to the power of the United States to so regulate commerce as to license passenger-carrying steam vessels, plying between different states, to navigate waters within the jurisdiction of a state, and *second*, as to the power of a state to so regulate commerce as to control the navigation of its waters by vessels engaged in interstate commerce. The judgment of the court sustained the power asserted for the government of the United States, and denied the existence of the power claimed to have been reserved to the state, and in reaching that result the court enunciated in clear terms the *criteria* of distinction between federal and state power over commerce. They held that the power to regulate commerce with foreign nations and among the several states "includes every species of commercial intercourse between the residents of any one state and the residents of a foreign nation, or the residents of another state," but that it does not "comprehend that commerce, which is completely internal, which is car-

but not broad enough for the occasion. It is not unlikely that the case would have been decided upon it, if you had not insisted that it should be put upon the broader constitutional ground of commerce and navigation. The court felt the application and force of your reasoning, and it made a decision releasing every creek and river, lake, bay, and harbour, in our country, from the interference of monopolies, which had already provoked unfriendly legislation between some of the states, and which would have been as little favourable to the interest of Fulton as they were unworthy of his genius." Mr. Webster, in his reply to Judge Wayne, said: "It is true, that, in the case of Gibbons *v.* Ogden, I declined to argue the case on any other ground than that of the great commercial question presented by it, the then novel question of the constitutional authority of Congress exclusively to regulate commerce in all its forms, on all the navigable waters of the United States, their bays rivers, and harbours, without any monopoly, restraint, or interference created by sta'e legislation. That question I regarded as all-important. Other grounds might have been sufficient for the disposal of this particular cause, but they were of no public or permanent importance. If that great point had then been waived or evaded, it is easy now to see what inferences unfavourable to the just authority of Congress might have been drawn." 2 Webster's Works, 399, 402.

ried on between man and man in a state, or between different parts of the same state, and which does not extend to or affect other states;" that, both as to foreign and interstate commerce, " the power of Congress does not stop at the jurisdictional lines of the several states," but may be exercised within the territory of a state wherever that which is at the time the subject of foreign or interstate commerce may be; that the power of regulating foreign and interstate commerce is exclusively vested in Congress, and no part of that power can be concurrently or to any extent, exercised by the states; that the power to regulate interstate and foreign commerce includes as an integral part thereof the regulation of the navigation of waters within the jurisdiction of any state in the prosecution of such commerce by the transportation of either passengers or goods in vessels propelled by any sort of motive power; that the grant to the United States of that power forbids the states to create monopolies to interfere with the free navigation of their waters in the prosecution of foreign or interstate commerce; and that, for these reasons, the statutes of New York granting to Fulton and his successors the exclusive rights under which they claimed were void for repugnancy to the Constitution. In The Daniel Ball,[1] a legitimate corollary of the main point established in Gibbons v. Ogden, was enunciated. The facts were, that the Acts of Congress of 7 July, 1838,[2] and 30 August, 1852,[3] having required, under a penalty, all steam vessels engaged in the transportation of passengers and goods upon "the bays, lakes, rivers, or other navigable waters of the United States, to be inspected and licensed," the Daniel Ball, a steamer engaged in navigating Grand river in the state of Michigan between the cities of Grand Rapids and Grand Haven was libeled

[1] 10 Wall. 557.   [2] 5 Stat. 304.   [3] 10 Stat. 61.

by the United States in the court of the proper district for violation of the statutes, it being admitted by stipulation that some of the goods she carried came from, or were destined for, places out of the state of Michigan. A decree of condemnation was made in the court below, and affirmed in the Supreme Court, on the ground that the vessel, though plying exclusively within the limits of a state, was engaged in interstate commerce, for as to each article of merchandise transported from a point without the state to a point within the state, or *vice versa*, interstate commerce began whenever the article commenced to move in trade from one state to another, and continued until the article reached its destination, and the vessel was, by reason of its participation in that transportation, subject to the regulating power of Congress.[1] The judgments in Sinnot *v.* Davenport,[2] and in Foster *v* Davenport,[3] were the necessary result of the principles upon which the judgment in Gibbons *v.* Ogden was based. These cases raised the question of the constitutionality of a statute of Alabama requiring the owners of steamboats navigating the waters of that state to file with the local authorities a statement in writing setting forth the name of the vessel, the name of its owners, their places of residence, and the amount of their respective interests in the vessel, as regulations of commerce affecting in Sinnot's case, vessels licensed

[1] 22 How. 227.     [2] 22 How. 244.
[3] Field, J., said very forcibly, p. 566, "we are unable to draw any clear and distinct line between the authority of Congress to regulate an agency employed in commerce between the states, when that agency extends through two or more states, and when it is confined in its action entirely within the limits of a single state. If its authority does not extend to an agency in such commerce, when that agency is confined within the limits of a state, its entire authority over interstate commerce may be defeated. Several agencies combining, each taking up the commodity transported at the boundary line at one end of a state, and leaving it at the boundary line at the other end, the federal jurisdiction would be entirely ousted, and the constitutional provision would become a dead letter."

under the Act of Congress to carry on the coasting trade and plying between a port in Alabama and ports in other states, and, in Foster's case, steamboats licensed by the United States and employed as lighters and towboats in the port and harbour of Mobile in aid of vessels engaged in commerce, either foreign or coastwise, with other states. In each case the court held the statute of Mobile to be void as an attempted regulation of commerce.[1] The case of Philadelphia and Southern Steamship Company v. Pennsylvania[2] follows in the same line, for it was therein held, that a state cannot tax the gross receipts of a steamship company incorporated by it and engaged in the transportation of persons and of goods in the prosecution of both foreign and interstate commerce. The principle established by Gibbons v. Ogden is further exemplified by Hall v. DeCuir,[3] in which the question was as to the validity of a Civil-Rights statute of Louisiana, which had been so construed by the Supreme Court of the state as to require " those engaged in the transportation of passengers among the states to give to all persons traveling within that state, upon vessels employed in such business, equal rights and privileges in all parts of the vessel, without distinction on account of race or colour," and to subject " to an action for damages the owner of such a vessel, who excludes coloured passengers, on account of their colour, from the cabin set apart by him for the use of whites during the passage." The Court held the statute to be void as an attempted regulation of interstate commerce, on the ground that the statute did not " act upon the business through the local instruments to be employed after coming within the

---

[1] The case of New York v. Miln. 11 Pet. 102, though cited and relied upon at the argument, was not noticed in the judgment of the court.
[2] 122 U. S. 326.   [3] 95 U. S. 485.

state, but directly upon the business as it comes into the state from without or goes out from within."[1] Waite, C. J., said,[2] "while it purports only to control the carrier when engaged within the state, it must necessarily influence his conduct to some extent in the management of his business throughout his entire voyage. His disposition of passengers taken up and put down within the state, or taken up within to be carried without, cannot but affect in a greater or less degree those taken up without and brought within, and sometimes those taken up and put down without. A passenger in the cabin set apart for the use of whites without the state must, when the boat comes within, share the accommodations of that cabin with such coloured persons as may come on board afterwards, if the law is enforced. It was to meet just such a case that the commercial clause in the Constitution was adopted. . . . If the public good requires such legislation, it must come from Congress, and not from the states."[3] The case of Veazie v. Moor[4] presents the converse of the main proposition enunciated in Gibbons v. Ogden and in The Daniel Ball. The facts were, that the river Penobscot being entirely within the state of Maine from its source to its mouth, the last eight miles from its source not being navigable by reason of dams, but there being higher up the stream an imperfect navigation, without outlet, or connection with any other waterway, the state of Maine, in consideration of improvements to be made to that navigation, granted to Moor and his associates an exclusive right of navigating by steamboats such portions of the stream as they should improve, and Veazie, having built and attempted to oper-

[1] Per Waite, C. J., at p. 488.     [2] p. 489.
[3] Clifford, J., delivered an elaborate concurring judgment.
[4] 14 How. 568.

ate within the limits of the grant to Moor a steamboat for which he had obtained an United States enrollment and license, was enjoined by a state court at the suit of Moor, and the decree of the state court was affirmed on appeal by the Supreme Court of the United States. The ground of decision was, that any commerce that could by possibility be conducted upon the upper Penobscot was of necessity purely internal, and in no sense interstate, commerce, and that as internal commerce it was properly a subject of state, and not of federal, regulation, and that a coasting license issued by the United States is "a warrant to traverse the waters washing or bounding the coast of the United States," but conveys no privileges to use the internal waters of a state in the prosecution of that which is not interstate commerce. Daniel, J., said, p. 574, "nor can it be properly concluded, that, because the products of domestic enterprise in agriculture or manufactures or in the arts may ultimately become the subject of foreign commerce, that the control of the means, or the encouragements, by which enterprise is fostered and protected, is legitimately within the import of the phrase foreign commerce, or fairly implied in any investiture of the power to regulate such commerce. . . . Such a pretension would effectually prevent or paralyze every effort at internal improvement by the several states ; for it cannot be supposed that the states would exhaust their capital and their credit in the construction of turnpikes, canals, and railroads, the remuneration derivable from which and all control over which might be immediately wrested from them, because such public works would be facilities for a commerce which, whilst availing itself of these facilities, was unquestionably internal, although intermediately or ultimately it might become foreign." The case of Lord *v.* G. N. & P. S. S. Co.[1] furnishes another illustration of the regulating power of Congress with regard to commerce. The facts were, that Section 4283 of the Revised Statutes of the United States, as defined in its application by Section 4289, having limited to the amount of their interest the liability of vessel-owners as common carriers of goods, and the steamer *Ventura*, owned by the G. N. & P. S. S. Co., and plying on the high seas between San Francisco and San Diego, both on the coast of, and in the state of California, having been totally lost while carrying goods for Lord, he brought suit; the company set up by plea their discharge from liability under the Revised Statutes, and the judge at the trial having directed the jury that the statutes exonerated the defendant, if they should find that the case came within the terms of the statute, a verdict was found for the defendant, and after judgment thereon, a bill of exceptions was taken to the judge's direction, but the Supreme Court affirmed the judgment of the court below, on the ground that as the vessel, though engaged in commerce between two ports in the same state, navigated the high seas, she necessarily became subject to the regulating power of Congress.[2] The commercial power as affecting navigation also authorizes congressional legislation with regard to the sale and mortgaging of ships and requires state regulations on that subject to yield when they conflict with those made by Congress. Thus in White's Bank *v.* Smith,[3] the facts were, that the Act of Congress of 29 July, 1850,[4] having declared that no mortgage of any vessel of the United States shall be valid against any

---

[1] 102 U. S. 541.
[2] See Norwich Co. *v.* Wright, 13 Wall. 104, and The City of Norwich, 118 U. S. 468, in further illustration of Sections 4282–4289 Revised Statutes of the United States.
[3] 7 Wall. 646.    [4] 9 Stat. 440.

person other than the mortgagor, his representatives, and persons having any actual notice thereof, unless such mortgage " be recorded in the office of the collector of customs where such vessel is registered or enrolled," and a statute of the state of New York having declared that no chattel mortgage should be valid as against the creditors of the mortgagor, or as " against subsequent mortgages in good faith" unless originally, and annually thereafter, filed in the clerk's office in " the town and city where the mortgagor shall then reside," " Hoyt, a resident of Buffalo in the state of New York, on 22 May, 1863, executed a mortgage to White's Bank of his schooner Emmett, and the mortgage was on 13 June, 1863, recorded in the office of the collector of customs at Buffalo, where the Emmett was duly enrolled, and on 5 June, 1863, the mortgage was also filed in the clerk's office of the city of Buffalo, but it was not filed therein annually thereafter. Hoyt sold the vessel to Zahm of Sandusky in the state of Ohio, and on 2 June, 1865, Zahm mortgaged her to Smith, and the Emmett having been duly enrolled in the office of the collector of customs at Sandusky, the mortgage to Smith was recorded in that office. Thereafter, the Emmett was sold under a paramount lien for sailors' wages, and the balance of the fund remaining after payment of the sailors' wages was claimed by both Smith and White's, Bank. The court below decided in favour of Smith, but the Supreme Court reversed that decree, and directed distribution to White's Bank, on the ground that ships or vessels being " the creations of the legislation of Congress" and instrumentalities of commerce, Congress has, as incidental to its power of regulating foreign and interstate commerce, the power of prescribing the manner of selling and encumbering ships, and the requisites to the validity of conveyances and encumbrances thereof, and the laws of the states, when conflicting with such federal regulations, must give way, and, therefore, the mortgage to White's Bank, being prior in point of time to the mortgage to Smith, and having been duly recorded under the act of Congress, was not invalidated by the failure to renew annually its registration in the clerk's office of Buffalo under the law of New York. In Aldrich v. Ætna Co.,[1] the ruling in White's Bank v. Smith was reiterated. In his judgment in the Lottawanna,[2] Bradley, J., intimates that under the power to regulate commerce, Congress might create a maritime lien for supplies and repairs furnished to vessels in their home ports. While state legislatures cannot create maritime liens, nor confer jurisdiction upon their courts for the enforcement of such liens, as *exempli gratia*, liens of shippers under contracts of affreightment to be performed on navigable waters within the general jurisdiction of admiralty,[3] nor can states authorize their courts to entertain suits for damages for the breach of contracts for the transportation of passengers on the high seas,[4] nor proceedings *in rem* in cases of collision on navigable waters,[5] yet, as the general maritime law does not recognize liens in favour of material men for supplies furnished to vessels in their home ports, or for materials furnished to ships in process of construction, the states may by statutes authorize such liens, and those liens may be enforced by proceedings *in rem* in the admiralty courts of the United States.[6] On the same principle, as both at common law and in admiralty, the right of action for a tort is personal and dies with the person injured,

---

[1] 8 Wall. 491.
[2] 21 Wall. 577.
[3] The Belfast, 7 Wall. 624.
[4] The Moses Taylor, 4 Wall. 411.
[5] The Hine v. Trevor, 4 Wall. 556.
[6] Edwards v. Elliott, 21 Wall. 532; The Lottawanna, *ibid.* 558.

and no action is maintainable for a tort causing death,[1] the right of action in such cases, when conferred by a state statute, is enforcible in a state court in case of death caused by collision in navigable waters, which are within the jurisdiction of the state and also within the admiralty jurisdiction of the United States,[2] and it is also enforcible in the common law courts of the United States[3] and in the admiralty courts of the United States,[4] In his judgment in Sherlock v. Alling[5] Field, J., says, "it is true that the commercial power conferred by the Constitution is one without limitation. It authorizes legislation with respect to all the subjects of foreign and interstate commerce, the persons engaged in it, and the instruments by which it is carried on. . . . The power to prescribe these and similar regulations necessarily involves the right to declare the liability which shall follow their infraction. Whatever, therefore, Congress determines, either as to a regulation or the liability for its infringement, is exclusive of state authority. But with reference to a great variety of matters touching the rights and liabilities of persons engaged in commerce, either as owners or navigators of vessels, the laws of Congress are silent, and the laws of the state govern. . . . Until Congress, therefore, makes some regulation touching the liabilities of parties for marine torts resulting in the death of the persons injured, we are of the opinion that the statute of Indiana applies, giving a right of action in such cases to the personal representatives of the deceased, and

---

[1] Higgins v. Bucher, Yelv. 89; Baker v. Boulton, 1 Camp. 493; *Ex parte* Gordon, 104 U. S. 515; Crapo v. Allen, 1 Sprague 184; *sed. cf.* Cutting v. Seabury, *ibid.* 522.

[2] American Steamboat Co. v. Chase, 16 Wall. 522; Sherlock v. Alling, 93 U. S. 99.

[3] C. & N. W. Ry. v. Whitton, 13 Wall. 270.

[4] *Ex parte* Gordon, 104 U. S. 515; *Ex parte* Ferry Co., *ibid.* 519.

[5] 93 U. S. 103.

that, as thus applied, it constitutes no encroachment upon the commercial power of Congress."

34. There are three cases which illustrate clearly the necessary limitations upon the exercise by Congress of its power over subjects of commerce, and the equally necessary limitation of the implied restrictions upon state action. In the Trade-Mark Cases,[1] the question was as to the constitutionality of the acts of Congress of 14 August, 1876,[2] and 8 July, 1870,[3] which authorize the registration in the Patent Office of devices in the nature of trade-marks, make the wrongful use of a registered trade-mark a cause of action in a civil suit for damages, and punish by fine and imprisonment the fraudulent use, sale, and counterfeiting of registered trade-marks. The court in a judgment read by Miller, J., declined to decide, "whether the trade-mark bears such a relation to commerce in general terms as to bring it within congressional control, when used or applied to the classes of commerce which fall within that control,[4] but held, that the statutes in question, not being limited in terms, or by the essential nature of their subject-matter, to the regulation of trade-marks in their relation to "commerce with foreign nations, and among the several states, and with the Indian tribes," they must be held to have been enacted in "the exercise of a power not confided to Congress," and are, therefore, unconstitutional. Prior to the judgment in the trade-mark cases, some of the Circuit Courts of the United States had sustained the constitutionality of the trade-mark legislation, and in McLean v. Fleming,[5] Clifford, J., had said, "protection for lawful trade-marks may be obtained by individuals, firms, or corporations entitled to the

---
[1] 100 U. S. 82.  [3] Rev. Stat. Sec. 4937 to 4947.  [5] 96 U. S. 248.
[2] 19 Stat. 141.  [4] p. 95.

same, if they comply with the requirements prescribed by the act of Congress. In Nathan *v.* Louisiana,[1] the facts were that the state of Louisiana having, by a statute, imposed an annual tax upon "money or exchange brokers," and the state having brought an action in one of its courts against Nathan, a broker dealing in foreign and interstate bills of exchange, for the collection of taxes unpaid, obtained a judgment against him, which was affirmed in the state court of last resort, and also by the Supreme Court, on the ground that a state has the right to tax its own citizens for the prosecution of any business within the state, although that business may consist in dealing in instruments of commerce.[2] In People *v.* Commissioners,[3] the facts were, that Haneman, a resident of New York, having been assessed for taxation under the laws of that state on his personal property as of 1 January, 1876, and having objected to the validity of the assessment as affecting the bulk of his property, on the ground that

---

[1] 8 How 73.

[2] McLean, J., said, p. 80, "this is not a tax on bills of exchange. Under the law, every person is free to buy or sell bills of exchange, as may be necessary in his business transactions; but he is required to pay the tax if he engage in the business of a money, or an exchange, broker. The right of a state to tax its own citizens for the prosecution of any particular business or profession, within the state has not been doubted. . . . He is not engaged in commerce, but is supplying an instrument of commerce. He is less connected with it than the ship builder, without whose labour foreign commerce could not be carried on. . . . The taxing power of a state is one of its attributes of sovereignty, and where there has been no compact with the federal government, or cession of jurisdiction for the purposes specified in the Constitution, this power reaches all the property and business within the state, which are

it properly denominated the means of the general government; and, as laid down by this court, it may be exercised at the discretion of the state. . . . Whatever exists within its territorial limits in the form of property, real or personal, with the exceptions stated, is subject to its laws; and also the numberless enterprises in which its citizens may be engaged. These are subjects of state regulation and state taxation, and there is no federal power under the Constitution which can impair this exercise of state sovereignty."

[3] 104 U. S. 466.

that property was "continuously employed in the business of exporting cotton from the United States of America to foreign countries," and "in purchasing and paying for cotton in different states of the United States," it was argued on his behalf "that products of the United States, which have passed the Customs Department, and are on shipboard, in the course of exportation to a foreign market, have become exports, and are no longer within the taxing power of the state; that to tax money invested in such products is, in effect, laying an impost or duty on exports; and that a tax on capital invested in the products of the United States in transit from one state to another for purposes of exportation, or on money used and employed in exporting such products, is an unauthorized interference by the state with the regulation of commerce."[1] The court, however, declined to determine those questions, but affirmed the judgment of the court below sustaining the assessment, on the ground that, if the capital assessed was, in fact, in money at the date of the assessment, a subsequent investment thereof in a subject-matter of commerce could not relieve that capital from liability to state taxation, and that the burden of proof resting on Haneman, he had failed to show that such investment of his capital had preceded its assessment for taxation.

35. The cases as to state taxation of ships establish the doctrine that while a state may tax the property of those persons, natural or corporate, who may be by residence subject to its jurisdiction, even if that property be invested in ships, yet a state may not tax ships whose owners are not personally subject to its jurisdiction, and which come within its territorial limits in the pursuit of commerce. Thus, in Hays v. The Pacific

[1] Per Harlan, J., p. 468.

Mail Steamship Co.,[1] the question was as to the liability to taxation under the laws of California of steamships, plying between the ports of New York and San Francisco, whose home port and the place of whose registry under the federal statutes, and the residence of whose owner was in the state of New York, and the court held them not to be so liable, the ground of decision being, as stated by Nelson, J.,[2] "that the state of California had no jurisdiction over these vessels for the purpose of taxation; they were there but temporarily engaged in lawful trade and commerce, with their *situs* at the home port, where the vessel belonged, and where the owners were liable to be taxed for the capital invested, and where the taxes had been paid." Daniel, J., dissented on the ground that the federal court had no jurisdiction. Campbell, J., concurred solely on the ground "that the vessels were *in transitu*, having no *situs* in California, nor permanent connection with its internal commerce." In Morgan v. Parham,[3] the facts raised the question that had been decided in Hays v. The Pacific Mail Steamship Co., and, in addition thereto, the further question as to the possible effect of a temporary enrollment, under the Act of 18 February, 1793,[4] of a steamship in a port other than its home port in subjecting it to state taxation in the port of temporary enrollment. The steamship, "The Frances," having been registered in the port of New York, was temporarily enrolled in the port of Mobile, was employed in the coasting trade between Mobile and New Orleans, and while the owner, Morgan, was a citizen of, and a resident in, New York, the master of the vessel and the agents, who managed its business, were residents of Mobile. The court reiterated the doctrine

[1] 17 How. 596.
[2] p. 599.
[3] 16 Wall. 471.
[4] 11 Stat. 306.

of the Hays Case, and held, also, that there was nothing in the temporary enrollment of the vessel "in the port of Mobile, that affected her registry in New York, or her ownership in that place, or that tended to subject her to the taxation of the state of Alabama."[1] St. Louis v. Wiggins Ferry Co.,[2] and Gloucester Ferry Co. v. Pennsylvania,[3] also follow the rule laid down in Hays v. The Pacific Mail Steamship Co., but the converse of the doctrine of that case is to be found in Transportation Co. v. Wheeling,[4] where the facts were, that the Transportation Company, being incorporated under the laws of West Virginia, having its principal office in the city of Wheeling in that state, and owning certain steamboats, which had been enrolled and licensed under the laws of the United States, and which were used by it in navigating the Ohio between Wheeling and other ports on that river in the states of West Virginia and Ohio, was taxed by the city of Wheeling on the assessed value of the boats as part of the personal property of the company under a statute of West Virginia authorizing the city to "assess, levy, and collect an annual tax for the use of the city on personal property in the city," and the company, having paid the tax under protest, brought an action against the city in a state court to recover the amount of the tax, and judgment for the defendant was rendered in the court below and affirmed in error, the court holding that the tax was not a duty on tonnage, because not graduated in proportion to the cubical capacity of the vessel, nor a regulation of commerce, because it was only assessed upon the owner's personal property invested in the vessel, nor an infringement upon the privilege conferred by the enrollment and licensing of

[1] Per Hunt, J., p. 476.
[2] 11 Wall. 423.
[3] 114 U. S. 196.
[4] 99 U. S. 273.

boats under the statutes of the United States, for such enrollment and licensing does not exempt the vessels so enrolled and licensed from taxation as the personal property of their owner. Wiggins Ferry Co. *v.* East St. Louis,[1] is to the same effect. A state cannot tax ships or vessels as instruments of commerce, though they be owned within its jurisdiction; thus, in Moran *v.* New Orleans,[2] the question was as to the power of a state to authorize municipal taxation of steam tow-boats licensed under the coasting laws of the United States and employed in towing vessels between the sea and the port of the municipality, and the court held, that the taxation was void as an attempted regulation of interstate commerce. On the same principle a state cannot by statute require the payment by every vessel coming into a port of the state to the port wardens of the sum of five dollars, whether the wardens be, or be not, called on to perform any service for the vessel.[3]

36. The Constitution in express terms forbids the states to impose duties on tonnage. Section 10 of article I of the Constitution declares that "no state shall, without the consent of Congress, lay any duty on tonnage." The word "tonnage," as applied to American shipping, means "their entire internal capacity, expressed in tons of 100 cubical feet each, as estimated and ascertained by those rules of admeasurement and computation[4] which are prescribed by the acts of Congress.[5] The constitutional prohibition prevents state taxation of " water-crafts plying in the navigable waters of the state " . . . . " at the rate of one dollar per ton of registered tonnage."[6] Nor can a state require

---

[1] 107 U. S. 365.           112 U. S. 69.
[3] Steamship Co. *v.* Port Wardens, 6 Wall. 31.
[4] State Tonnage Tax Cases, 12 Wall. 212.     [5] 13 Stat. 70; *ibid.* 444.
[6] State Tonnage Tax Cases, 12 Wall. 204.

that every vessel arriving at a port of the state shall pay to the port wardens a fixed sum whether the wardens be, or be not, called on to perform any services for the vessel;[1] nor compel every vessel arriving at any quarantine station on the coast of the state to pay a fixed sum per ton;[2] nor require every steamboat mooring in any port of the state to pay a sum regulated by the tonnage of the boat;[3] nor require all vessels entering a certain port to load or unload, or making fast to any wharf therein, to pay a sum regulated by the registered tonnage of the vessel.[4] In each one of these cases, the taxation imposed by the state would have been void as an attempted regulation of interstate commerce, had there been no express prohibition of state tonnage duties.

37. The cases as to taxation of water transportation of passengers and goods further illustrate the principle. In the Head Money Cases,[5] the facts were that Congress having by the Act of 3 August, 1882,[6] imposed a duty of fifty cents payable " for each and every passenger not a citizen of the United States who shall come by steam or sail vessel from a foreign port to any port within the United States," certain steamship companies, having landed passengers at the port of New York, and having paid the duty under protest, brought actions at law against the collector of the port in a circuit court of the United States to recover back the amounts so paid, and judgments rendered for the defendant were affirmed in the Supreme Court, on the ground that the statute imposing the duty was a rightful exercise by Congress of the power vested in it to regulate foreign

[1] Steamship Co. v. Port Wardens, 6 Wall. 31.
[2] Peete v. Morgan, 19 Wall. 581.
[3] Cannon v. New Orleans, 20 Wall. 577.
[4] I. S. S. Co. v. Tinker, 94 U. S. 238.
[5] 112 U. S. 580.       [6] 23 Stat. 214.

commerce, and that, while the burden imposed on the shipowner being, not a tax, but an incident of a regulation of commerce, is not subject to the constitutional requirement of uniformity of operation throughout the United States, it is, nevertheless, in fact uniform, for " it operates with the same force and effect in every place where the subject of it is found."[1] The correlative of the principle enunciated in that case is illustrated by a series of cases, in which, after considerable variance of judicial opinion, the court has finally so settled the rule as to leave it no longer an open question. In New York v. Miln,[2] it was held, that a state may require, under a penalty, the master of every passenger-carrying vessel, on arriving at any port within the state, to report to the state authorities the name, place of birth, last legal settlement, age, and occupation of every passenger, the statute under consideration being one enacted by New York in 1824, and the court affirmed its validity on the ground that it was a regulation, not of commerce, but of police, and as such falling within the reserved powers of the state. The authority of the case is, however, much shaken by the admirably reasoned dissenting judgment of Story, J., with whose conclusions Marshall, C. J., concurred,[3] and the result reached by the court on the precise question before it is with difficulty reconcilable with the later cases of Sinnot v. Davenport,[4] and Foster v. Davenport.[5] The next cases are Smith v. Turner, Health Commissioner of the Port of New York, and Norris v. The City of Boston, reported together under the title of the Passenger Cases,[6] wherein was brought into question the validity of statutes of the states of New York and Massachusetts imposing taxes

---

[1] Per Miller, J., at p. 594.
[2] 11 Pet. 102.
[3] p. 161.
[4] 22 How. 227.
[5] 22 How. 244.
[6] 7 How. 283.

upon the landing of alien passengers in the ports of those states. In the first of the Passenger Cases, Smith *v.* Turner, the question was as to the validity of a statute of New York, authorizing the Health Commissioner to demand, and, if not paid, to sue for and recover, from the master of every vessel arriving in the port of New York from a foreign port "$1.50 for each cabin passenger, and $1.00 for each steerage passenger, mate, sailor, or mariner, and from the master of each coasting vessel 25 cents for each person on board." In the second of the passenger cases, Norris *v.* The City of Boston, the question was as to the validity of a statute of Massachusetts enacted in 1837, and imposing a duty of $2.00 per capita on alien passengers landed at any port in the state. The effect of those cases can best be stated, in the words of Miller, J., who, in Henderson *v.* Mayor of New York,[1] after referring to the fact that one of the statutes under consideration in the Passenger Cases, though not the same statute considered in New York *v.* Miln, was part of the New York system of regulation of, and taxation upon, the landing of passengers from vessels, said that the New York statute "authorized the Health Commissioner to demand, and, if not paid, to sue for and recover, from the master of every vessel arriving in the port of New York from a foreign port one dollar and fifty cents for each cabin passenger, and one dollar for each steerage passenger, mate, sailor, or mariner, and from the master of each coasting vessel twenty-five cents for each person on board. . . . . The defendant Smith, who was sued for the sum of $295, for refusing to pay for 295 steerage passengers on board the British ship 'Henry Bliss,' of which he was master, demurred to the declaration on the ground that the act

[1] 92. U. S. 266, 269.

was contrary to the Constitution of the United States, and void. From a judgment against him affirmed in the Court of Errors of the state of New York, he sued out a writ of error, on which the question was brought to this court. It was here held, at the January Term, 1849, that the statute was repugnant to the Constitution and laws of the United States, and therefore, void." [1] Miller, J., added,[2] "so far as the authority of the cases of New York v. Miln and the Passenger Cases can be received as conclusive, they decide, that the requirement of a catalogue of passengers, with statements of their last residences and other matters of that character, is a proper exercise of state authority, and that the requirement of the bond, or the alternative of money of such passenger is void, because forbidden by the Constitution and laws of the United States. But the Passenger Cases . . . were decided by a bare majority of the court. Justices McLean, Wayne, Catron, McKinley, and Grier held both statutes void, while Chief Justice Taney and Justices Daniel, Nelson, and Woodbury held them valid. Each member of the court delivered a separate opinion, giving the reasons for his judgment, except Judge Nelson, none of them professing to be the authoritative opinion of the court. Nor is there to be found in the reasons given by the judges, who constituted the majority, such harmony of views as would give that weight to the decision, which it lacks by reason of the divided judgments of the members of the court." Therefore, after as before the decision of the Passenger Cases, the question remained an open one until it was authoritatively determined by the unanimous judgment of the court in the case of Henderson v. The Mayor of New York.[3] In that case the question was as to the validity of the New York statutes,

[1] 7 How. 572.   [2] 92 U. S. 269.   [3] 92 U. S. 259.

which had been so amended as to require from the owner, or consignee, of every vessel bringing from a foreign port into a port of the state passengers not being citizens of the United States a bond, in a substantial penalty, conditioned to indemnify the state against any expenditure for the relief or support of the particular passenger, or, in default of such bond, the payment of a duty of $1.50 on the importation of each passenger. The argument was that "the requirement of the bond is but a suitable regulation under the power of the state to protect its cities and towns from the expense of supporting persons who are paupers or diseased, or helpless women and children, coming from foreign countries," and that the payment of the duty in lieu of giving the bond was a voluntary payment, and not a tax. But the court held, that the intent of the statute was to compel, by the imposition of a burdensome alternative, the payment of the duty; that the duty was in effect, imposed upon, because ultimately payable by, the passengers, and it was therefore, a tax upon foreign commerce, and, as such, void. In the case of the Commissioner of Immigration *v.* North German Lloyd,[1] a similar statute of Louisiana was held to be void. In Chy Lung *v.* Freeman,[2] it was held, that a statute of California, requiring under similar conditions a bond or a commutation in money, not for all passengers, but only for certain classes of passengers, and in particular for "lewd and debauched women," was, on the like reasoning, void. In People *v.* Compagnie Générale Transatlantique,[3] the question was as to the validity of a statute of New York, entitled "an act to raise money for the exercise of the inspection laws of the state of New York," and levying "a duty of one dollar for each and every alien passenger, who shall come

[1] 92 U. S. 259.     [2] 92 U. S. 275.     [3] 107 U. S. 59.

by vessel from a foreign port to the port of New York, for whom a tax has not heretofore been paid," and the court held the statute to be void, on the grounds that the words "inspection laws," "imports," and "exports," as used in the Constitution, refer not to the persons, but to property, and that the case, therefore, came within the ruling of the cases which have been cited. The rule, therefore, as to the taxation of passengers coming by water into the ports of a state from foreign countries and from other states is that the United States may, and the states may not, directly or indirectly, tax such passengers. The application of the same principles determined the case of the Philadelphia and Southern Steamship Co. v. Pennsylvania,[1] in which the question was as to the liability of the gross receipts of a steamship company derived from the foreign and interstate transportation of persons and property to taxation by the state incorporating the company, and the court decided against the liability, overruling the case of the State Tax on Railway Gross Receipts.[2]

38. The cases as to state taxation of goods, as subjects of interstate commerce, follow in the same line. The first case is Almy v. California,[3] in which the facts were that a statute of California having imposed a stamp duty "on bills of lading for the transportation from any point or place within that state to any point or place without the state," of gold or silver coin, and bars, and gold dust, and Almy having been indicted and convicted in the state court of last resort for violation of that law, in that he, as master of the ship Rattler, then lying in the port of San Francisco, received on board certain gold dust for transportation to New York, and issued therefor an unstamped bill of lading; the judgment was reversed in the Supreme Court of the

[1] 122 U. S. 326.     [2] 15 Wall. 284.     [3] 24 How. 169.

United States, on the grounds that the statute of the state was void for repugnancy to the constitutional prohibition of state duties on imports and exports, a duty on a bill of lading being in substance a duty on the merchandise represented by that instrument. In Woodruff v. Parham,[1] Miller, J., in delivering the judgment of the court says, "it seems to have escaped the attention of counsel on both sides, and of the Chief Justice who delivered the opinion, that the case was one of interstate commerce. No distinction of the kind is taken by counsel, none alluded to by the court, except in the incidental statement of the *termini* of the voyage. . . . . The case, however, was well decided on the ground taken by Mr. Blair, counsel for the defendant, namely, that such a tax was a regulation of commerce, a tax imposed upon the transportation of goods from one state to another, over the high seas, in conflict with that freedom of transit of goods and persons between one state and another, which is within the rule laid down in Crandall v. Nevada,[2] and with the authority of Congress to regulate commerce among the states." The next case is Woodruff v. Parham,[3] in which the facts were that the city of Mobile having, under the legislative authority of the state of Alabama, imposed a tax upon "sales at auction," and Woodruff having, as an auctioneer, sold in their original and unbroken packages merchandise, the product of states other than Alabama, resisted payment of the tax, and an action having been brought in a court of the state against him, to recover the amount of the tax, judgment was entered against him, and affirmed in the Supreme Court, on the ground that, as the constitutional prohibition of duties on imports and exports has reference not to articles imported from one state to another, but

[1] 8 Wall. 137.   [2] 6 Wall. 35.   [3] 8 Wall. 123.

only to articles imported from a foreign country into one of the United States, or from one of those states to a foreign country, the tax in question was not a duty on imports or exports; and that as the tax had an uniform application to all "sales at auction" within the city of Mobile, and did not discriminate as against "sales at auction" of the products of other states, it was not open to objection as an attempted regulation of interstate commerce.[1] In Brown v. Houston,[2] the question was as to the liability to taxation in New Orleans under the authority of the state of Louisiana of certain coal which had been consigned by a resident of Pennsylvania to his agent in New Orleans for sale, the assessment for taxation being made under a statute of Louisiana taxing at the rate of "six mills on a dollar of the assessed valuation hereafter to be made of all property situated within the state," and the coal, when assessed, being afloat in the port of New Orleans in the vessel in which it had been transported from Pennsylvania. The court held that the coal was properly taxed, inasmuch as, under the authority of Woodruff v. Parham, it was not an "import," and by reason of its consignment for sale at New Orleans and its delivery at that port for that purpose, it had become merged in the mass of property within the jurisdiction of the state of Louisiana. In Coe v. Errol,[3] the question was, "whether the products of a state, in this case timber cut in its forests, are liable to be taxed like other property within the state, though intended for exportation to another state, and partially prepared for that purpose by being deposited at a place of shipment, such products being owned by persons residing in another state."[4] The court held, that, as "a

---

[1] Nelson, J., dissented, on the ground that the tax was a duty on imports, and as such wrongfully imposed.
[2] 114 U. S. 622.      [3] 116 U. S. 517.
[4] Per Bradley, J., at p. 524.

state has jurisdiction of all persons and things within its territory which do not belong to some other jurisdiction," such as the persons and the property of representatives of foreign governments, and "property belonging to, or in the use of, the government of the United State," the mere fact of non-resident ownership does not exempt property from state taxation; and that property, the product of a state, though intended for transportation to another state, is subject to taxation in common with the mass of property in the state until " actually started in the course of transportation to another state, or delivered to a carrier for such transportation,"[1] but such property is not, at any point, subject to state taxation based upon its intended, or actual, transportation to another state. In the Daniel Ball,[2] Field, J., said, " whenever a commodity has begun to move as an article of trade from one state to another, commerce in that commodity between the states has commenced." Bradley, J., in Coe v. Errol,[3] quoted this *dictum* of Field J., and added, " but this movement does not begin until the article has been shipped, or started for transportation from one state to another. . . . . Until shipped, or started on its final journey out of the state, its exportation is a matter altogether *in fieri*, and not at all a fixed and certain thing."

39. The rule on this subject is further illustrated by those cases which hold that a state cannot by taxation discriminate against either the natural products of, or the goods manufactured in, other states. Thus in Ward v. Maryland,[4] a statute of Maryland having required all traders resident within the state to take out licenses, and to pay therefor fees varying from $12 to $15, and all non-resident traders, as a prerequisite to their sale of any goods, wares, or merchandise whatsoever, other than

[1] p. 525.   [2] 10 Wall. 565.   [3] 116 U. S. 528.   [4] 12 Wall. 418.

agricultural products of and articles manufactured in Maryland, to take out a license and to pay therefor annually a fee of $300, and Ward, a citizen and resident of New Jersey, having been indicted in a court of the state of Maryland and convicted of selling, without a license, goods manufactured in a state other than Maryland, the judgment was affirmed in the state court of last resort, and, on a writ of error, reversed in the Supreme Court, on the grounds that the license tax was, by reason of its discrimination against goods grown or manufactured in other states, an attempted regulation of interstate commerce, and as such void, and that it was also in contravention of the constitutional declaration, that "the citizens of each state shall be entitled to all the privileges and immunities of citizens in the several states." Clifford, J., delivered the judgment of the court. Bradley, J., concurred; but held [1] that the license fee would be equally void, "although it imposed upon residents the same burden for selling goods by sample as is imposed on non-residents. Such a law would effectually prevent the manufacturers of the manufacturing states from selling their goods in other states unless they established commercial houses therein, or sold to resident merchants, who chose to send their orders. It is, in fact, a duty upon importation from one state to another, under the name of a tax."

Following in the line of Ward v. Maryland, state laws have been held void, requiring payment of a tax or license fee by vendors of merchandise "not the growth, produce, or manufacture" of the state, no tax or license fee being required of vendors of domestic merchandise;[2] authorizing a municipality to impose on vessels laden with the products of other states a fee for

[1] p. 432.
[2] Welton v. Missouri, 91 U. S. 275; Webber v. Virginia, 103 U. S. 344.

their use of the public wharves, when vessels laden with the products of the state are permitted to use such wharves without charge;[1] or requiring a "non-resident merchant, desiring to sell by sample in the state, to pay for a license to do that business a sum to be ascertained by the amount of his stock in trade in the state where he resides, and in which he has his principal place of business."[2] In Walling v. Michigan,[3] the facts were, that a statute of Michigan, enacted in 1875, having required payment of a license tax by every person making sale within the state of spirituous or malt liquors for account of persons not having their principal places of business within the state, there being no such requirement of agents of domestic dealers, and a statute of 1879, as amended by a statute of 1881, having taxed to a greater amount the manufacturers of or dealers in domestic liquors, and Walling having been convicted in a court of the state of Michigan under the statute of 1875 of selling without a license, spirituous liquors in the state of Michigan on behalf of a firm having its principal place of business in Chicago in the state of Illinois, and the judgment having been affirmed in the state court of last resort, he brought the record to the Supreme Court of the United States, where the judgment was reversed, on the ground that the statute of 1875, by its imposition of a tax on each selling agent of a foreign dealer, discriminated "against persons for selling goods brought into the state from other states or countries,"[4] and that as the statute of 1881 imposed a single tax only on the manufacturer or dealer, and did not tax his selling agents, "the tax im-

[1] Guy v. Baltimore, 100 U. S. 434.

[2] Corson v. Maryland, 120 U. S. 502. The statement as to the effect of the Maryland statute is quoted from the concurring judgment of Waite, C. J., at p. 506.

[3] 116 U. S. 446.          [4] Per Bradley, J., at p. 454.

posed by the Act of 1875 is not imposed on the same class of persons as is the tax imposed by the Act of 1831,"[1] and the later statute, therefore, cannot operate to relieve the discrimination created by the earlier statute. In Machine Co. v. Gage,[2] the facts were, that the laws of Tennessee, as construed by the Supreme Court of that state, having levied a "tax upon all pedlars of sewing-machines, without regard to the place of growth or produce of material or manufacture," and an agent of the Howe Machine Co., of Bridgeport in the state of Connecticut, having made sales in Tennessee of sewing-machines manufactured by his company in Connecticut, and having paid the tax under protest, the company brought suit in a state court to recover back the amount of the tax, and judgment against the company in the state court of last resort was affirmed in the Supreme Court on the ground, as stated by Swayne, J.,[3] that the law of the state made no discrimination. "It applies alike to sewing-machines manufactured in the state and out of it. . . . . The state, putting all such machines upon the same footing with respect to the tax complained of, had an unquestionable right to impose the burden." Of course, if discrimination against the sale within a state of articles of non-domestic growth or manufacture be the test of the invalidity of a tax, it is not material that the mode of collecting the tax differ, if its amount be the same, on articles of domestic, and of foreign, produce and make; thus in Hinson v. Lott,[4] it was held that there was no discrimination in a statute requiring from vendors of liquor introduced from another state prepayment of a tax of fifty cents per gallon and imposing on manufacturers of domestic liquors a tax of the same

[1] Per Bradley, J., at p. 459.
[2] 100 U. S. 676.
[3] p. 679.
[4] 8 Wall. 148.

amount per gallon, on returns made from time to time.¹ The case of Robbins v. Shelby County Taxing District² gives the sanction of the judgment of the court to the *dictum* of Bradley, J., in his concurring opinion in Ward v. Maryland,³ and in so doing establishes a principle very different from that on which the judgment in Machine Co. v. Gage was based. The facts in the Robbins case were, that a statute of Tennessee having required all drummers, etc., under a penalty to pay a license fee before selling goods in Shelby county, and Robbins, a drummer acting on behalf of a firm doing business in Cincinnati in the state of Ohio, having been convicted in a court of the state of Tennessee of selling goods without a license, in violation of the statute, and the state court of last resort having affirmed the judgment, the Supreme Court of the United States reversed the judgment, for the reasons, as stated by Bradley, J., that a state statute levying a tax or imposing any other restrictions "upon the citizens or inhabitants of other states, for selling, or seeking to sell their goods in such state before they are introduced therein"⁴ is an attempted regulation of interstate commerce, and as such void. The ground of the decision, therefore, is that the license fee in question is not a tax upon goods brought from another state within the jurisdiction of the taxing state, and there subjected to taxation in common with the mass of property in that state, but it is a tax which stands as a barrier in the way of the manufacturer or merchant of another state, and hinders him in the introduction of his goods into the taxing state. In this view, it is no answer to say, as Waite, C. J., and Field

---

[1] Nelson, J., dissented on the grounds stated in his dissenting judgment in Woodruff v. Parham, 8 Wall. 140.
[2] 120 U. S. 489.   [3] 12 Wall. 432.   [4] p. 494.

and Gray, JJ., said in the dissenting judgment of the Chief Justice,[1] that "if citizens of other states cannot be taxed in the same way for the same business, there will be discrimination against the inhabitants of Tennessee and in favour of those of other states," for the conclusive reply is, that, while a state may, without discrimination against interstate commerce, regulate its internal commerce, it cannot, with or without discrimination, regulate that interstate commerce which has not been terminated by the delivery of its subject within the jurisdiction of the taxing state. In Tiernan *v.* Rinker,[2] the facts were, that a statute of Texas having imposed an annual tax on the sale of "spirituous, vinous, malt, and other intoxicating liquors," with a *proviso* that the tax should not operate upon "wines or beer manufactured in this state," Tiernan, being engaged in selling "spirituous, vinous, malt, and other intoxicating liquors," including "wines and beers," "not of the manufacture of the state," brought suit in an equity court of the state to enjoin the enforcement of the tax, on the ground "that the statute is invalid in that it discriminates in favour of wines and beers manufactured in the state and against those which are manufactured elsewhere," and judgment on demurrer against the plaintiff was affirmed in the state court of last resort and in the Supreme Court, on the grounds, as stated by Field, J., that while "the statute of Texas is inoperative, so far as it makes a discrimination against wines and beer imported from other states when sold separately from other liquors," yet the plaintiff, being engaged in the sale of liquor other than beer or wines, and the statute making no discrimination in favour of other liquors of home manufacture, the plaintiff was rightfully taxed. Of course, he who claims, under the cases

[1] p. 501.   [2] 102 U. S. 123.

cited, exemption from the burden of state taxation, must prove his case; thus, in Downham *v.* Alexandria Council,[1] the council of the city of Alexandria in the state of Virginia having imposed a license tax of $200 upon dealers in beer and ale not manufactured in the city but brought there for sale, and Downham asserting the invalidity of the tax as affecting ale and beer manufactured in a foreign country, or in another state of the Union, but having proved only that the ale and beer, in which he dealt, were not manufactured in the city of Alexandria, the court dismissed the writ of error to the judgment of the state court which had held him liable to the payment of the tax, on the ground that the record raised no federal question.

40. The United States are expressly forbidden to tax exports by section 9 of article I of the Constitution, which declares that "no tax or duty shall be laid on articles exported from any state." This constitutional restraint upon the federal power has been subjected to judicial consideration in only two cases. In Pace *v.* Burgess[2] the question was, whether or not the charge for stamps required by the act of Congress of July 20, 1868,[3] and 6 June, 1872,[4] to be placed by the manufacturers upon snuff and tobacco manufactured, not for domestic use, but for exportation to foreign countries, constituted, in the constitutional sense of the term, "a tax or duty" "on articles exported from any state," and the court held, that the requirement of such stamps was not a method of imposing an export tax or duty, but was simply the means devised for the prevention of fraud by separating and identifying the tobacco intended for exportation from that which was intended for domestic use, and of relieving the former from the inter-

[1] 10 Wall. 173.
[2] 92 U. S. 372.
[3] 15 Stat. 157.
[4] 17 *id.* 254.

nal revenue taxation to which the latter was subjected, and that the price of such stamps was, in effect, nothing more than a charge for the services rendered by the government in effecting the segregation of the tobacco intended for exportation, and, therefore, in no sense a tax or duty on exports. In Turpin *v.* Burgess,[1] the court re-affirmed the doctrine of Pace *v.* Burgess, and decided further, that the stamps being required to be affixed to the tobacco before it left the factory could not constitute a tax on exports because the tobacco was not then in course of exportation, however much the manufacturer might then intend to ultimately export it; and in support of that view, Bradley, J., referred to Coe *v.* Errol,[2] wherein it was held that "goods intended for exportation to another state are liable to taxation as part of the general mass of property of the state of their origin until actually started in a course of transportation to the state of their destination, or delivered to a common carrier for that purpose."

41. Section 10 of article I of the Constitution declares, that "no state shall, without the consent of Congress, lay any imposts or duties on imports or exports, except what may be absolutely necessary for executing its inspection laws, and the net proceeds of all duties and imposts laid by any state on imports and exports shall be for the use of the treasury of the United States and all such laws shall be subject to the revision and control of Congress." In Brown *v.* Maryland,[3] it was held that a state statute, requiring all importers of foreign goods by the bale or package, etc., and other persons selling the same by wholesale, bale, or package, etc., to take out a license, paying $50 therefor, and, for neglect or refusal to take out the license, subjecting them to certain forfeitures and penalties, was void for repug-

---

[1] 117 U. S. 504.   [2] 116 U. S. 517.   [3] 12 Wheat. 419.

nancy both to the commerce clause of the Constitution, and to the express prohibition of state duties on imports and exports save under the specific exception in the 10th section of article I of the Constitution, the ground of decision being that the power to regulate commerce with foreign nations includes the power to impose duties on the importation of goods therefrom, and, on condition of the payment of the duties, to license the importation and sale of the goods within any state, and that a penalty inflicted by a state on the importer for selling the goods as importer in the original form and package in which they are imported, and before they are incorporated with the mass of the property in the country, is an interference with the freedom of importation, and as such an usurpation of power vested by the Constitution exclusively in the government of the United States.[1] The doctrine of Brown *v.* Maryland has been applied in later cases. Thus it has been held, in Low *v.* Austin,[2] that a state cannot impose an *ad valorem* tax on imported goods remaining in their original cases in the hands of the importer, though a similar tax be imposed on all merchandise in the state; and, in Cook *v.* Pennsylvania,[3] that a state cannot tax an auctioneer's sales of imported goods in their original cases sold by him for the account of the importers thereof.[4] In The State

---

[1] Marshall. C. J., said, p. 446, "Commerce is intercourse: one of its most ordinary ingredients is traffic. It is inconceivable that the power to authorize this traffic, when given in the most comprehensive terms, with the intent that its efficacy should be complete, should cease at the point when its continuance is indispensable to its value. . . . . Sale is the object of importation, and is an essential ingredient of that intercourse, of which importation constitutes a part. It is as essential an ingredient, as indispensable to the existence of the entire thing, then, as importation itself. It must be considered as a component part of the power to regulate commerce. Congress has a right, not only to authorize importation, but to authorize the importer to sell."

[2] 13 Wall. 29.    [3] 97 U. S. 566.

[4] In Groves *v.* Slaughter, 15 Pet. 449, it was argued that interstate traffic in

Tax on Railway Gross Receipts,[1] it was held, that state taxation of the gross receipts of a railway is not taxation of imports or exports, although those gross receipts include freights from the transportation of merchandise, which has come into a state from a foreign country, or which is in course of transportation within the state, for the purpose of being exported therefrom, but that case, having been shaken, as an authority, by the case of Fargo v. Michigan,[2] has been overruled by Philadelphia and Southern Steamship Co. v. Pennsylvania,[3] and state taxation of the gross receipts of the transportation of imported or exported goods, either by land or water, is no longer permissible. In Almy v. California,[4] the court held that a stamp duty imposed by a state on bills of lading for gold or silver fell within the constitutional prohibition of duties on exports, not noticing in the judgment the argument which had been made at the bar, that the stamp duty in question was also unconstitutional as a regulation of commerce. Miller, J., in his judgment in Woodruff v. Parham,[5] pointed out that the question in Almy v. California was really one of interstate, and not of foreign, commerce, and he added, "the case, however, was well decided on the ground taken by Mr. Blair, counsel for defendant, namely:—that such a tax was 'a regulation of commerce,' a tax imposed upon the transportation of goods from one state to another, over the high seas, in conflict with that freedom of transit of goods and persons between one state and another, which is within the rule laid down in Crandall v. Nevada,[6] and with the

slaves was, as interstate commerce, subject to regulation by Congress and exempt from state regulation, but the court did not decide the question, for the case went off on other points.

[1] 15 Wall. 284.
[2] 121 U. S. 230.
[3] 122 U. S. 326.
[4] 24 How. 169.
[5] 8 Wall. 138.
[6] 6 Wall. 35.

authority of Congress to regulate commerce among the states." It must also be remembered that the words "imports" and "exports" include only merchandise brought from foreign countries into the United States or carried from the United States to foreign countries, and not merchandise moved from one state into another state, and therefore a state may tax merchandise of the latter description, provided there be in such taxation no discrimination as against the growth or products of other states nor any regulation of interstate commerce.[1] The word "imports" in the constitutional sense of the term, as applied to goods brought from a foreign country, does not include merchandise, which, by the terms of the contract of purchase, is not to be at the risk of the purchaser until delivered to him in the port of entry, and such goods, though in their original packages, may be taxed by a state in whose port their contract of purchase is completed by delivery.[2] The power vested in Congress to regulate commerce carries with it also, by implication, the power of punishing the commission of acts within the territory of a state which interfere with, obstruct, or prevent the transportation of goods by sea from foreign countries. Thus in United States v. Coombs,[3] the ninth section of the Act of Congress of 3 March, 1825, having forbidden under penalty of fine and imprisonment, the plundering of merchandise from any ship in distress or cast away in any place within the admiralty or maritime jurisdiction of the United States, and Coombs, on an indictment under that law, having been convicted, on proof that he had stolen goods from the ship Bristol cast away above high-water mark at Rockaway Beach in the state of New York, the conviction was sustained,

[1] Woodruff v. Parham, 8 Wall. 123; Brown v. Houston, 114 U. S. 622.
[2] Waring v. The Mayor, 8 Wall. 110.   [3] 12 Pet. 72.

the court holding that the statute in question was rightfully enacted in the exercise of the power to regulate commerce.

In Gibbons v. Ogden,[1] Marshall, C. J., said, "the object of inspection laws is to improve the quality of articles produced by the labour of a country; to fit them for exportation; or, it may be, for domestic use. They act upon the subject before it becomes an article of foreign commerce, or of commerce among the states, and prepare it for that purpose. They form a portion of that immense mass of legislation which embraces everything within the territory of a state, not surrendered to the general government; all which can be most advantageously exercised by the states themselves."[2] In Turner v. Maryland,[3] Blatchford, J., said, that the "recognized elements of inspection laws have always been quality of the article, form, capacity, dimensions, and weight of package, mode of putting up and marking and branding of various kinds, all these matters being supervised by a public officer having authority to pass, or not pass, the article as lawful merchandise, as it did, or did not, answer the prescribed requirements. It has never been regarded as necessary, and it is manifestly not necessary, that all those elements should coexist in order to make a valid inspection law. Quality alone may be the subject of the inspection without other requirement, or the inspection may be made to extend to all the above matters. When all are prescribed, and then inspection as to quality is dropped out, leaving the rest in force, it cannot be said to be a necessary legal conclusion that the law has ceased to be an inspection law."

[1] 9 Wheat. 203.
[2] For a reference to state inspection laws, see note to Gibbons v. Ogden, 9 Wheat. 119, and note to Turner v. Maryland, 107 U. S. 51 et seq.
[3] 107 U. S. 55.

## INSPECTION LAWS. 87

In Turner v. Maryland,[1] the question was as to the constitutionality of a statute of the state of Maryland, prohibiting under a penalty the exportation in hogsheads of tobacco raised in the state, without delivery at a state tobacco warehouse, there to be inspected, numbered, recorded, weighed, and marked, and without payment of certain specified fees, called "outage," as charges for the performance of service by the state's officials. The court decided in favour of the validity of the statute, on the ground that it was enacted in the exercise of the state's power to lay such duties on exports as "may be absolutely necessary for executing its inspection laws," similar laws having been at various times enacted by many of the states, and Congress never having claimed the net proceeds of such duties, nor exercised its revisory and controlling power. The words "inspection laws," "imports," and "exports" as used in the Constitution having exclusive reference to property as distinguished from persons,[2] a state *per capita* tax on immigrants cannot be sustained as a means of executing the inspection laws of a state.[3]

42. The result of the cases with regard to improvements of navigation is that, while Congress may, in the exercise of its power to regulate commerce, authorize or prohibit improvements to the waterways of foreign or interstate commerce, a state may, if Congress does not prohibit, improve such waterways within its jurisdiction, and a state may exercise exclusive control over such other waterways as are within its territory, and are not used in the transportation of foreign or interstate commerce. Thus in South Carolina v. Georgia,[4] the facts were, that the states of South Carolina and Georgia hav-

---

[1] 107 U. S. 38.  
[2] Crandall v. Nevada, 6 Wall. 35.  
[3] People v. Compagnie Générale Transatlantique, 107 U. S. 59.  
[4] 93 U. S. 4.

ing on 24 April, 1787,[1] entered into a compact stipulating, *inter alia*, that the boundary line between the two states should be the northern branch of the Savannah river, and that the navigation of the river along a specified channel should be forever free to the citizens of both states, Congress by the Act of 23 June, 1874,[2] appropriated certain sums of money "to be expended under the direction of the Secretary of War, . . . for continuing the improvement of the harbour at Savannah," and that officer, for the purpose of securing a greater depth of water in that harbour, authorized the construction of a crib, which had the effect of diverting the water from the northern branch of the river, referred to in the compact of 1787. The state of South Carolina then filed its bill in equity in the Supreme Court of the United States against the state of Georgia, the Secretary of War, Mr. Taft, and his subordinates, General Humphries and Colonel Gilmore, praying an injunction to restrain them from obstructing the navigation of the Savannah river in violation of the compact between South Carolina and Georgia. At the hearing the court dismissed the bill, holding that whatever might have been the rights of South Carolina and Georgia under the compact of 1787, the Constitution of the United States vested in Congress the power of regulating foreign and interstate commerce, and thereby authorized Congress to do whatever in its discretion, or in the discretion of its agents, might be expedient in the improvement of the navigation of the harbours and rivers which are waterways of commerce, foreign and interstate, even to the extent of changing the established channels of such rivers.

---

[1] The Constitution of the United States went into effect on the first Wednesday in March, 1789. Owings *v.* Speed, 5 Wheat. 420.

[2] 18 Stat. 240.

In Wisconsin v. Duluth,[1] the facts were, that Congress having directed, and appropriated the money for, the improvement of the harbour of Duluth, a town in the state of Minnesota, and situated upon Lake Superior, the state of Wisconsin apprehending, as the result of the improvements contemplated and in progress of construction, a diversion of trade from the town of Superior City, also on Lake Superior, but in the state of Wisconsin, by reason of alterations in the channel of a river flowing into the lake, filed a bill in equity in the Supreme Court of the United States to enjoin the continuance of the work by the city of Duluth. The answer set up as an affirmative defense, that the work had been done with the approval and under the control of the United States, and with money appropriated therefor by Congress, and the court at the hearing, on bill, answer, and proofs, sustained the defense as set up in the answer and dismissed the bill. Miller, J., said,[2] " while this court has maintained, in many cases, the right of the states to authorize structures in and over the navigable waters of the states, which may either impede or improve their navigation, in the absence of any action of the general government in the same matter, the doctrine has been laid down with unvarying uniformity, that when Congress has, by any expression of its will, occupied the field, that action was conclusive of any right to the contrary asserted under state authority. . . . . . . . . If then, Congress, in the exercise of a lawful authority, has adopted and is carrying out a system of harbour improvements at Duluth, this court can have no lawful authority to forbid the work. . . . . While the engineering officers of the government are, under the authority of Congress, doing all they can to make this canal useful to com-

[1] 96 U. S. 379.      [2] p. 387.

merce, and to keep it in good condition, this court can owe no duty to a state which requires it to order the city of Duluth to destroy it."

On the other hand, in the County of Mobile *v.* Kimball,[1] the facts were, that a statute of Alabama having created a Board of Commissioners for the improvement, deepening, and widening of the harbour of Mobile, and having authorized an issue of bonds to defray the cost of the improvements, and certain of the bonds having been stipulated to be issued to Kimball, a contractor for a portion of the work, Kimball filed a bill in equity to compel a delivery of certain bonds remaining due to him, and the defendants set up, among other defenses, the unconstitutionality of the statute by reason of its infringement upon the power of Congress over commerce. The court, however, affirmed the constitutionality of the statute, on grounds which can be best stated in the words of Field, J.,[2] who said, "the uniformity of commercial regulations, which the grant to Congress was designed to secure against conflicting state provisions, was necessarily intended only for cases where such uniformity is practicable. Where from the nature of the subject or the sphere of its operations the case is local and limited, special regulations adapted to the immediate locality could only have been contemplated. State action upon such subjects can constitute no interference with the commercial power of Congress, for when that acts the state authority is superseded. Inaction of Congress upon these subjects of a local nature or operation, unlike its inaction upon matters affecting all the states and requiring uniformity of regulation, is not to be taken as a declaration that nothing shall be done with respect to them, but it is rather to be deemed a declara-

[1] 102 U. S. 691.      [2] p. 698.

tion that for the time being, and until it sees fit to act, they may be regulated by state authority. The improvement of harbours, bays, and navigable rivers within the states falls within this last category of cases. The control of Congress over them is to insure freedom in their navigation so far as that is essential to the exercise of its commercial power. Such freedom is not encroached upon by the removal of obstructions to their navigability, or by other legitimate improvements. The states have as full control over their purely internal commerce as Congress has over commerce among the several states and with foreign nations; and to promote the growth of that internal commerce and insure its safety they have an undoubted right to remove obstructions from their harbours and rivers, deepen their channels, and improve them generally if they do not impair their free navigation as permitted under the laws of the United States, or defeat any system for the improvement of their navigation provided by the general government." The case of Huse *v.* Glover,[1] follows in the same line. The facts in that case were that the state of Illinois, having by statute authorized the improvement of the navigation of the Illinois river in that state, including the construction of locks and dams, and the imposition of tolls proportioned to the tonnage of the vessels passing through the locks, the complainants, as owners of steamboats engaged in the navigation of the river, filed a bill in equity in the Circuit Court of the United States for the Northern District of Illinois to enjoin the Commissioners from exacting tolls for the passage of the complainants' steamboats, and from interfering with their free and uninterrupted navigation of the river. The cause was argued in the court below on demurrer to the bill,

[1] 119 U. S. 543.

and a decree entered dismissing it, which on appeal was affirmed by the Supreme Court, on the ground that the state could rightfully make the improvement, in the exercise of its legislative discretion, "although increased inconvenience and expense may thereby result to the business of individuals," and charge tolls therefor, whose exaction is "compensation for the use of artificial facilities constructed," and not "an impost for the navigation of the stream," and the fixing of whose rate in proportion to the tonnage of the vessel and the amount of freight carried by them is not a duty on tonnage within the meaning of the constitutional prohibition, because it is not "a charge upon a vessel, according to its tonnage, as an instrument of commerce, for entering or leaving a port or navigating the public waters of the country."[1] The doctrine of Huse v. Glover was reiterated in Sands v. Manistee River Improvement Company,[2] in which case it was further held, that the exaction of tolls for the use of an improved waterway is not a deprivation of property without due process of law, within the meaning of the XIV Amendment. So also in Withers v. Buckley,[3] Withers being the owner of a plantation on Old river, which was within the state of Mississippi, and the state having by statute authorized a diversion of the water from that river, filed a bill in a court of the state to enjoin the prosecution of the work: the defendant demurred and at the hearing a decree was entered dismissing the plaintiff's bill, and on appeal that decree was affirmed. Veazie v. Moor[4] involves the same principle.

43. The deduction to be drawn from the cases as to dams and bridges is that the ultimate power of bridging, or otherwise obstructing, navigable waters is vested

---

[1] See the Wharfage Cases, Sec. 45.
[2] 123 U. S. 288.
[3] 20 How. 84.
[4] 14 How. 568.

in Congress, and as navigable waters are no longer the sole, nor, indeed, the main channels of commerce, and as that volume of trade which is carried over such waters by bridges or viaducts is in some cases entitled, by reason of its magnitude, to greater consideration than that which is moved in boats upon the water, it must be determined in the case of any bridge, whose erection or the method of whose construction is called into question, whether or not the public interest will be promoted by its construction in the particular manner, and such a matter is primarily one for the decision of the legislature rather than of any courts, and until Congress has exercised its paramount power in the premises, the state or states within whose jurisdiction navigable waters are situated may, at its or their pleasure, authorize by legislation the complete obstruction of those waters by dams, or their partial obstruction by bridges. The leading case is Willson v. The Black Bird Creek Marsh Co.,[1] in which the facts were, that the Black Bird Creek being a navigable stream wholly within the state of Delaware, and that state having enacted a statute authorizing the company to construct a dam across the creek, and the dam having been built, and a sloop, enrolled and licensed under the navigation laws of the United States, and owned by Willson, having broken and injured the dam, the company brought an action of trespass *vi et armis* against Willson in a court of the state of Delaware, and he raised, by plea, the question of the right of the state to authorize the obstruction of a navigable stream. A verdict having been found for the plaintiff, judgment thereon was affirmed by the Supreme Court, the ground of decision being,[2] that, while Congress could authorize or prohibit

[1] 2 Pet. 245.
[2] Marshall, C. J., p. 252, said;—"if Congress had passed any act which

the obstruction of a navigable river, yet if that body did not act, the state, within whose territory the navigable river in question was situated, was free in its discretion to authorize the obstruction. The next case in the order of time is Pennsylvania *v.* The Wheeling and Belmont Bridge Co.[1] The facts were that, when the state of Kentucky was created by the severance of its territory from that of Virginia, the two states entered into a compact stipulating that the navigation of the Ohio "shall be free and common to the citizens of the United States," and that compact received the sanction of Congress. Congress thereafter neither licensed nor prohibited the obstruction of the navigation of the Ohio by a bridge, nor made any statutory regulations of commerce on the Ohio, other than such as were applicable to the navigable waters of the United States in general. The state of Virginia thereafter by statute authorized the construction of a bridge over the Ohio river from Wheeling to an island in the river belonging to Virginia, the manner of construction designated in the statute necessarily interfering with the navigation of the river by steamboats plying on the river between Pittsburg in the state of Pennsylvania and the points below the bridge on the Ohio and on the Mississippi. At that time the state of Pennsylvania was the proprietor of certain lines of railway and canal, connecting Pittsburg with the eastern portion of the state. While the bridge

bore upon the case; any act in execution of the power to regulate commerce, the object of which was to control state legislation over those small navigable reeks into which the tide flows, and which abound throughout the lower country of the middle and southern states; we should feel not much difficulty in saying that a state law coming in conflict with such act would be void. But Congress has passed no such act. The repugnancy of the law of Delaware to the Constitution is placed entirely on its repugnancy to the power to regulate commerce with foreign nations and among the several states; a power which has not been so exercised as to affect the question."

[1] 9 How. 647, 11 *id.* 528, 13 *id.* 518, 18 *id.* 421.

was in progress of construction, the state of Pennsylvania filed its bill in equity in the Supreme Court of the United States against the bridge company, praying an injunction to restrain the erection of the bridge and a decree for its abatement as a nuisance. Various interlocutory proceedings were had, and the court held that the state of Pennsylvania had, by virtue of its ownership of an interest in its lines of railway and canal, a standing in court; that the bridge was an obstruction to the navigation of the Ohio, and, as such, a violation of the compact between Virginia and Ohio, and that it must be abated as a nuisance, unless so modified in construction as not to obstruct the navigation. Further proceedings in the suit were, however, prevented by the passage of an act of Congress declaring the bridge as constructed to be a lawful structure, and the constitutional validity of this act having been sustained by the court, it necessarily followed that nothing more could be done by the court than to insist that so much of its final decree as awarded costs to the plaintiff in the suit should be carried into effect. The case, as presented to the court for a decree on the merits, was simply that of a bridge over navigable waters which were wholly within the jurisdiction of the state of Virginia, the erection and manner of construction of the bridge having been sanctioned by the state of Virginia, and not prohibited by the United States, and yet on this state of facts the court held that the bridge was abatable as a nuisance. This conclusion is certainly not reconcilable with the doctrine of either Willson *v.* Black Bird Creek Marsh Company, or with that of the later cases.[1] Indeed, the only possible distinction upon the facts to be drawn between the Wheeling Bridge

[1] See the dissenting judgment of Clifford, J., in which Wayne and Davis, JJ., concurred, in Gilman *v.* Philadelphia, 3 Wall. 732.

Case and the other cases on the subject to which reference has been, or will be, made, is to be found in the facts that the Ohio river constituted a waterway of interstate commerce between Pennsylvania and the states between which the Mississippi flows, and that by compact between Virginia and Kentucky the navigation of the Ohio was declared "to be free and common to all the states;" but neither of these distinguishing facts could afford any ground for denying the right of Virginia to control the navigation of so much of the river as is within its jurisdiction so long as Congress, the constituted guardian of the rights of the citizens of all the states, deemed it unnecessary to interfere. The next case is M. & M. R. R. *v.* Ward,[1] in which Ward filed his bill in the District Court of the United States for the District of Iowa, as the owner and the navigator of steamboats plying on the Mississippi river between St. Louis in the state of Missouri and St. Paul in the state of Minnesota, praying a decree for the abatement as a nuisance of a bridge over the Mississippi erected by the railroad company between Rock Island in the state of Illinois and Davenport in the state of Iowa under the authority of statutes of the two states. The court below entered a decree, directing the abatement of so much of the bridge as was within the limits of the state of Iowa, and on appeal by the railroad company, the Supreme Court reversed the decree and dismissed the plaintiff's bill.[2] The reasons for the decree of reversal, as stated by Catron, J., were, that the middle of the Mississippi river between Illinois and Iowa being the boundary dividing the one state from the other, and the territorial jurisdiction of the District Court of the

---

[1] 2 Bl. 485.
[2] Catron, J., delivered the opinion of the court, and Nelson, Wayne, and Clifford, JJ., dissented.

United States for the District of Iowa being restricted to the limits of that state, and a bill in equity to enjoin a nuisance being a remedy local in its character and operation, the court below had no jurisdiction to abate as a nuisance so much of the bridge as was within the jurisdiction of Illinois, and that on the proofs, the main channel of the river being on the Illinois side, it could not be held that the bridge by its obstruction to navigation on the Iowa side constituted so serious a nuisance as to justify the prostration of so much of the bridge as was on the Iowa side.[1]

The next cases that follow in the order of time are The Albany Bridge Case[2] and The Passaic Bridge Case,[3] and, in each of these cases, a decree of a Circuit Court dismissing a bill filed to enjoin the construction under state authority of a bridge over a navigable stream within the jurisdiction of a state was affirmed in the Supreme Court by an equally divided court, and, therefore, these cases, though technically authorities in favour of the right of the state,[4] have not that moral weight which attaches to judgments which are pronounced by all, or a majority of, the members of the tribunal, and which state the reasoning which has led the court to its conclusions. The next case is Gilman v. Philadelphia,[5] in which the facts were that Gilman, a citizen of New Hampshire, and the owner of coal wharves on the river Schuylkill in the state of Pennsylvania, filed his bill in equity in the Circuit Court of the United States to enjoin the construction under the

---

[1] Nelson, Wayne, and Clifford, JJ., dissented on the ground that the rule, as established by the Wheeling Bridge Case, being that riparian states have no power to obstruct the free navigation of a navigable river, it must in every case be found as a fact whether or not the bridge, whose abatement is sought as a nuisance, does so obstruct, and if that finding be in favour of the plaintiff, a decree of abatement follows.

[2] 2 Wall. 403.
[3] 3 Wall. Appendix 782.
[4] Queen v. Millis, 10 Cl. & Fin. 534.
[5] 3 Wall. 713.

authority of that state, of a bridge over the Schuylkill river which would obstruct the navigation of that river and prevent the approach of boats to his wharves. A decree dismissing the plaintiff's bill was affirmed,[1] the court holding that there was no distinction in principle between the case at bar and the case of Wilson v. The Blackbird Creek Marsh Co.,[2] and that the rule laid down in the earlier case was decisive of the controversy. The later cases of Pound v. Turck,[3] Escanaba Co. v. Chicago,[4] Cardwell v. American Bridge Co.,[5] Hamilton v. V. S. & P. R. R.,[6] and Huse v. Glover,[7] follow in the same line and require but slight comment. It is, however, to be noticed that the court held in Escanaba Co. v. Chicago, and in Huse v. Glover, and also in Sands v. M. R. & I. Co.,[8] that the pre-constitutional ordinance of 1787 for the government of the northwestern territory, providing for the free navigation of the waters leading into the Mississippi and the St. Lawrence, "without any tax, impost, or duty therefor," could not limit the powers of the states under the Constitution, and that if it could, the privilege of free navigation without tax, impost, or duty was not impaired by the construction of bridges over these waters.[9] In Cardwell v. Bridge Co., it was decided that the act of Congress admitting California to the Union, and declaring, in terms almost identical with those of the ordinance of 1787, that the navigable waters of the state should be forever free, did not affect the state's rights to bridge those navigable waters, and, in Hamilton v. V. S. & P.

---

[1] Chase, C. J., and Nelson, Grier, Swayne, Miller, and Field, JJ., concurring, and Clifford, Wayne, and Davis, JJ., dissenting.
[2] 2 Pet. 250.     [3] 95 U. S. 459.     [4] 107 U. S. 678.     [5] 113 U. S. 205.
[6] 119 U. S. 280.     [7] 119 U. S. 543.     [8] 123 U. S. 288.
[9] That case also rules that a state may delegate to a municipal corporation created by it the power to construct, repair, and regulate the use of bridges under state authority.

R. R., the court refused to give any greater effect to a similar declaration with regard to the navigation of the Mississippi and its tributaries contained in the act of Congress admitting the state of Louisiana to the Union. Nevertheless, while the states may in the absence of congressional action upon the subject, in their discretion partially obstruct by bridges, or wholly obstruct by dams, navigable waters within their limits, yet the ultimate power over the matter is vested in Congress, Bridge Co. v. United States,[1] and Congress may forbid, or permit upon conditions, the erection of a bridge under state authority,[2] or it may legalize a bridge already erected, pending a suit to enjoin its construction,[3] or even after the Supreme Court of the United States has entered a final decree declaring the bridge as constructed to be an unlawful obstruction to navigation.[4] It is also competent for Congress to declare that a bridge over navigable waters, if constructed in a specified way, shall not be held to be a nuisance, but shall be deemed to be a lawful structure, and to delegate to the Secretary of War, or to other officers of the government, the duty of determining whether or not the required method of construction has been adopted.[5]

44. The result of the cases as to ferries is, that interstate ferries are primarily subjects of state regulation, and that a state may tax a ferry franchise granted by it, and that it may tax the ferry-boats owned by a person, natural or corporate, who, by reason of residence

---

[1] 105 U. S. 470. For a reference to the acts of Congress, which have been passed in the exercise of this power, see the judgment of Waite, C. J., 105 U. S. 476.

[2] Bridge Co v. United States, 105 U. S. 470.

[3] The Clinton Bridge, 10 Wall. 454.

[4] Pennsylvania v. W. & B. Bridge Co., 18 How. 421.

[5] Miller v. New York, 109 U. S. 385, 393.

within the territory, is subject to its jurisdiction; but a state may not tax ferry-boats owned by a person, natural or corporate, who is not by residence within its territory subject to its jurisdiction, and which only come within its jurisdiction in the prosecution of interstate commerce. In Gibbons v. Ogden,[1] Marshall, C. J., enumerates "turnpike roads, ferries," etc., as "component parts" of "that immense mass of legislation, which embraces everything within the territory of a state not surrendered to the general government," yet as Field, J., has clearly shown in Gloucester Ferry Co. v. Pennsylvania,[2] these words, fairly taken, do not mean that a state can so regulate ferries plying between its ports and the ports of another state as to obstruct interstate or foreign commerce, but they mean only that, as the privilege of keeping a ferry has been from earliest times "a franchise grantable by the state, to be exercised within such limits and under such regulations as may be required for the safety, comfort, and convenience of the public,"[3] the state may annex conditions to the grant of the franchise. A ferry is a franchise entitling him to whom it is granted to exercise at a designated point on the bank of some navigable water the privilege of embarking and landing passengers for and from some other point. Thus it is said in Viner's Abridgment,[4] "a Ferry is in Respect of the Landing Place, and not of the Water; the Water may be to one and the Ferry to another; as 'tis of Ferries on the Thames, where the Ferry in some Place belongs to the Arch Bishop of Canterbury, when the Mayor of London has the interest in the Water; and in every Ferry the Land of both Sides of the Water ought to be to the Owner of the Ferry, or

---

[1] 9 Wheat. 203.
[2] 114 U. S. 196.
[3] per Field, J., 114 U. S. 196.
[4] Vol. XIII, 208, tit. Ferry.

otherwise he cannot land on the other Part." A ferry is therefore, the subject of grant and regulation under state authority. Thus in Conway *v.* Taylor,[1] the state of Kentucky having granted to the appellees an exclusive ferry at the town of Newport in that state situated on the Ohio river, and the appellees having under that license maintained the ferry between Newport and Cincinnati in the state of Ohio, and the appellants having undertaken, by means of a steamboat licensed as a coasting vessel of the United States, to carry passengers between Cincinnati and Newport and to land them at the latter port in derogation of the exclusive ferry right vested in the appellees, and having been at the suit of the appellees enjoined from so doing by the decree of the court below, that decree was affirmed, on the ground that the ferry franchise, being granted in respect of the landing, was a matter of state regulation, that so far as regards rights exercised in one state under such a franchise, though as a means to the end of transportation, to or from another state, the concurrent action of the two states was not necessary, and that the United States coasting license granted to the appellant's boat, while entitling them to navigate in the prosecution of commerce, did not empower them to invade the appellee's ferry franchise, nor to participate in the exercise of that privilege, for " the vitality of such a franchise lies in its exclusiveness," and "the moment the right becomes common, the franchise ceases to exist."[2] The

---

[1] 1 Bl. 603.
[2] per Swayne, J., p. 634. In Fanning *v.* Gregoire, 16 How. 524, where the question was as to the exclusive character of a ferry franchise under the terms of a certain grant and the decision was adverse to its exclusiveness, McLean, J., said, p. 534, "the argument that the free navigation of the Mississippi river, guaranteed by the ordinance of 1787, or any right which may be supposed to arise from the exercise of the commercial power of Congress, does not apply in this case. Neither of these interferes with the police power of the states, in granting ferry licenses. When navigable rivers, within the

right of a riparian state to grant franchises to ferries engaged in the transportation of passengers to and from its shore to that of another state, includes both the right to grant such ferries on condition, that is, to license them on payment of a fee, or tax them for, and also, under certain limitations, to tax the boats and other property used in the business of the ferry. Thus, in Wiggins Ferry Co. *v.* East St. Louis,[1] the facts were, that the state of Illinois having by a statute of 1819 granted to Wiggins the franchise of establishing and running a ferry upon the Mississippi, and having by a statute of 1853 incorporated the Wiggins Ferry Company with power to hold, use, and enjoy the franchise theretofore granted to Wiggins and to run a ferry from East St. Louis in Illinois to St. Louis in Missouri, and the company having in the exercise of its franchise employed boats which had been duly licensed as coasting vessels of the United States, and the city of East St. Louis having, under the powers conferred upon it by its charter, imposed, by an ordinance of 1878, a license fee of $100 *per annum* for each boat of the Wiggins Ferry Company, and, on the company's refusal to make payment thereof, having brought an action to recover the amount of the annual license then due, judgment was rendered in the court below against the ferry company and affirmed in the Supreme Court, the ground of decision being that the tax, being imposed not on the boats but on their owner, and being assessed at a fixed rate and not graduated in proportion to the carrying capacity of the boats, was not a tonnage tax, and being taxation of the personal property of the owner, who was admittedly resident within the jurisdiction of the state

commercial power of the Union, may be obstructed, one or both of these powers may be invoked."

[1] 107 U. S. 365.

and, therefore, subject to taxation by it, it was not a regulation of commerce, nor an infringement upon any rights conferred by the enrollment and licensing of the boats under the statutes of the United States. Transportation Co. v. Wheeling,[1] lays down the same principles. In St. Louis v. The Wiggins Ferry Co.,[2] the sole question was whether the company was taxable by the city of St. Louis under a statute permitting that city to tax "all property within the city," the facts as found in the case being that the company was incorporated under the laws of Illinois, but its principal office was in St. Louis in the state of Missouri, while the boats when not in actual use were laid up on the Illinois shore, and when in use were permitted by the ordinances of St. Louis to remain not longer than ten minutes at a time at their St. Louis landing. On these facts the court held, that the boats "did not so abide within the city as to become incorporated with and form part of its personal property," and, "hence they were beyond the jurisdiction of the authorities by which the taxes were assessed," and were not within the meaning of the statute "within the city." In Gloucester Ferry Co. v. Pennsylvania,[3] the facts were that the company having been incorporated by a statute of the state of New Jersey, maintained a ferry on the Delaware river between Gloucester in that state, and Philadelphia in the state of Pennsylvania, owning a dock at Gloucester and leasing one at Philadelphia, and owning or leasing the boats which it used in the operation of the ferry, those boats being registered at the port of Camden in the state of New Jersey, and when not in use being laid up on the New Jersey bank of the Delaware, and when in use only remaining at the dock on the Pennsylvania side sufficiently long to discharge and load passengers

[1] 99 U. S. 273.     [2] 11 Wall. 423.     [3] 114 U. S. 196.

and freight. The state of Pennsylvania having assessed the capital stock of the company for taxation under a statute of the state subjecting to taxation the capital stock of companies incorporated by other states and " doing business in " that state, and the Supreme Court, of the state having held the company liable to taxation under that statute, the Supreme Court of the United States reversed the decree of the state court, holding that while the company did business within the state of Pennsylvania within the meaning of the statute imposing the tax, yet, the business being interstate commerce, inasmuch as it was the interstate transportation of passengers and freight, and the capital of the company being invested in its boats and in that business, that capital was not subject to taxation by the state of Pennsylvania, for the reason that such taxation was in practical effect the imposition of a burden on, and an obstruction to, and, therefore, a regulation of, interstate commerce, and as such void. Field, J., said,[1] " the company has no domicile in Pennsylvania, and its capital stock representing its property is held outside of its limits. It is solely, therefore, for the business of the company in landing and receiving passengers at the wharf in Philadelphia that the tax is laid, and that business, as already said, is an essential part of the transportation between the states of New Jersey and Pennsylvania, which is itself interstate commerce. While it is conceded that the property in a state belonging to a foreign corporation engaged in foreign and interstate commerce may be taxed equally with like property of a domestic corporation engaged in that business, we are clear that a tax or other burden imposed on the property of either corporation because it is used to carry on that commerce, or upon the transportation of persons or

[1] p. 211.

property, or for the navigation of the public waters over which the transportation is made, is invalid and void as an interference with, and an obstruction of, the power of Congress in the regulation of such commerce." The doctrine of this case is further supported by that of P. & S. S. S. Co. v. Pennsylvania.[1]

45. The validity of charges imposed on vessels by reason of their use of the facilities afforded by wharves and piers constructed under state authority on the banks of navigable waters depends upon the same principles as those which have been laid down in the cases of improvements to navigation; and the result of the cases is, that the states may build wharves on navigable rivers, and collect reasonable dues for the use thereof, provided that such dues are not so charged as to discriminate against interstate commerce. It has already been said,[2] that the title to the land under navigable waters is vested in the riparian state subject only to the paramount power of the United States over navigation. While the title of the individual riparian owner, in general, stops at high-water mark, the state has the power to build wharves and piers on the bank of the stream below high-water mark,[3] and it may charge and collect wharfage dues therefor. Thus in Packet Co. v. Keokuk,[4] the facts were that the municipal council of the city of Keokuk, situated on the Mississippi river, having under legislative authority constructed wharves on the river-front of the city, and having imposed as wharfage fees the sum of "$1 if the tonnage of the boat was less than 50 tons," and larger sums for heavier tonnage, and the Packet Co., as owner of steamboats licensed and enrolled under the act of Congress, and plying on the Mississippi river between St. Louis

[1] 122 U. S. 326.
[2] Section 32.
[3] Barney v. Keokuk, 94 U. S. 324.
[4] 95 U. S. 80.

and St. Paul, and in the course of their voyages landing at the city wharves at Keokuk, having refused to pay the wharfage charges, which were admittedly reasonable in amount, the city brought in a state court an action at law against the Packet Co. to recover the amount due for wharfage charges, and judgment was rendered against the Packet Co. and successively affirmed in the state court of last resort and in the Supreme Court of the United States, the ground of decision being, that wharfage dues are not taxes, that is, "impositions by virtue of sovereignty," but they are "a charge for services rendered, or for conveniences provided," and they are "claimed in right of proprietorship."[1] This case is followed and supported by Packet Co. v. St. Louis,[2] Vicksburg v. Tobin,[3] Packet Co. v. Catlettsburg,[4] Transportation Co. v. Parkersburg,[5] and Ouachita Packet Co. v. Aiken.[6] The last two cases are also authorities for the proposition, that wharfage dues, like the charges of common carriers, must be reasonable, but whether they be in fact reasonable is not a question of federal law, nor as such cognizable in a court of the United States in cases other than those in which the federal court has acquired jurisdiction by reason of the citizenship of the parties. Nevertheless, clear as is the right of a state to erect wharves on navigable waters and collect tolls or dues for their use, that right cannot be so exercised as to discriminate in favour of the products of its own territory and against interstate commerce. Thus, in Guy v. Baltimore,[7] the facts being, that the city of Baltimore having, under legislative authority, constructed public wharves, and imposed wharfage dues upon, *inter alia*,

[1] per Strong, J., p. 84.
[2] 100 U. S. 423.
[3] 100 U. S. 430.
[4] 105 U. S. 559.
[5] 107 U. S. 69.
[6] 121 U. S. 444.
[7] 100 U. S. 434.

potatoes not grown in the state of Maryland, and Guy, a resident and citizen of the county of Accomac in the state of Virginia, having arrived at Baltimore with a schooner laden with potatoes grown in the state of Virginia, and having, after landing his cargo at the city wharves, declined to pay the wharfage dues, the city of Baltimore brought an action against Guy in a state court to recover the statutory penalty for the non-payment of the wharfage dues, judgment was rendered against Guy, but reversed in the Supreme Court of the United States, on the ground that, under the circumstances of the case, the wharfage dues were exacted not as compensation for the use of the city's property, but "as a mere expedient or device to accomplish by indirection what the state could not accomplish by a direct tax, namely, build up its domestic commerce by means of unequal and oppressive burdens upon the industry and business of other states."[1]

46. The result of the cases as to pilotage is, that that subject being one primarily of local concern, the states may regulate and control it so long as, and to the extent that, Congress does not legislate with regard to it; but when Congress does legislate on the subject its regulation thereof will be of paramount authority. As the thirteen original states were existing governments when the Constitution was ratified, they all, with the exception of New Hampshire, had, before the adoption of the Constitution, enacted laws regulating pilotage. The act of Congress of 7 August, 1789, section 4,[2] pro-

[1] per Harlan, J., at p. 443. Waite, C. J., dissented. p. 444, saying, "the state of Maryland has seen fit to prohibit the City of Baltimore from making any such charge for landing and depositing the products of the state. That was all the state undertook to do. I am unable to bring my mind to the conclusion that the Constitution of the United States makes this the equivalent of a provision that all wharfage at the public wharves belonging to the city shall be free so long as the law as it now stands is in force."
[2] 1 Stat. 54.

vided, "that all pilots in the bays, inlets, rivers, harbours, and ports of the United States shall continue to be regulated in conformity with the existing laws of the states respectively wherein such pilots may be, or with such laws as the states may respectively hereafter enact for the purpose, until further legislative provision shall be made by Congress." The act of Congress of 2 March, 1837,[1] declared it "lawful for the master or commander of any vessel coming in or going out of any port, situate upon the waters which are the boundary between two states, to employ any pilot duly licensed or authorized by the laws of either of the states." In his judgment in the License Cases,[2] Taney, C. J., said that this act was "intended, as it is understood, to alter only a single provision of the New York law, leaving the residue of its provisions entirely untouched." The act of Congress of 30 August, 1852, section 9,[3] provided, *inter alia*, that "instead of the present system of pilotage" of vessels propelled in whole or in part by steam, certain designated inspectors shall license and "classify all" "pilots of steamers carrying passengers," and declares it "unlawful for any person to employ, or any person to serve, as engineer or pilot on any such vessel who is not licensed by the inspectors."[4] In Gibbons *v.* Ogden,[5] Marshall, C. J., said, "it has been said that the Act of 7 August, 1789, acknowledges a concurrent power in the states to regulate the conduct of pilots, and hence is inferred an admission of their concurrent right with Congress to regulate commerce with foreign nations and among the states. But this inference is not, we think, justified by the fact. Although Congress

---

[1] 5 Stat. 153.  [2] 5 How. 580.  [3] 10 Stat. 61.
[4] Sections 4235 *et seq.*, Revised Statutes of the United States, re-enact the Act of 1789.
[5] 9 Wheat. 207.

cannot enable a state to legislate, Congress may adopt the provisions of a state on any subject. When the government of the Union was brought into existence, it found a system for the regulation of its pilots in full force in every state. The act, which has been mentioned, adopts this system, and gives it the same validity as if its provisions had been specially made by Congress. But the act, it may be said, is prospective also, and the adoption of the laws to be made in future presupposes the right in the maker to legislate on the subject. The act unquestionably manifests an intention to leave this subject entirely to the states, until Congress should think proper to interpose; but the very enactment of such a law indicates an opinion that it was necessary: that the existing system would not be applicable to the new state of things, unless expressly applied to it by Congress. But this section is confined to the pilots within the "bays, inlets, rivers, harbours and ports of the United States," which are, of course, in whole or in part, also within the limits of some particular state. The acknowledged power of a state to regulate its police, its domestic trade, and to govern its own citizens may enable it to legislate on this subject to a considerable extent; and the adoption of its system by Congress, and the application of it to the whole subject of commerce, does not seem to the court to imply a right in the states so to apply it of their own authority. But the adoption of the state system being temporary, being only "until further legislative provisions shall be made by Congress," shows conclusively an opinion that Congress could control the whole subject, and might adopt the system of the states, or provide one of its own." In his judgment in the License Cases,[1] Taney, C. J., referring to the pilotage laws,

[1] 5 How. 580.

said, "they are admitted on all hands to belong to foreign commerce, and to be subject to the regulations of Congress. .... Yet they have been continually regulated by the maritime states, as fully and entirely since the adoption of the Constitution as they were before; and there is but one law of Congress, making any specified regulation upon the subject, and that passed as late as 1837, and intended, as it is understood, to alter only a single provision of the New York law, leaving the residue of its provisions entirely untouched. It is true, that the Act of 1789 provides that pilots shall continue to be regulated by the laws of the respective states then in force, or which may thereafter be passed, until Congress shall make provisions on the subject. And undoubtedly Congress had the power, by assenting to the state laws then in force, to make them its own, and thus make the previous regulations of the states the regulations of the general government. But it is equally clear that, as to all future laws by the states, if the Constitution deprived them of the power of making any regulations on the subject, an act of Congress could not restore it. For it will hardly be contended that an act of Congress can alter the Constitution, and confer upon a state a power which the Constitution declares it shall not possess. And if the grant of power to the United States to make regulations of commerce is a prohibition to the states to make any regulation upon the subject, Congress could no more restore to the states the power of which they were thus deprived, than it could authorize them to coin money or make paper money a tender in the payment of debts, or to do any other act forbidden to them by the Constitution. Every pilot law in the commercial states has, it is believed, been either modified or passed since the Act of 1789 adopted those then in force; and the provisions since made are all void if the restriction on the power of the states now contended for should be maintained; and the regulations made, the duties imposed, the securities required, and penalties inflicted by these various state laws are mere nullities, and could not be enforced in a court of justice. It is hardly necessary to speak of the mischiefs which such a construction would produce to those who are engaged in shipping, navigation, and commerce. Up to this time their validity has never been questioned. On the contrary, they have been repeatedly recognized and upheld by the decision of this court." Taney, C. J., in thus saying, did not, of course, mean that the Supreme Court had ever up to that time judicially passed upon the validity of state pilotage laws; he meant only that, in his opinion, the constitutionality of such laws was established by the principles on which were based the judgments in the cases of Willson v. The Blackbird Creek Marsh Co.,[1] New York v. Miln,[2] Houston v. Moore,[3] Sturges v. Crowninshield,[4] and Chirac v. Chirac.[5] In Hobart v. Drogan,[6] where the question at issue was as to the right of a pilot to claim salvage, it was argued, " that the act of Congress, so far as it adopts the future laws to be passed by the states on the subject of pilotage is unconstitutional and void, for Congress cannot delegate their powers of legislation to the states," but the court holding the case to be one of salvage, and not of pilotage, declined to express any opinion as to the power of the states over pilotage. It was not until 1851, that, in the case of Cooley v. The Board of Wardens,[7] the question came before the court for judicial determination. The facts of the case were, that a statute of Pennsylvania, enacted on 2 March, 1803, having, with regard

---

[1] 2 Pet. 251.    [3] 5 Wheat. 1.    [5] 2 id. 269.    [7] 12 How. 299.
[2] 11 id. 130.    [4] 4 id. 196.    [6] 10 Pet. 109.

to the port of Philadelphia and the navigation of the river Delaware, imposed the duty of taking a pilot on "every ship or vessel arriving from or bound to any foreign port or place, and every ship or vessel, of the burden of seventy-five tons or more, sailing from or bound to any port not within the river Delaware," and provided, in case of the master's refusal or neglect to take a pilot, that half pilotage should be forfeited, and recovered as pilotage, and the masters of two vessels, the Undine and the Consul, having refused to take a pilot under the statute, two actions at law were brought in a state court by the Board of Wardens against Cooley, the consignee of both vessels, and on pleadings, which raised the question of the power of a state to regulate pilotage by a statute enacted after the adoption of the Constitution, judgment was rendered against Cooley in the court of the first instance, and affirmed in the state court of last resort and in the Supreme Court of the United States, on the grounds, that the regulation of pilotage "demanding that diversity which alone can meet the local necessities of navigation," and the Act of 1789 being an authoritative declaration "that the nature of this subject is such that until Congress should find it necessary to exert its power, it should be left to the legislation of the states," the states may, by legislation after as well as before the adoption of the Constitution, continue to regulate pilotage, until Congress, in its discretion, shall make regulations which shall govern pilotage to and from all the ports of the country. Curtis, J., said, in the judgment of the court,[1] pilotage laws "rest upon the propriety of securing lives and property exposed to the perils of a dangerous navigation, by taking on board a person peculiarly skilled to encounter or avoid them ; upon the policy of discourag-

[1] p. 312.

ing the commanders of vessels from refusing to receive such persons on board at the proper times and places; and upon the expediency, and even intrinsic justice, of not suffering those who have incurred labour, and expense, and danger, to place themselves in a position to render important services generally necessary, to go unrewarded, because the master of a particular vessel either rashly refuses their proffered assistance or, contrary to the general experience, does not need it. There are many cases in which an offer to perform, accompanied by present ability to perform, is deemed by law equivalent to performance. The laws of commercial states and countries have made an offer of pilotage service one of those cases. . . . . The purpose of the law being to cause masters of such vessels, as generally need a pilot, to employ one, and to secure to the pilots a fair remuneration for cruising in search of vessels, or waiting for employment in port, there is an obvious propriety in having reference to the number, size, and nature of employment of vessels frequenting the port, and it will be found, by an examination of the different systems of their regulations, which have from time to time been made in this and other countries, that the legislative discretion has been constantly exercised in making discriminations, founded on differences both in the character of the trade, and the tonnage of vessels engaged therein."[1] . . . . "If the law of Pennsylvania, now in question, had been in existence at the date of this act of Congress, 1789, we might hold it to have been adopted by Congress, and thus made a law of the United States, and so valid. Because this act does, in effect, give the force of an act of Congress to the then existing state laws on this subject, so long as they should continue unrepealed by the state which enacted

[1] p. 317.

them. But the law on which these actions are founded was not enacted until 1803. What effect then can be attributed to so much of the Act of 1789 as declares, that pilots shall continue to be regulated in conformity 'with such laws as the states may respectively hereafter enact for the purpose, until further legislative provisions shall be made by Congress? If the states were divested of the power to legislate on this subject by the grant of the commercial power to Congress, it is plain that this act could not confer upon them power thus to regulate. . . . . The grant of commercial power to Congress does not contain any terms which expressly exclude the states from exercising an authority over its subject-matter. If they are excluded it must be because the nature of the power, thus granted to Congress, requires that a similar authority should not exist in the states. . . . . Now the power to regulate commerce embraces a vast field, containing not only many, but exceedingly various subjects, quite unlike in their nature; some imperatively demanding a single uniform rule, operating equally on the commerce of the United States in every port; and some, like the subject now in question, as imperatively demanding that diversity, which alone can meet the local necessities of navigation. . . . . The Act of 1789 contains a clear and authoritative declaration by the first Congress, that the nature of this subject is such, that until Congress should find it necessary to exert its power, it should be left to the legislation of the states; that it is local and not national; that it is likely to be best provided for, not by one system or plan of regulations, but by as many as the legislative discretion of the several states should deem applicable to the local peculiarities of the ports within their limits. . . . . It is the opinion of the majority of the court that the mere grant to Congress of the power to regulate commerce did not deprive the states of power to regulate pilots, and that, although Congress has legislated on this subject, its legislation manifests an intention, with a single exception, not to regulate this subject, but to leave its regulation to the several states. . . . . We are of opinion that this state law was enacted by virtue of a power, residing in the state to legislate: that it is not in conflict with any law of Congress: that it does not interfere with any system which Congress has established by making regulations, or by intentionally leaving individuals to their own unrestricted action; that this law is, therefore, valid, and the judgment of the Supreme Court of Pennsylvania in each case must be affirmed."[1] The later cases follow in the line laid down by Curtis, J.[2] In the Steamship Co. v. Joliffe,[3] the court held that the act of Congress of 30 August, 1852,[4] does not establish pilotage regulations for ports, and that a state statute, imposing half pilotage fees upon a steam vessel neglecting or refusing to take a pilot when coming into a port of the state is not in conflict with that act of Congress, but Spraigue v. Thompson[5] decides that the Revised Statutes of the United States[6] prevent a state from discriminating in its pilotage regulations in favour of some states, and against others, as by requiring vessels of

[1] McLean and Wayne, JJ., dissented, holding that the states could not by statutes enacted subsequently to the adoption of the Constitution, regulate pilotage; and Daniel, J., while concurring in the judgment of affirmance, did not agree in the reasoning of the majority of the court, as stated by Curtis, J., but, on the contrary, held that the regulation of pilotage, being a subject local in its nature, was not delegated to Congress by the grant of the power to regulate commerce, but remained as an original and inherent power in the states.

[2] Steamship Co. v. Joliffe 2 Wall. 450; The China, 7 *id.* 53; *Ex parte* McNeil, 13 *id.* 236; Wilson v. McNamee, 102 U. S. 572; Spraigue v. Thompson, 118 *id.* 90.

[3] 2 Wall. 450.

[4] 10 Stat. 61.

[5] 118 U. S. 90.

[6] Sections 4237, 4401 and 4444.

some states to pay half pilotage fees and exempting vessels of other states from that requirement, and that a vessel under the lawful control and direction of a pilot licensed under the laws of the United States, cannot be required to take a pilot under the laws of a state, nor be subjected to a penalty for the failure or neglect so to do. The points of minor importance which have been adjudicated in the pilotage cases are, that a state may impose upon a vessel neglecting or refusing to take a pilot the forfeiture of half pilotage fees, and it may exempt from such forfeitures the vessels engaged in a particular trade.[1] The forfeiture of half pilotage fees being not in the nature of a penalty, but of compensation under an implied contract,[2] those fees must be paid, though the pilot's services were tendered and refused before the vessel had come within the jurisdiction of the state,[3] and although the statute authorizing the recovery shall have been repealed after the services of the pilot were tendered, and refused, but before the action was brought to recover therefor.[4] Such a statute may impose a compulsory obligation on foreign vessels.[5] Pilotage fees being matters of admiralty jurisdiction,[6] the Supreme Court of the United States will not by prohibition restrain the admiralty courts from hearing and deciding such causes.[7]

47. The doctrine of the cases as to state quarantine and sanitary regulations is, that a state may prohibit the entry into its territory of infected persons or goods, and it may provide for an examination of all persons

[1] Cooley v. Board of Wardens, 12 How. 299; Steamship Co. v. Joliffe, 2 Wall. 450; Ex parte MacNeil, 13 id. 236; Wilson v. McNamee, 102 U. S. 572.
[2] Ex parte MacNeil, 13 Wall. 236.
[3] Wilson v. McNamee, 102 U. S. 572.
[4] Steamship Co. v. Joliffe, 2 Wall. 450.
[5] The China, 7 Wall. 53.
[6] Hobart v. Drogan, 10 Pet. 108; Ex parte MacNeil, 13 Wall. 236.
[7] Ex parte Hagar, 104 U. S. 520; Ex parte Pennsylvania, 109 id. 174.

or goods coming into its territory in order to determine whether or not they be infected, and in order to defray the expenses of such sanitary inspection it may collect charges, provided that such charges be not in form duties on tonnage, and that they do not unnecessarily interfere with foreign and interstate transportation. Marshall, C. J., in his judgment in Gibbons v. Ogden,[1] enumerates "quarantine laws" and " health laws of every description" as "component parts of that immense mass of legislation, which embraces everything within the territory of a state, not surrendered to the general government: all which can be most advantageously exercised by the states themselves;" and he adds,[2] " the acts of Congress, passed in 1796 and 1799,[3] empowering and directing the officers of the general government to conform to, and assist in the execution of the quarantine and health laws of a state, proceed, it is said, upon the idea that these laws are constitutional. It is, undoubtedly, true, that they do proceed upon that idea; and the constitutionality of such laws has never, so far as we are informed, been denied. But they do not imply an acknowledgment that a state may rightfully regulate commerce with foreign nations, or among the states; for they do not imply that such laws are an exercise of that power, or enacted with a view to it. On the contrary, they are treated as quarantine and health laws, are so denominated in the acts of Congress, and are considered as flowing from the acknowledged power of a state to provide for the health of its citizens. But, as it was apparent that some of the provisions made for this purpose, and in virtue of this power, might interfere with, and be affected by, the laws of the United States, made for the regulation of commerce, Congress, in that spirit of harmony and conciliation, which ought always to

[1] 9 Wheat. 203.     [2] p. 205.     [3] 2 Stat. 545; 3 id. 126.

characterize the conduct of governments standing in the relation which that of the Union and those of the states bear to each other, has directed its officers to aid in the execution of these laws; and has, in some measure, adapted its own legislation to this object by making provisions in aid of those states. But, in making these provisions, the opinion is unequivocally manifested that Congress may control the state laws, so far as it may be necessary to control them for the regulation of commerce." Title LVIII, of the Revised Statutes of the United States, as Miller, J., says, in Morgan v. Louisiana,[1] referring to state quarantine regulations, shows "very clearly the intention of Congress to adopt these laws, or to recognize the power of the states to pass them." A state may, therefore, in the absence of conflicting federal legislation, make and enforce a quarantine regulation requiring all vessels coming into a port of the state, to stop at a designated quarantine station, there submit to a sanitary examination, and pay therefor a fee rated in amount in proportion to the marine class to which the vessel may belong,[2] and equal in amount for all vessels of the same class. On the other hand, a state cannot, for the purpose of defraying the expenses of enforcing her quarantine regulations, impose on vessels owned in ports of other states, and entering her harbours in the pursuit of commerce, a tax which is based on the tonnage of the vessel, as *ex gr.* a tax at the rate of \$5 for the first hundred tons and 1½ cents for each additional ton,[3] for such a tax is a duty on tonnage, and as such prohibited.[4] So apprehensive was Congress that its legislation in 1799,[5] directing the

---

[1] 118 U. S. 465      [2] Morgan v. Louisiana, 118 U. S. 455.
[3] Peete v. Morgan, 19 Wall. 581.
[4] In Peete v. Morgan, 19 Wall. 583, Davis, J., said, the power of imposing tonnage duties cannot be exercised without the permission of Congress, and Congress has never consented that the states should lay any duty on tonnage.
[5] 1 Stat. 619.

collectors of customs and officers commanding forts and revenue cutters to aid in the execution of the quarantine and health laws of the states, rendered necessary on account of the prevalence of yellow fever in New York, might be construed into an admission of the right of the states to lay this duty, that it used the following words of exclusion, "that nothing herein shall enable any state to collect a duty of tonnage or impost without the consent of the Congress of the United States thereto."[1] Nor can a state, under the form of sanitary regulations, enact statutes which are, in effect, regulations of commerce, either foreign or interstate; thus, in R. R. *v.* Husen,[2] the facts being that the state of Missouri having, by a statute, prohibited the driving or conveyance of Texan, Mexican, or Indian cattle into the state between the first day of March and the first day of November in any year, and having permitted the transportation of such cattle through the state only on condition that the transporting agent "shall be responsible for all damages which may result from the disease called Spanish or Texan fever, should the same occur along the line of transportation, and the existence of such disease along such route shall be *prima facie* evidence that such disease has been communicated by such transportation," and the statute having further provided that a liability "for all damages sustained on account of disease communicated by said cattle" should follow from a violation of the statute; and Husen, having brought suit in a state court against the H. & St. J. R. R. to recover damages under the statute and having obtained judgment, the Supreme Court reversed the judgment, holding that the statute was void as an attempted regulation of interstate commerce, inasmuch as it prohibited the introduction into the state, not merely of diseased

---

[1] See *supra*, Tonnage Duties, Sec. 36.   [2] 95 U. S. 465.

cattle, but of all Texan, Mexican, and Indian cattle during eight months of each year, and it imposed a burden on the transportation of cattle through the state in the prosecution of interstate commerce, by subjecting the transporting agent to liability for damages caused by the communication of disease from such cattle, though there might not be any negligence on the part of such agent.

48. Port dues, that is, charges imposed on vessels as instruments of commerce, and payable by all vessels entering, remaining in, or leaving a port, by reason of such entry, stay, or departure, and without regard to services rendered to or received by the vessel, are regulations of commerce, and as such cannot be rightfully imposed under state authority.[1] Under this rule, as expounded in Steamship Co. *v.* Port Wardens,[2] a charge of $5 per vessel payable to the wardens "whether called on to perform any service or not, for every vessel arriving in" the port of New Orleans, was held to be a wrongful imposition. So also, under pretence of making port regulations, a state cannot rightfully vest in the master and wardens of a port, or in his deputies, a monopoly of the survey of the hatches of sea-going vessels coming to the port, or of damaged goods, on such vessels, for such a monopoly is a burden upon, and therefore a regulation of, foreign and interstate commerce.[3] The prohibition of state duties on tonnage[4] forbids the imposition by a state of port dues in the form of a tax of $5 for the first hundred tons and 1½ cents for each additional ton payable by vessels owned in another state and entering a harbour of the taxing

---

[1] Such dues are also open to objection as duties on tonnage. Sec. 36.
[2] 6 Wall. 31.
[3] Foster *v.* Master and Wardens of the Port of New Orleans, 94 U. S. 246.
[4] Section 36.

state in the pursuit of commerce,[1] and also of a tax similarly proportioned on "all steamboats which shall moor or land in any part of" a state port.[2]

49. A state may establish port regulations, prescribing where a vessel may lie in harbour, how long she may remain there, and what lights she must show at night; thus in the James Gray v. The John Frazer,[3] an admiralty cause of damage resulting from a collision of the two vessels in Charleston harbour, that one was held to be in fault, which had by its failure to display lights in conformity with the regulations of the port imposed under authority of the state, been the cause of the collision. Taney, C. J., said,[4] "regulations of this kind are necessary and indispensable in every commercial port, for the convenience and safety of commerce, and the local authorities have a right to prescribe at what wharf a vessel may lie, and how long she may remain there, where she may unload or take on board particular cargoes, where she may anchor in the harbour, and for what time, and what description of light she shall display at night to warn the passing vessels of her position, and that she is at anchor and not under sail. They are like to the local usages of navigation in different ports, and every vessel, from whatever part of the world she may come, is bound to take notice of them and conform to them. And there is nothing in the regulations referred to in the port of Charleston, which is in conflict with any law of Congress regulating commerce, or with the general admiralty jurisdiction conferred on the courts of the United States." Ostensibly, on the same principle, it was held in New York v. Miln,[5] that a state may require under

---
[1] Peete v. Morgan, 19 Wall. 581.
[2] Cannon v. New Orleans, 20 Wall. 577.
[3] 21 How. 184.  [4] p. 187.  [5] 11 Pet. 102.

a penalty the master of every passenger-carrying vessel on arriving at any port within the state to report to the state authorities the name, place of birth, last legal settlement, age, and occupation of every passenger, the statute under consideration being one enacted by New York in 1824, and the court affirming its validity on the ground that it was a regulation, not of commerce, but of police, and as such falling within the reserved powers of the state. The authority of the case is, however, much shaken by the admirably reasoned dissenting judgment of Story, J., with whose conclusions Marshall, C. J., concurred,[1] and the result reached by the court is possibly inconsistent with the later cases of Sinnot v. Davenport,[2] Foster v. Davenport,[3] and the yet later cases, which hold that a state cannot, directly or indirectly, tax the transportation of passengers coming from foreign countries.[4]

50. Section 9 of article I of the Constitution declares that "no preference shall be given by any regulation of commerce or revenue to the ports of one state over those of another." This prohibition is, obviously, a restraint upon the exercise of power by the United States and not by the states; and it is intended to guard against partiality and favoritism in customs regulations. It has, therefore, been held that the diversion of water from one navigable river to another, as the result of congressional legislation in the exercise of the power to regulate commerce, is not a preference to the ports of one state over those of another,[5] and that the legalization by an act of Congress of a bridge over navigable waters, though indirectly obstructing the commerce of

---

[1] p. 161.
[2] 22 How. 227.
[5] South Carolina v. Georgia, 93 U. S. 4.
[3] 22 How. 224. *Supra*, sec. 33.
[4] *Supra*, sec. 37.

a port in another state, is not a violation of the constitutional prohibition.[1]

51. The construction of railways, and the development of systems of through transportation have required the court to consider in several cases the restrictive powers of the government of the United States and of the states with regard to the interstate transportation of passengers and goods by railway. In 1824, Marshall, C. J., incidentally referring in Gibbons v. Ogden[2] to the then ordinary appliances of interstate transportation, enumerated "turn-pike roads," etc., as "component parts" of "that immense mass of legislation, which embraces everything within the territory of a state, not surrendered to the general government." In the same case,[3] Johnson, J., said, "as to laws affecting ferries, turnpike roads, and other subjects of the same class, so far from meriting the epithet of commercial regulations, they are, in fact, commercial facilities, for which, by the consent of mankind, a compensation is paid, upon the same principle, that the whole commercial world submit to pay light money to the Danes." In Searight v. Stokes;[4] Neil v. Ohio,[5] and Achison v. Huddleson,[6] it was held that a state, through which the Cumberland Road passed,[7] could not tax the coaches carrying the mail, nor the persons traveling in the coaches thereon on the service of the United States, but the exemption from taxation was, in the several judgments of the court, based exclusively upon the terms of the contracts between the United States, and the states of Pennsylvania, Maryland, and Ohio, as made by the

[1] Penna. v. W. & B. Bridge Co., 18 How. 421, 423.
[2] 9 Wheat. 203.
[3] p. 235.
[4] 3 How. 151.
[5] 3 How. 720.
[6] 12 How. 293.
[7] That road having been originally constructed by the government of the United States with the consent of the states through which it passed.

statutes of those states authorizing the construction of the road within their respective territories. The result of the cases which have directly dealt with the subject of the interstate transportation of passengers and goods by railways is, that, while a state may, directly or indirectly, provide facilities of transportation, and charge tolls for the use of such facilities, and while a state may, in the exercise of the police power, reasonably regulate interstate transportation by railways, so far as is necessary for the protection of its citizens, provided that such police regulations do not unnecessarily obstruct the commerce thus regulated, and while a state may make the payment of a license fee a condition precedent to the transaction within the state of the business of making contracts for interstate transportation; and while a state may tax the capital stock of corporations created by it, and authorized to transport passengers and freight to and from the state; a state, nevertheless, cannot obstruct or embarrass interstate transportation by its taxation of passengers *per capita*, or of freight by the pound moved, or of the appliances of transportation permitted to be used by a foreign corporation within the state, or of the gross receipts of transportation as received either by a foreign corporation or a corporation created by the state.

52. The first branch of the proposition, that which affirms the right of the state, as the owner of an artificial highway, to charge tolls for the use of that highway, is supported by the case of B. & O. R. R. *v.* Maryland,[1] in which the facts were, that a statute of the state of Maryland having authorized the B. & O. R. R. to construct a line of railway between Baltimore in that state to Washington in the District of Columbia, and to transport passengers thereon for a charge not exceeding $2.50 for each person and to pay semi-annually to the

[1] 21 Wall. 456.

state "one-fifth of the whole amount which may be received for the transportation of passengers during the preceding six months," and the state having brought in one of its courts an action against the company to recover the amount of a semi-annual payment which the company had refused to make, judgment was rendered in favour of the state, and affirmed by the court, on the ground, as stated in the judgment of Bradley, J.,[1] that the payment required of the company was not a tax on the interstate transportation of persons, but a charge of toll for the use of improved facilities of travel which the state by its agent, the railroad company, had constructed, and for whose use it had a right to charge. Miller, J., dissented,[2] on the ground, that the state statute "was intended to raise a revenue for the state from all persons coming to Washington by rail," and, therefore, "void within the principle laid down by the court in Crandall *v.* Nevada."[3] If, in connection with this case, the case of the State Freight Tax[4] be considered, the distinction will be clearly apprehended between a toll charged in virtue of ownership, and a tax imposed in the exercise of sovereignty.

53. As to the second branch of the proposition, that which relates to the exercise by the states of the power of police regulation with regard to interstate commerce conducted by railways, there has been some variance of judicial opinion; but the deduction to be drawn from the cases is, that while a state may, in the exercise of its police power, reasonably regulate interstate transportation by railway, so far as may be necessary for the protection of the safety, health, and comfort of its citizens, it may not by such regulations unnecessarily embarrass or obstruct interstate railway transportation. In Railway

[1] p. 470 to 473.
[2] p. 475.
[3] 6 Wall. 35, *infra*, sec. 54.
[4] 15 Wall. 232, *infra*, sec. 54.

Company v. Fuller,[1] the facts were, that the state of Iowa having, by a statute of 1862, required, under a penalty, all railroad companies to fix annually their rates of fare and freight, to post the same in their stations and depots, and not to charge in excess thereof, and the C. & N. W. R. R., a corporation chartered by the state of Illinois, and operating under due authority a line of railway through Illinois, Iowa, and other states, having duly posted its rates of freight at its station at Marshalltown in Iowa, having transported certain goods for Fuller from Chicago in Illinois to Marshalltown, and having charged him therefor freight in excess of its posted rate, Fuller brought an action against the company to recover the statutory penalty, and the company defended on the ground that the state statute was void as an attempted regulation of interstate commerce, but the court sustained the constitutionality of the statute as a police regulation. Swayne, J., said,[2] "no discrimination is made between local and interstate freights, and no attempt is made to control the rates that may be charged. It is only required that the rates shall be fixed, made public, and honestly adhered to. In this there is nothing unreasonable or onerous. The public welfare is promoted without wrong or injury to the company. The statute was deemed to be called for by the interests of the community to be affected by it, and it rests upon a solid foundation of reason and justice." The court having held in Munn v. Illinois,[3] that a state might regulate the rates charged by a private warehouse for the storage of grain, notwithstanding the fact that grain was stored therein in course of interstate transportation, the same doctrine was in C., B. & Q. R. R. v. Iowa,[4] applied to interstate transportation by railway.

[1] 17 Wall. 560.    [2] p. 567.    [3] 94 U. S. 113.    [4] 94 U. S. 155.

The facts were that the C. B. & Q. R. R. Co., a corporation created by the laws of the state of Illinois, and operating, as lessee, a line of railway constructed by the B. & M. R. R. in the state of Iowa, and carrying on that line goods and passengers to and from states other than Iowa, filed its bill in equity in the federal court of the first instance to enjoin the Attorney-General of Iowa from proceeding against it for charges made in violation of a statute enacted by the state of Iowa in 1874, which fixed the maximum rates of fare and freight for all railways within the state, and the court affirmed a decree dismissing the bill, *inter alia*, on the ground, as stated by Waite, C. J.,[1] that the B. & M. line, like the warehouse in Munn *v.* Illinois, "is situated within the limits of a single state. Its business is carried on there, and its regulation is a matter of domestic concern. It is employed in state as well as in interstate commerce, and, until Congress acts, the state must be permitted to adopt such rules and regulations as may be necessary for the promotion of the general welfare of the people within its own jurisdiction, even though in so doing those without may be indirectly affected."[2] The view expressed in this case was reiterated in Peik *v.* C. & N. W. Ry.[3] The next case is R. R. *v.* Husen,[4] in which the court held void as an attempted regulation of interstate commerce a statute of the state of Missouri, prohibiting the driving of Texan, Mexican, or Indian cattle into the state between the first day of March and the first day of November in any year, and permitting the transportation of such cattle through the state only on condition that the transporting agent "shall be responsible for all damages which may result from the

[1] p. 163.  [2] Field and Strong, JJ., dissented.
[3] 94 U. S. 164, Field and Strong, JJ., dissenting.
[4] 95 U. S. 465.

disease called the Spanish or Texan fever, should the same occur along the line of trasportation."[1] In the first of the Railroad Commission Cases, Stone *v.* Farmers' Loan and Trust Co.,[2] Stone *v.* I. C. R. R.,[3] and Stone *v.* N. O. & N. E. R. R.,[4] wherein the question was as to the validity of a statute of Mississippi, forbidding discriminations in railway transportation, and constituting a commission with power to revise the tariff of railway charges and to enforce the statute, Waite, C. J., said,[5] "the statute makes no mention of persons or property taken up without the state, and delivered within, nor of such as may be taken up within and carried without. As to this, the only limit on the power of commissioners is the constitutional authority of the state over the subject. Precisely all that may be done, or all that may not be done, it is not easy to say in advance. The line between the exclusive power of Congress, and the general powers of the state in this particular, is not everywhere distinctly marked, and it is always easier to determine when a case arises whether it falls on one side or on the other, than to settle in advance the boundary, so that it may be, in all respects, strictly accurate. As yet the commissioners have done nothing. There is, certainly, much they may do in regulating charges within the state, which will not be in conflict with the Constitution of the United States. It is to be presumed they will always act within the limits of their constitutional authority. It will be time enough to consider what may be done to prevent it when they attempt to go beyond." In W. St. L. & P. Ry. *v.* Illinois,[6] the facts were, that a statute of Illinois having enacted that "if any railroad corporation shall charge, collect, or receive for the

---

[1] *Supra*, sec. 47.
[2] 116 U. S. 307.
[3] 116 U. S. 347.
[4] 116 U. S. 352.
[5] p. 335.
[6] 118 U. S. 557.

transportation of any passenger or freight of any description upon its railroad, for any distance within the state, the same or a greater amount of toll or compensation than is at the same time charged, collected, and received for the transportation in the same direction of any passenger or like quantity of freight of the same class over a greater distance of the same road, all such discriminating rates, charges, collections, or receipts, whether made directly, or by means of rebate, drawback, or other shift or evasion, shall be deemed and taken against any such railroad corporation as *prima facie* evidence of unjust discrimination," and the W. St. L. & P. Ry. having charged Elder & McKinney at the rate of 15 cents per 100 pounds for the transportation of certain goods from Peoria in the state of Illinois to New York in the state of New York, and having on the same day charged Bailey at the rate of 25 cents per 100 pounds for the transportation of like goods from Gilman in the state of Illinois to the city of New York, the distance between Gilman and New York being less by 86 miles than that between Peoria and New York, an action at law was brought in the name of the state of Illinois against the railway company to recover the amount of a statutory penalty in a court of the state, and a judgment rendered therein in favour of the state was reversed by the court, on the grounds, as stated by Miller, J., that "the right of continuous transportation from one end of the country to the other is essential in modern times to that freedom of commerce from the restraints which the state might choose to impose upon it," and that, the power of regulating interstate commerce vested by the Constitution in Congress would fail of its intended object, " if, at every stage of the transportation of goods and chattels through the country, the state, within whose limits a part of this transportation must be done, could impose regulations concerning the price, compensation, or taxation, or any other restrictive regulation interfering with and seriously embarrassing this commerce,"[1] and that "a statute of a state, which attempts to regulate the charges by railroad companies within its limits, for a transportation which constitutes a part of commerce among the states," cannot be a " valid law,"[2] because " this species of regulation is one which must be, if established at all, of a general and national character, and cannot be safely and wisely remitted to local rules and local regulations." In the judgment in this case, Miller, J., disposed of the case of Munn v. Illinois and the Granger Cases by saying,[3] that, " although as incidental to the question of an impairment of the obligation of a contract alleged to subsist between the state and the railway, the question of the exclusive right of Congress to make such regulations of charges as any legislative power had the right to make, to the exclusion of the states, was presented, it received but little attention at the hands of the court," and he added,[4] that " it is not, and never has been, the deliberate opinion of a majority of this court that a statute of a state, which attempts to regulate the fares and charges by railroad companies within its limits for a transportation, which constitutes a part of commerce among the states, is a valid law." Waite, C. J., and Bradley and Gray, JJ., dissented, on the grounds, as stated by Bradley, J.,[5] that "all local arrangements and regulations respecting highways, turnpikes, railroads, bridges, canals, ferries, dams, and wharves, within the state, their construction and repair, and the charges to be made for their use, though materially affecting

[1] p. 573.
[2] p. 575.
[3] p. 569.
[4] p. 575.
[5] p. 581.

commerce, both internal and external, and thereby incidentally operating to a certain extent as regulations of interstate commerce, were within the power and jurisdiction of the several states," and that Peik v. C. & N. W. Ry., was a conclusive authority in support of the judgment of the court below.

54. In considering the limits within which a state may tax the interstate transportation of passengers and goods by railway, those cases will first be cited in which state taxation has been sustained. In the State Tax on Railway Gross Receipts,[1] the question was as to the validity of a statute of Pennsylvania, imposing on all transportation companies a "tax of three-fourths of one per centum upon the gross receipts of said company," payable semi-annually, so far as such gross receipts were derived from interstate transportation of goods, and the majority of the court in a judgment, read by Strong, J., sustained the tax in question because by its being "laid upon a fund which has become the property of the company, mingled with its other property, and possibly expended in improvements, or put out at interest," it was not taxation of the goods carried, nor the freight received therefor, nor in any sense a regulation of interstate commerce. Miller, Field, and Hunt, JJ., dissented, on the ground that, while railways may be taxed [2] "on their capital stock, on their property, real and personal, and in any other way, that does not impose a burden on transportation between one state and another," yet their business, so far as regards the transportation of persons and property to and from other states, being in itself commerce, is by the Constitution exempted from taxation, or other regulation under state authority. Miller, J., added,[3] "I lay down the broad proposition that by no device or evasion, by no form of

[1] 15 Wall. 284.     [2] p. 299.     [3] p. 299.

statutory words, can a state compel citizens of other states to pay to it a tax, contribution, or toll, for the privilege of having their goods transported through that state by the ordinary channels of commerce. And that this was the purpose of the framers of the Constitution I have no doubt; and I have just as little doubt that the full recognition of this principle is essential to the harmonious future of this country now, as it was then. The internal commerce of that day was of small importance, and the foreign was considered as of great consequence. But both were placed beyond the power of the states to control. The interstate commerce to-day far exceeds in value that which is foreign, and it is of immense importance that it should not be shackled by restrictions imposed by any state in order to place on others the burden of supporting its own government, as was done in the days of the helpless confederation. I think the tax on gross receipts is a violation of the federal Constitution, and, therefore, void." It must be observed that the authority of this case was shaken by Fargo v. Michigan,[1] and that it has been overruled by the case of the P. & S. S. S. Co. v. Pennsylvania.[2]

The next case is Osborne v. Mobile,[3] in which the facts were, that an ordinance of the city of Mobile, in the state of Alabama, requiring under a penalty every express or railway company doing in that city a business extending beyond the limits of the state to pay an annual license fee of $500, and requiring such companies doing business not extending beyond the state or the city to pay lesser license fees, and Osborne, an agent resident in Mobile of the Southern Express Company, a corporation chartered by the state of Georgia, but doing in Mobile business within the terms of the ordinance by making contracts and receiving goods for

[1] 121 U. S. 230.   [2] 122 U. S. 326.   [3] 16 Wall 479.

transportation from Mobile to points without the state of Alabama, having been fined for transacting business for his company in violation of the ordinance, the court sustained the validity of the ordinance in a judgment, read by Chase, C. J., on the ground that the license fee in question was not a burden on interstate commerce, but was an exercise by the state of its general authority to tax persons, property, business, or occupations within its limits. In the Delaware R. R. Tax Case,[1] the facts were, that the P., W. & B. R. R. having been duly formed by the consolidation of companies severally incorporated by the states of Pennsylvania, Delaware, and Maryland, and having constructed and operated a line of railroad running through the state of Delaware, and a statute of that state, having required each of its railroads to pay an annual "tax of one-fourth of one per cent. of the actual cash value of every share of its capital stock," the P., W. & B. R. R. resisted payment of the tax on several grounds, and, *inter alia*, on the ground that the tax imposed a burden on interstate commerce, but the court held, in a judgment, read by Field, J., that[2] while the tax indirectly affected commerce in "just the same way and in no other, that taxation of any kind necessarily increases the expenses attendant upon the use or possession of the thing taxed," yet that "the exercise of the authority which every state possesses to tax its corporations and all their property, real and personal, and their franchises, and to graduate the tax upon the corporations according to their business or income, or the value of their property, when this is not done by discriminating against rights held in other states, and the tax is not on imports, exports, or tonnage, or on transportation to other states, cannot be regarded as conflicting with any

[1] Minot v. P., W. & B. R. R. *et al.*, 18 Wall. 206.   [2] p. 232.

constitutional power of Congress." The cases in which taxation of transportation has been held to be invalid will now be cited. The first case is Crandall *v.* Nevada,[1] in which the question was as to the validity of a statute of Nevada, imposing "a capitation tax of one dollar upon every person leaving the state by any railroad, stage, coach, or other vessel engaged or employed in the business of transporting passengers for hire," the court unanimously held the statute to be void, the majority of the judges, in a judgment read by Miller, J., intimating, as was subsequently decided in Woodruff *v.* Parham,[2] that the constitutional prohibition of state taxation of imports or exports has exclusive reference to foreign commerce, and also expressing the opinion, which has been overruled in all the subsequent cases, that "as the tax does not itself institute any regulation of commerce of a national character or which has an uniform operation over the whole country, it is not easy to maintain, in view of the principles on which those cases[3] were decided, that it violates the commerce clause of the Constitution," but resting the conclusions as to the invalidity of the statute on the ground, that a state tax on the interstate transportation of passengers was void as an interference with the freedom of transit of citizens to the seat of government of the United States, and to the federal offices and the ports of entry in the several states, and as a consequent infringement upon the federal supremacy. Chase, C. J., and Clifford, J., while concurring in the judgment of the court, dissented from the reasoning on which the majority of the court were agreed, and held that the statute was unconstitutional

---

[1] 6 Wall. 35.      [2] 8 Wall. 123.
[3] The Passenger Cases. 7 How. 283; Cooley *v.* Board of Wardens, 12 *id.* 299; Gilman *v.* Philadelphia, 3 Wall. 713.

because it imposed "a burden upon commerce among the several states." Curiously enough, Crandall *v.* Nevada is constantly referred to in the later judgments of the court as if it had been decided on the ground taken in the dissenting judgment of Chase, C. J., and Clifford, J. Next comes the case of The State Freight Tax,[1] in which a statute of Pennsylvania having imposed on all freight transporting companies a tax, varying according to the character of freight transported in rate from 2 to 5 cents for each 2,000 pounds of freight moved without regard to distance, the question was whether the statute was constitutional, so far as it affected freight taken up within the state and carried out of it, or taken up without the state and brought within it, and the court held that the statute was void as an attempted regulation of interstate commerce. Strong, J., in delivering the judgment of the court, said,[2] " we concede the right and power of the state to tax the franchises of its corporations, and the right of the owner of artificial highways, whether such owners be the state, or grantees of franchises from the state, to exact what they please for the use of their ways. That right is an attribute of ownership. But this tax is not laid upon the franchises of the corporation, nor upon those who hold a part of the state's eminent domain. It is laid upon those who deal with the owners of the highways or means of conveyance. The state is not herself the owner of the roadways, nor of the motive power. The tax is not compensation for services rendered by her, or by her agents. It is something beyond the cost of transportation or the ordinary charges therefor. Having no ownership in the railroads or canals, the state has no title to their incomes, except so far as she has reserved it in the charters of the companies. Tolls and freights

[1] 15 Wall. 232.      [2] p. 277.

are a compensation for services rendered or facilities furnished to a passenger or transporter. These are not rendered or furnished by the state. A tax is a demand of sovereignty; a toll is a demand of proprietorship. The tax levied by this act is, therefore, not a toll. It is not exacted in compensation for the use of the roadway; and if it were, the right to make terms for the use of the roadway is in the grantee of the franchises, not in the grantor. But, in truth, the state has no more right to demand a portion of the tolls which the grantees of her franchises may exact, than she would have to demand a portion of the rents of the land which she had sold. She may tax by virtue of her sovereignty, and measure the tax by income, but the income itself is beyond her reach." Swayne and Davis, JJ., dissented, on the grounds that the tax in question was "imposed on the business of those required to pay it," and that the specification of tonnage was "only the mode of ascertaining the extent of the business," no discrimination being "made between freight carried wholly within the state, and that brought into or carried out of it." In Erie Railway *v.* Pennsylvania,[1] the question was as to the validity of the same tax as affecting a railway corporation chartered by the state of New York, but authorized by statutes of Pennsylvania to construct a portion of its line within that state, and the court held the tax void. In Pickard *v.* Pullman Southern Car Co.,[2] the facts were that the Constitution of the state of Tennessee, having authorized the state legislature to tax "privileges" in its discretion, and a statute of the state having declared "the running and using of sleeping-cars or coaches on railroads in Tennessee not owned by the railroads upon which they are run or used" to be a "privilege," and as such to be subject to an annual tax

---

[1] 15 Wall. 282, *note.*  [2] 117 U. S. 34.

of $50 for each car, and the Pullman Southern Car Co., a corporation created by the state of Kentucky and having its principal office at Louisville in that state, being the owner of certain sleeping-cars, leased them to certain railroad companies who used them in the transportation of passengers into, through, or out of the state of Tennessee, the car company receiving the extra fare paid by the passengers for berths and seats in the cars. The state of Tennessee having demanded from the Car Co. payment of the " privilege " tax, it was paid under protest, and the company having brought an action against the State Comptroller to recover the amount of the tax, a judgment in its favour was affirmed by the court, on the grounds, as stated by Blatchford, J., that the tax was a charge upon the interstate transportation of passengers, and, therefore, void as an attempted regulation of interstate commerce.[1] In Fargo v. Michigan,[2] the facts were that the state of Michigan having by statute imposed a tax on the gross receipts of corporations "engaged in the business of running cars over any of the railroads of this state," and the Merchants' Dispatch Transportation Co., a corporation organized under the laws of the state of New York, being the owner of certain freight cars which were used for the transportation of freight from points without the state of Michigan to points within that state, and from points within that state to points without that state, and also between other states but passing through the state of Michigan, and having, under protest, made return to the commissioner of railroads of the state of Michigan of its gross receipts, including *inter alia* a sum of $28,890.01 "received for

[1] In Tennessee v. P. S. C. Co., 117 U. S. 51, the doctrine was reiterated with regard to an annual "privilege" tax of $75 on each sleeping-car imposed by the Tennessee statute of 1881.
[2] 121 U. S. 230.

the transportation of freight from points without to points within the state of Michigan, and from points within to points without that state," filed in a court of the state of Michigan, its bill in equity against the Auditor-General of Michigan, praying an injunction to restrain him from collecting the tax on those gross receipts, and a decree dismissing the plaintiff's bill was reversed by the court, in a judgment delivered by Miller, J., on the ground that the statute of Michigan was, so far as it taxed receipts from interstate commerce, void as an attempted regulation thereof, the case of the State Tax on Railway Gross Receipts [1] being distinguished by the facts, that the corporation taxed in that case was a corporation exercising a franchise granted to it by the taxing state, and, as such, taxable by that state, and its gross receipts having passed into the treasury of the corporation were as much subject to taxation as any other money within the state, whereas, in the case at bar, the corporation whose gross receipts were sought to be reached was a corporation of a state other than the taxing state, and, "the money which it received for freight carried within the state probably never was within the state, being paid to the company, either at the beginning or the end of its route, and certainly, at the time the tax was levied, it was neither money nor property of the corporation within the state of Michigan." The case of the Philadelphia and Southern Steamship Co. *v.* Pennsylvania,[2] though not a case of railway transportation, must be here referred to, for it overrules the case of the State Tax on Railway Gross Receipts.[3] The facts were, that a statute of Pennsylvania enacted in 1877, having imposed upon, *inter alia*, steamboat companies, doing business in the Commonwealth and in any way engaged in the business of

[1] 15 Wall. 284.   [2] 122 U. S. 326.   [3] 15 Wall. 284.

transporting freight or passengers, a tax upon the gross receipts of the company for tolls and transportations, and the Philadelphia and Southern Steamship Company, a corporation created by the state of Pennsylvania, and engaged in the business of operating sea-going steamships enrolled, registered, and licensed under the laws of the United States for the coasting or foreign trade of the United States, and engaged in the business of ocean transportation of passengers and freight between different states of the United States and between the United States and foreign countries, having resisted payment of the tax in question, the court held that on the facts thus stated the company was not liable, Bradley, J. delivering judgment, and holding that taxation of ocean transportation "either by its tonnage, or its distance, or by the number of trips performed, or in any other way, would certainly be a regulation of the commerce, a restriction upon it, a burden upon it;"[1] that foreign commerce having been fully regulated by Congress, "any regulations imposed by the states upon that branch of commerce would be a palpable interference," and that in whatever respects Congress has not regulated interstate commerce, "its inaction . . . is equivalent to a declaration that it shall be free, in all cases where its power is exclusive; and its power is necessarily exclusive wherever the subject-matter is national in its character and properly admits of only one uniform system;" that "interstate commerce carried on by ships on the sea is surely of this character;" and that the state cannot tax such transportation, nor the fares and freights received therefor. Bradley, J., then dealt with the case of the State Tax on Railway Gross Receipts,[2] and quoting in substance, the first ground on which the judgment in that case was based,

[1] p. 336.   [2] 15 Wall. 234.

namely, "that the tax being collectible only once in six months, was laid upon a fund which had become the property of the company, mingled with its other property, and incorporated into the general mass of its property, possibly expended in improvements, or otherwise invested," he replied,[1] "the tax in the present case is laid upon the gross receipts from transportation as such. Those receipts are followed and caused to be accounted for by the company, dollar for dollar. It is those specific receipts, or the amount thereof, which is the same thing, for which the company is called on to pay the tax. They are taxed not only because they are money, or its value, but because they were received for transportation. . . . If such a tax is laid, and the receipts taxed are those derived from transporting goods and passengers in the way of interstate or foreign commerce, no matter when the tax is exacted, whether at the time of realizing the receipts, or at the end of six months or a year, it is an exaction aimed at the commerce itself, and it is a burden upon it, and seriously affects it." Bradley, J., next met the second ground taken in the case of the "State Tax on Railway Gross Receipts," namely that the tax was imposed "upon the franchise of the corporation granted to it by the state," and, in reply to that, while conceding, that [2] "the corporate franchises, the property, the business, the income of corporations created by a state may undoubtedly be taxed by the state," he pointed out, that "a tax on the franchise of doing business, which, in this case, is the business of transportation in carrying on interstate and foreign commerce, would clearly be unconstitutional."[3]

55. Congress, by the Act of 24 July, 1866,[4] authorized

---

[1] p. 341.
[2] p. 345.
[3] p. 342.
[4] 14 Stat. 221, Rev. Stat. Sec. 5263 et seq.

any telegraph company organized under the laws of any state, "to construct, maintain, and operate lines of telegraph, through and over any portion of the public dominion of the United States, over and along any of the military or post roads of[1] the United States which may have been, or may hereafter be declared such by act of Congress, and over, under, or across the navigable streams or waters of the United States," upon certain conditions, including, *inter alia*, a concession by the company of priority to government messages at rates to be fixed annually by the Postmaster General, a reservation to the government of the privilege of purchasing the lines, property, and effects of the company at an appraised value, and a written acceptance by the company of the restrictions and obligations of the act. This act has been subjected to judicial consideration in three cases. In P. T. Co. *v.* W. U. T. Co.,[2] the facts were that the state of Florida had by an act of 1866 granted to the P. T. Co. a monopoly of the business of telegraphing, and the W. U. T. Co., having in 1867 accepted the terms imposed by the act of Congress, had in 1874 begun under a license from the P. & L. R. R. Co. the erection of a telegraph line upon the right of way of that railway, the railway having also assigned to the W. U. T. Co. rights vested in it by statutes of the state of Florida enacted in 1873 and 1874, and authorizing it to construct, maintain, and operate a telegraph line along the line of the railway. Before the W. U. T. Co. had completed the construction of its line, the P. T. Co. filed a bill in equity in a Circuit Court of the United States to restrain the W. U. T. Co. from interfering with the monopoly vested in the

---

[1] Congress, by Act of 8 June, 1872, c. 335, 17 Stat. 308, Rev. Stat. Sec. 3964 *et seq.*, declares all railway lines in the United States to be post roads.
[2] 96 U. S. 1.

plaintiff by the Florida statute of 1866, and the Circuit Court having dismissed the bill, its decree was affirmed in the Supreme Court, the ground of decision being that the power to regulate commerce is not confined to the instrumentalities of commerce, known or in use when the Constitution was adopted; that telegraphic communication is commercial intercourse and, as such, subject to congressional regulation; that the Act of Congress of 24 July, 1866, is a legitimate regulation of interstate commercial intercourse, in that it declares in substance "that the erection of telegraph lines shall, so far as state interference is concerned, be free to all who will submit to the conditions imposed by Congress,"[1] that, as the statute confers a right to use public property and authorizes the use of private property only by the consent of its owner, there is therein no interference with the reserved rights of the states; and that the exclusive monopoly vested by the Florida Act of 1866 in the P. T. Co. was void as an attempted regulation of interstate commerce. In W. U. T. Co. *v.* Texas,[2] the only question was as to the right of the state of Texas to tax the telegraph company, upon the messages transmitted by it, the company relying upon its acceptance of the act of Congress, and resisting the tax so far as concerned the messages transmitted to points outside of the state, and the messages sent over its lines by officers of the United States on public business; and the court held, that the burden of the tax being imposed on the messages sent, it was void, as a regulation of interstate commerce, so far as regarded the messages sent to points without the state, and as an interference with the means employed by the government of the United States in the execution of its constitutional powers, so far as regarded the messages of the govern-

---

[1] per Waite, C. J., 96 U. S. 11.  [2] 105 U. S. 460.

ment. In W. U. T. Co. *v.* Pendleton,[1] the question was as to the validity of a statute of Indiana, which undertook to regulate the delivery in other states of messages transmitted from places in the state of Indiana, by requiring under certain conditions a delivery of the messages to the person addressed by special messenger, and the court held the statute void as an interstate regulation of commerce, so far as regarded its intended extra-territorial effect. It may, therefore, be regarded as settled, that the trasmission of messages by telegraph is, within the meaning of the Constitution, "commerce;"[2] and that as interstate commerce, it is subject to congressional regulation and exempt from state control or interference.

56. The Indian tribes are not foreign, but domestic and dependent nations; their relation to the United States resembles that of a ward to his guardian; and they are completely under the sovereignty and dominion of the United States. They, therefore, cannot sue in the courts of the United States as foreign states. The reg-

[1] 122 U. S. 347.
[2] Waite, C. J., said in Telegraph Co. *v.* Texas, 105 U. S. 460, 464, "a telegraph company occupies the same relation to commerce as a carrier of messages, that a railroad company does as a carrier of goods. Both companies are instruments of commerce, and their business is commerce itself. They do their transportation in different ways, and their liabilities are in some respects different, but they are both indispensable to those engaged to any considerable extent in commercial pursuits." In W. U. T. Co. *v.* Pendleton, 122 U. S. 356, Field, J., said, "although intercourse by telegraphic messages between the states is thus held to be interstate commerce, it differs in material particulars from that portion of commerce with foreign countries and between the states which consists in the carriage of persons and the transportation and exchange of commodities. . . . . It differs not only in the subjects which it transmits, but in the means of transmission. Other commerce deals only with persons, or with visible and tangible things. But the telegraph transports nothing visible and tangible; it carries only ideas, wishes, orders, and intelligence. Other commerce requires the constant attention and supervision of the carrier for the safety of the persons and property carried. The message of the telegraph passes at once beyond the control of the sender, and reaches the office to which it is sent instantaneously."
[3] Cherokee Nation *v.* Georgia, 5 Pet. 1; Worcester *v.* Same, 6 *id.* 515.

ulation of the relation between the several states and the Indian tribes is exclusively vested in the United States, and state laws cannot operate within an Indian reservation.[1] Congress, under the power to regulate commerce with the Indian tribes, may constitutionally forbid the sale of spirituous liquors to all persons belonging to Indian tribes within the territorial limits of a state, even outside the bounds of an Indian reservation,[2] and it is competent for the United States, in the exercise of the treaty-making power, to stipulate in a treaty with an Indian tribe, that the introduction and sale of spirituous liquors shall be prohibited within certain territories ceded by the tribe to the United States, and such stipulation operates *proprio vigore*, and is binding though the ceded territory be within the limits of an organized county of one of the United States.[3]

[1] Worcester *v.* Georgia, 6 Pet. 515.
[2] United States *v.* Holliday; Same *v.* Haas, 3 Wall. 407.
[3] U. S. *v.* 43 gallons of whisky, 93 U. S. 188. As to the term "Indian country," see *Ex parte* Crow Dog, 109 U. S. 556; U. S. *v.* Le Bois, 121 *id.* 278. The subject of the exercise by the states of their powers of taxation, and of police regulation, as affecting commerce, is more fully treated in other chapters of this book.

# CHAPTER V.

## THE IMPAIRMENT OF THE OBLIGATION OF CONTRACTS.

57. The prohibition affects only laws passed by states.
58. The term "law" defined.
59. Judgments of state courts not conclusive either as to the non-existence, or non impairment, of contracts.
60. The obligation of a contract defined.
61. Legislation as to remedies.
62. The term "contracts" defined.
63. State insolvent laws.
64. Judgments as contracts.
65. Municipal taxation.
66. History of the prohibition.
67. State grants.
68. Express contracts of exemption from taxation.
69. Express grants of peculiar privileges.
70. Contracts between a state and its political subdivisions.
71. Implied contracts in charters of incorporation.
72. Implied corporate exemption from taxation.
73. Implied grants of peculiar privileges.
74. Implied exemption from the operation of the police power.
75. Implied contracts as to matters of public concern.
76. The withdrawal by a state of its consent to be sued.
77. The force and effect of the prohibition as construed by the Supreme Court.

57. Section 10 of article I of the Constitution declares that "no state shall . . . pass any . . . law impairing the obligation of contracts." This prohibition does not in terms affect the exercise of legislative power by the government of the United States, and not only is there not in the Constitution any similar prohibition with regard to the United States, but by the grant of power to Congress, "to establish . . . uniform laws on the subject of bankruptcies throughout the United

States,"[1] authority is expressly conferred to impair the obligation of contracts between debtors and creditors;[2] and under the doctrine of the implied powers, as construed by the court, Congress may impair the obligation of contracts by authorizing the issue of notes which shall be a legal tender in satisfaction of antecedently contracted debts.[3] The constitutional prohibition is likewise inoperative with regard to the acts of any political organization, which at the time of the adoption of the act in question, is not one of the United States; thus, the Constitution having, under the resolution of the Convention of 1787 and the Act of Congress of February, 1788, gone into effect on the first Wednesday of March, 1789, a statute enacted by the state of Virginia in 1788 was not affected by the constitutional prohibition.[4] So, also, a statute enacted by the republic of Texas before its admission into the United States as the state of Texas could not be held to be void for repugnancy to this clause of the Constitution.[5]

58. The prohibition of the passage by a state of any "law impairing the obligation of contracts," would, if strictly construed, include under the word "law" only statutes enacted by state legislatures, but it has been determined that the word "law" comprehends, in addition to acts of legislation, state constitutions and constitutional amendments;[6] judicial decisions of state

---

[1] Article I, Section 9.
[2] Sturges v. Crowninshield, 4 Wheat. 122, 194.
[3] *Supra*, Chapter II.
[4] Owings v. Speed. 5 Wheat. 420.
[5] League v. De Young, 11 How. 185, 203. See also Scott v. Jones, 5 How. 343, 378.
[6] O. & M. R. R v. McClure, 10 Wall. 511; White v. Hart, 13 id. 646; Osborn v. Nicholson, ibid. 654; Gunn v. Barry, 15 id. 610; County of Moultrie v. Rockingham T. C. S. Bank, 92 U. S. 631; Edward v. Kerzey, 96 id. 595; Keith v. Clark, 97 id. 454; N. O. Gas Co. v. Louisiana Light Co., 115 id. 650; Fisk v. Jefferson Police Jury, 116 id. 031.

courts of last resort, rendered subsequently to the making of the contract in question, and antecedently to the suit in which the court determines the invalidity of the contract, and altering by construction the Constitution and statutes of the state in force when the contract was made;[1] and, in general, any act or order, from whatever source emanating, to which a state, by its enforcement thereof, gives the force of a law; as, for instance, a statute enacted by the congress of the Confederacy and enforced during the war of the rebellion by a court of a state within the insurgent lines.[2] Obviously the law, which is alleged to have impaired the obligation of the contract must have been enacted subsequently to the making of the contract, for a law enacted antecedently to the making of the contract can be said to have entered into, and become part of, the contract.[3] The judgment of the state court in the cause, determining the particular contract to be invalid, cannot be said to be a law impairing the obligation of the contract, for otherwise the federal court of last resort would be called upon to "re-examine the judgments of the state courts in every case involving the enforcement of contracts." As Harlan, J., said in Lehigh Water

---

[1] Gelpcke v. Dubuque, 1 Wall. 175; Olcott v The Supervisors, *ibid.* 678; Chicago v. Sheldon, 9 *id.* 50; The City v. Lamson, *ibid.* 477; Douglass v. The County of Pike, 101 U. S. 677; County of Rolls v. Douglass, 105 *id.* 728; Havemeyer v. Iowa County, 3 Wall. 29 l. This doctrine was first suggested by Taney, C. J., who said in Ohio L. I. & T. Co. v. Debolt, 16 How. 432, "the sound and true rule is, that if the contract when made was valid by the laws of the state, as then expounded by all the departments of its government and administered in its courts of justice, its validity and obligation cannot be impaired by any subsequent act of the legislature of the state, or decision of its courts, altering the construction of the law;" and in Gelpcke v. Dubuque, 1 Wall. 206, Swayne, J, quoted the *dictum* of Taney, C. J., and declared it to be "the law of this court."

[2] Williams v. Bruffy, 96 U. S. 176; Stevens v. Griffith, 111 U. S. 48; Ford v. Surget, 97 U. S. 594.

[3] L. W Co. v. Easton, 121 U. S. 388, 391.

Co. v. Easton,[1] "the state court may erroneously determine questions arising under a contract, which constitutes the basis of the suit before it; it may hold a contract to be void, which, in our opinion, is valid; it may adjudge a contract to be valid, which, in our opinion, is void; or its interpretation of the contract may, in our opinion, be radically wrong; but, in neither of such cases, would the judgment be reviewable by this court under the clause of the Constitution protecting the obligation of contracts against impairment by state legislation, and under the existing statutes defining and regulating its jurisdiction, unless that judgment in terms, or by its necessary operation, gives effect to some provision of the state Constitution, or some legislative enactment of the state, which is claimed by the unsuccessful party to impair the obligation of the particular contract in question."[2] It must, therefore, appear in any cause in which it is sought to reverse in the Supreme Court of the United States, a decree or judgment of a state court for contravention of the constitutional prohibition of the impairment of contracts, that in the particular case the state court enforced to the prejudice of the plaintiff in error some act of state, either in the form of a state Constitution, or an act of the state legislature, or a judgment of a court in another case, or an act of an extrinsic authority to which the state by its adoption thereof gave the force of law, and that the act of state, whatever its form, was as affecting the contract put into operation subsequently to the making of that contract.

59. In questions under this clause of the Constitution

[1] 121 U. S. 388, 392.
[2] See also: R. R. v. Rock. 4 Wall. 177, 181; R. R. v. McClure, 10 Wall. 511, 515; Knox v. Exchange Bank, 12 id. 379, 383; Delmas v. Ins Co., 14 id. 661, 665; University v. People, 99 U. S. 309, 319; C. L. Ins. Co. v. Needles, 113 id. 574, 582.

the courts of the United States do not accept as conclusive upon them the judgment of the state court either as to the non-existence of contracts or as to their non-impairment,[1] for, if the decision of the state court were to be accepted without inquiry or examination, the constitutional prohibition would be nugatory.

60. The obligation of a contract is the duty of performance which the law imposes on one, or other, or both of the parties to the contract.[2] As Marshall, C. J., said in the case last cited, "any law which releases a part of this obligation must in the literal sense of the word impair it." Of course, the application of the constitutional prohibition is not dependent on the extent of the impairment.[3]

61. A state may, without impairment of the obligation of a contract, regulate, or even limit, the remedies for the enforcement of that contract, provided that it does not take away all remedies therefor, and that it leaves in force a substantial remedy. Thus a state may in the case of a corporation whose charter requires that service of process on the corporation shall be made only at its principal office provide by subsequent legislation that such process may be served on any officer, clerk, or agent of the corporation.[4] A state may abolish imprisonment for debt as a remedy for breach of contract;[5] it may validate technically defective mortgages,[6] or conveyances by femes covert;[7] it may by statute

---

[1] State Bank v. Knopp, 16 How. 369; Ohio L. I. & T. Co. v. De Bolt, ibid. 416; J. B. Bank v. Skelly. 1 Black. 436; Bridge Proprietors v. Hoboken Co., 1 Wall. 116; Delmas v. Insurance Co., 14 id. 661; Wright v. Nagle, 101 U. S. 791; Williams v. Louisiana, 103 id. 637; L. & N. R. R. v. Palmes, 109 id. 244.
[2] Sturges v. Crowninshield, 4 Wheat. 197.
[3] Green v. Biddle, 8 Wheat. 1.   [4] Railroad v. Hecht, 95 U. S. 168.
[5] Mason v. Haile, 12 Wheat. 327; Penniman's Case, 103 id. 714.
[6] Gross v. U. S. Mortgage Co., 108 U. S. 477.
[7] Randall v. Kreiger, 23 Wall. 137.

grant new trials and create new tribunals to set aside grants or reverse judgments alleged to be fraudulent;[1] it may provide speedy and equitable methods for determining the title to lands under patents granted by the state;[2] it may authorize at the request of all parties in interest the discharge of testamentary trustees of real estate;[3] it may change the rate of interest to be paid to the purchaser in the case of the redemption of mortgaged premises sold under foreclosure;[4] it may repeal usury laws which unrepealed would have avoided the contract;[5] it may prescribe a scheme for the reorganization of an embarrassed corporation and provide that creditors who have notice of and do not dissent from the scheme shall be bound thereby;[6] it may reduce the limitation of time for bringing suit provided that a reasonable limit elapses after the enactment before the limitation bars a suit upon existing contracts;[7] it may require registration as a prerequisite to the legal enforcement of existing mortgages, provided that a reasonable period be allowed before the law goes into effect;[8] it may require holders of tax sale certificates to give notice to the occupant of the land, if any there be, before taking a tax deed;[9] it may require registration with municipal officials of judgments against a municipality;[10] it may free shareholders of a corporation from individual liability for debts of the corporation to an

---

[1] League v. De Young, 11 How. 202.
[2] Jackson v. Lamphiere, 3 Pet. 208.
[3] Williamson v. Suydam, 6 Wall. 723.
[4] C. M. L. Ins Co. v. Cushman, 108 U. S. 51.
[5] Ewell v. Daggs, 108 U. S. 143.
[6] Gilfillan v. Union Canal Co., 109 U. S. 401.
[7] Terry v. Anderson, 95 U. S. 628; Barrett v. Holmes, 102 *id.* 651; Koshkonong v. Burton, 104 *id.* 660.
[8] Vance v. Vance, 108 U. S. 514.
[9] Curtis v Whitney, 13 Wall. 68.
[10] Louisiana v. New Orleans, 102 U. S. 203.

amount greater than their shares, for such legislation does not impair the direct liability of the corporation;[1] it may, after a state bank has obtained judgment against a party, authorize that party to set off against the judgment circulating notes of the bank procured by him after the entry of the judgment;[2] and, a disseised tenant for years being entitled to sue on the landlord's covenant for quiet possession and also on a statutory remedy for forcible entry and detainer, the state may take away the statutory remedy, provided that the action on the covenant be left unimpaired.[3] A state, having issued bonds, and having by a subsequent statute provided for the funding of those bonds on certain terms at a reduced rate of interest, may, by a later statute, prohibit the funding of a specified class of those bonds until by judicial decree their validity shall have been determined, for the original remedy of the bondholder is not thereby impaired.[4]

So also, a state, which has contracted to receive its taxes in the notes of a certain bank, may, by statute, provide that the only remedy for taxpayers, whose tender of such notes may be refused, shall be to pay in legal money and within a time limited to bring suit against the tax collector, judgment against whom shall be a preferred claim against the state.[5] So also where the laws of a state permit coupons of state bonds to be received in payment of state taxes, provided that in case of the refusal of such coupons when tendered the holder thereof might enforce his rights under the contract by suing out an alternative *mandamus* against the officer refusing the coupons, and if judgment should be rendered

[1] Ochiltree v. I. R. C. Co., 21 Wall. 249.
[2] Blount v. Windley, 95 U. S. 173. [3] Drehman v. Stifle, 8 Wall. 595.
[4] Guarantee Company v. Board of Liquidation, 105 U. S. 622.
[5] Tennessee v. Sneed, 96 U. S. 69.

in favour of the holder of the coupons that he could then have forthwith a peremptory writ of *mandamus* for the recovery of damages and costs, the obligation of the contract was not impaired by a subsequent statute which required in case of the refusal of the tender of the coupons a payment of the state taxes in lawful money and a lodging of the coupons in a state court of competent jurisdiction, and the subsequent framing of an issue to determine whether or not the coupons were genuine and legally receivable for taxes, with a right of appeal to the state court of last resort.[1] On the other hand, a state, in acting upon the remedy, cannot take away all, or a substantial part, of the power for the enforcement of a contract. It, therefore, cannot prohibit its courts to entertain jurisdiction of a suit to enforce or obtain damages for the breach of a class of contracts, legally valid when made;[2] nor can a state forbid its courts, after the abolition of slavery, to take jurisdiction of actions upon contracts made before that abolition and the consideration for which was the price of slaves;[3] nor could a state, after the restoration of peace, declare void a contract made between its citizens during the war of the rebellion stipulating for payment in confederate notes;[4] nor can a state, after the making of a contract, change to the prejudice of either party the measure of damages for its breach;[5] nor can a state, by subsequent legislation, impose as a condition precedent to the legal enforcement of a contractual right, that he who seeks to enforce that right shall prove an extrinsic and independent fact that has no necessary connection with the right to be enforced; as for instance that he

[1] Antoni *v.* Greenhow, 107 U. S. 769; Moore *v.* Same, 114 *id.* 338.
[2] Van Hoffman *v.* Quincy, 4 Wall. 552.
[3] Wright *v.* Hart, 13 Wall. 646.
[4] Delmas *v.* Insurance Co., 14 Wall. 661.
[5] Effinger *v.* Kenney, 115 U. S. 566; W. & W. R. R. *v.* King, 95 *id.* 3.

## CONTRACTS DEFINED. 153

never bore arms in support of, or never aided, the rebellion against the United States;[1] or that he has paid certain taxes; nor can it permit the defendant to set off damages not caused by the plaintiff; as for instance the defendant's loss of property resulting from the war of the rebellion;[2] nor can a state, after a judgment has been enrolled, materially increase the debtor's exemption;[3] nor can a state after the making of a mortgage enlarge the period of time allowed for the redemption after foreclosure;[4] nor forbid a sale in foreclosure at which less than two-thirds of the value of the mortgaged premises as fixed by appraisement shall be realized;[5] nor take away the right to compound interest, if given by the law existing at the time of the making of the contract;[6] nor repeal a statute in force at the time of making the contract which renders the stock of a shareholder liable for the debts of the corporation.[7]

62. The term "contracts," as used in the constitutional prohibition, includes both executory and executed contracts,[8] comprehending, within the former class,

[1] Pierce v. Carskadon, 16 Wall. 234.
[2] Walker v. Whitehead, 16 Wall. 314.
[3] Gunn v. Barry, 15 Wall. 610. [4] Howard v. Bugbee, 24 How. 461.
[5] Bronson v. Kinzie, 1 How. 311; McCracken v. Hayward, 2 id. 608; Gartly v. Ewing, 3 id. 707.
[6] Koshkonong v. Burton, 104 U. S. 668.
[7] Hawthorn v. Calef, 2 Wall. 210.
[8] "Contract" is, as Field, J., said in Louisiana v. Mayor of New Orleans, 109 U. S. 285, 288, "used in the Constitution in its ordinary sense as signifying the agreement of two or more minds for consideration proceeding from one to the other to do or not to do certain acts." In Sturges v. Crowninshield, 4 Wheat. 122, 197, Marshall, C. J., said, "a contract is an agreement in which a party undertakes to do or not to do a particular thing." Marshall, C. J., said in Fletcher v. Peck, 6 Cr. 87, 136, "a contract is a compact between two or more parties, and is either executory or executed. An executory contract is one in which a party binds himself to do, or not to do, a particular thing. . . . . A contract executed is one in which the object of contract is performed, and this, says Blackstone, differs in nothing from a grant. . . . . Since then, in fact, a grant is a contract executed, the obligation of which still continues, and since the Constitution uses the general term 'contracts,'

promissory notes and bills of exchange,[1] corporate bonds,[2] municipal bonds,[3] and municipal contracts for the payment of the salaries of their employés[4] and, generally, all legally enforcible contracts to do, or not to do, any particular act; and, within the latter class, grants and judgments founded upon contracts,[5] but not judgments founded upon torts.[6]

There can be no impairment of the obligation of a contract which has not been legally made. Thus a vote of the majority of the qualified voters of a county at an election held under a statute incorporating a railway and authorizing an issue of the bonds of the county in payment for the stock of the railway, if the qualified voters so decide it, does not constitute a contract whose obligation can be impaired by an amendment of the state Constitution,[7] or by a repeal of the statute,[8] before the subscription be made or the bonds issued. On the same

---

without distinguishing between those which are executory and those which are executed, it must be construed to comprehend the latter as well as the former." In Dartmouth College v. Woodward, 4 Wheat. 629, Marshall, C. J., said, "the provision of the Constitution never has been understood to embrace other contracts than those which respect property or some object of value and confer rights which may be asserted in a court of justice." Daniel, J., said in Butler v. Pennsylvania, 10 How. 402, 416, "the contracts designed to be protected . . . . are contracts by which perfect, certain, definite, fixed, private rights of property are vested."

[1] Sturges v. Crowninshield, 4 Wheat. 122; McMillan v. McNeil, ibid. 209; F. & M. Bank v. Smith, ibid. 131; Ogden v. Saunders, 12 id. 624; Boyle v. Zacharie, 6 Pet. 635; Suydam v. Broadnax, 14 id. 67; Cook v. Moffatt, 5 How. 295; Baldwin v. Hale, 1 Wall. 223.

[2] Case of State Tax on Foreign-held Bonds, 15 Wall. 300.

[3] County of Moultrie v. R. T. C. S. Bank 92 U. S. 631; Mobile v. Wattson, 116 U. S. 289; sed cf. Merriwether v. Garrett, 102 id. 472.

[4] Fiske v. J. Police Jury, 116 U. S. 131.

[5] Blount v. Windley, 95 U. S. 173; Memphis v. U. S., 97 U. S. 293; Mobile v. Wattson, 116 id. 298; Wolff v. New Orleans, 103 id. 358; Nelson v. St. Martin's Parish, 111 id. 716; Rolls County Court v. U. S., 105 id. 733; Louisiana v. Pillsbury, ibid. 278.

[6] Louisiana v. New Orleans, 109 U. S. 285.

[7] Aspinwall v. Daviess County, 22 How. 364.

[8] Wadsworth v. Supervisors, 102 U. S. 534.

principle, a state statute, which is void by reason of repugnancy to the Constitution of the United States, cannot constitute a contract of exemption from state taxation; as for instance, a statute imposing taxation on national banks to an extent not permitted by the National Banking Act, and, therefore, a subsequent state statute imposing on national banks a taxation which though a heavier burden than that imposed by the earlier statute is yet within the limits permitted by the National Banking Act, does not impair the obligation of any contract.[1] On the same principle, a statutory exemption from state taxation, if granted in violation of the Constitution of the state, does not bind the state as a contract.[2]

63. There was, for some time, a controversy as to the effect of the constitutional prohibition upon state insolvent laws; in Sturges v. Crowninshield,[3] the action being brought in a federal court within the state of Massachusetts, and the plaintiff being a citizen of New York, and the defendant a citizen of Massachusetts, it was held that a discharge under an insolvent law of Massachusetts, enacted subsequently to the making within that state of a contract to be performed within the state, was void as an impairment of the obligation of that contract. In McMillan v. McNeil,[4] the action being brought in a court of the state of Louisiana, the plaintiff and defendant both being citizens of South Carolina, and the contract having been made and stipulated to be performed in that state, it was held that a discharge under an antecedently enacted law of Louisiana impaired the obligation of the contract, and was no bar to its enforce-

---

[1] People v. Commissioners of Taxes, 94 U. S. 415.
[2] R. R. v. Gaines, 97 U. S. 697; Trask v. Maguire, 18 Wall. 391; Morgan v. Louisiana, 93 U. S. 217; Shields v. Ohio, 95 id. 319.
[3] 4 Wheat. 122.    [4] 4 Wheat. 209.

ment. In F. & M. Bank *v.* Smith,[1] the action being brought in a court of the state of Pennsylvania, and both plaintiff and defendant being residents of that state, and the contract having been made, and to be performed, in that state, it was held that a discharge under a subsequently enacted insolvent law of that state was no bar to the action. In Ogden *v.* Saunders,[2] the plaintiff being a citizen of Kentucky and the defendant a citizen of New York, the contract having been made in New York to be performed in that state, and the action having been brought in a federal court in the state of Louisiana, it was held that a discharge under an antecedently enacted insolvent law of the state of New York was no bar to the action; and in Shaw *v.* Robbins,[3] the same ruling was made, the action being brought in a court of the state of Ohio, the plaintiff being a citizen of Massachusetts, the defendant a citizen of New York, and the discharge set up being one that had been obtained under an antecedently enacted insolvent law of the last-mentioned state. In Boyle *v.* Zacharie,[4] Story, J., said, "the effect of the discharge under the insolvent act is of course at rest, so far as it is covered by the antecedent decisions made by this court. The ultimate opinion delivered by Mr. Justice Johnson in the case of Ogden *v.* Saunders,[5] was concurred in and adopted by the three judges, who were in the minority upon the general question of the constitutionality of state insolvent laws, so largely discussed in that case," and [6] Marshall, C. J., expressed the same view as to the effect of the judgment in Ogden *v.* Saunders. In Sudyam *v.* Broadnax,[7] the action having been brought in a court of the state of Alabama, the plaintiff

---

[1] 6 Wheat. 131.
[2] 12 Wheat. 213.
[3] 12 Wheat. 369.
[4] 6 Pet. 643.
[5] 12 Wheat. 213, 358.
[6] at p. 635.
[7] 14 Pet. 67.

being a citizen of New York, it was held that a judicial declaration of the insolvency of a decedent's estate under the terms of an antecedently enacted statute of Alabama was powerless to discharge a contract made by the decedent in his lifetime in New York and stipulated to be performed in that state. In Cook *v.* Moffat,[1] the action being brought in a federal court in the state of Maryland, the plaintiff being a citizen of New York and the defendant a citizen of Maryland, and the contract having been made in New York to be performed in that state, it was held that a discharge under an antecedently enacted statute of Maryland was no bar to the action. In Baldwin *v.* Hale,[2] the action having been brought in a federal court in the state of Massachusetts, the plaintiff being a citizen of Vermont and the defendant a citizen of Massachusetts, and the contract having been made in Massachusetts, to be performed in that state, it was held that a discharge under an antecedently enacted statute of Massachusetts did not bar the action. The result of the cases is, that a discharge under the insolvent laws of a state is not a bar to an action on a contract for the payment of money, *first:* when the law under which the discharge has been granted has been enacted subsequently to the making of the contract;[3] *second:* when, although the discharge has been granted under a law enacted antecedently to the making of the contract, the contract was made in another state to be performed in that other state;[4] *third:* when, although the discharge has been granted under a law enacted antecedently to the making of the contract, and although the contract was made and to be performed in the state in which the discharge has been granted, the action upon

---

[1] 5 How. 295.      [2] 1 Wall. 223.
[3] Sturges *v.* Crowninshield, 4 Wheat. 122; F. & M. Bank *v.* Smith, 6 *id.* 131.
[4] McMillan *v.* McNeil, 4 Wheat. 209; Cook *v.* Moffat, 5 How. 295.

the contract is brought in another state, by a party who is not a citizen of the state granting the discharge, and who has not made himself a party to the proceedings in insolvency;[1] and *fourth*, when, although the discharge has been granted under a law enacted antecedently to the making of the contract, and although the contract was made and to be performed in the state in which the discharge has been granted, the action upon the contract is brought in the state granting the discharge by one who is not a citizen of that state, and who has not made himself a party to the proceedings in insolvency.[2] The questions, as yet not concluded by the authority of the court, are as to the effect of the discharge as regards creditors, who, though not citizens of the state granting the discharge, voluntarily become parties to the insolvency proceedings, or, who, being citizens of the state granting the discharge, and being duly notified of the insolvency proceedings, neglect or refuse to become parties thereto.

64. Contracts for the payment of money being within the protection of the constitutional prohibition of the impairment of their obligation, judgments upon such contracts are equally entitled to protection.[3] Therefore, a judgment against a municipal corporation founded upon a breach of contract is not affected by a subsequent legislative abolition of the municipality's power to levy taxes for the payment of its debts.[4] But judgments founded upon *torts* are not contracts whose obligation will be protected against subsequent legislation; as, for instance, against a statutory diminution of

---

[1] Ogden *v.* Saunders, 12 Wheat. 213; Shaw *v.* Robbins, *ibid.* 369, note.
[2] Baldwin *v.* Hale, 1 Wall. 223.
[3] Blount *v* Windsley, 95 U. S. 173.
[4] Memphis *v.* U. S., 97 U.S. 293; Mobile *v.* Wattson, 116 *id.* 298; Wolff *v.* New Orleans, 103 *id.* 358; Nelson *v.* St. Martin's Parish, 111 *id.* 716; Rolls County Court *v.* United States, 105 *id.* 733; Louisiana *v.* Pillsbury, *ibid.* 278.

the taxing power of the municipality against which the judgment in *tort* has been obtained.[1]

65. A state cannot take away from a municipality existing powers of taxation so as to deprive of his compensation an officer who has served his term.[2] County bonds issued by public officers under authority of law either upon the subscription, or upon the agreement to subscribe to the stock of a railway constitute a contract between the county and the bondholders, whose obligation cannot be impaired by a subsequent legislative repeal of the statute authorizing the subscription, or by a subsequent amendment to the state Constitution prohibiting such a subscription.[3] But where public officers are by statute authorized to issue bonds in aid of railway construction only upon the fulfillment of a condition precedent which is not fulfilled before the adoption of an amended state Constitution prohibiting the issue of such bonds there is no contract whose obligation is impaired by the adoption of the state Constitution.[4] On the same principle a statutory authorization of borrowing of money by a municipality is not a contract between the state and the municipal creditors whose obligation can be impaired by the subsequent exercise by the state of the power of modifying the rate of taxation or of exempting certain property from taxation,[5] but a state cannot dissolve an existing municipal corporation having a bonded debt, for whose payment powers of taxation have been granted and specifically pledged, for that dissolution interferes with the exercise of such power of taxation.[6] Nor can a state withdraw or

[1] Louisiana *v.* New Orleans, 109 U. S. 285.
[2] Fiske *v.* J. Police Jury, 116 U. S. 131.
[3] County of Moultrie *v.* R. T. C. S. Bank, 92 U. S. 361.
[4] D. & J. R. R. *v.* Falconer, 103 U. S. 821.
[5] Gilman *v.* Sheboygan, 2 Bl. 510.
[6] Mobile *v.* Wattson, 116 U. S. 289; *sed cf.* Merriweather *v.* Garrett, 102 *id.* 472.

restrict the taxing power of a municipality so as to impair the obligation of contracts which have been made on the pledge, express or implied, that that taxing power shall be exercised for their fulfillment.[1] A statutory prohibition of the issuing by the courts of the state of a *mandamus* to compel the levying of a tax for the payment of the interest upon, or the principal of, municipal bonds, whose issue had been legally authorized, impairs the contract between the municipality and the bondholder.[2] In general, the statutory authorization of the contracting by a municipality of an extraordinary debt by the issue of negotiable securities therefor conclusively implies a power in the municipality to levy taxes sufficient to pay the accruing interest upon, and the matured principal of, the debt unless the statute conferring the authority, or the Constitution of the state, or some general law in force at the time, clearly manifests a contrary legislative intent.[3]

66. It has never been doubted that contracts between individuals were protected by the constitutional provision, but it was formerly a matter of grave doubt whether or not contracts, to which a state was a party, were likewise entitled to protection. The history of the Constitution shows clearly, that the mischiefs, which the framers of the Constitution intended to remedy by this prohibition, were, primarily, those caused by state legislation enabling debtors to discharge their debts otherwise than as stipulated in their contracts, and that the prohibition was not intended by its originators to interfere with the exercise of state sovereignty in cases of other than private contracts. This restriction on

---

[1] Wolff *v.* New Orleans, 103 U. S. 358; Nelson *v.* St. Martin's Parish, 111 *id.* 716; Rolls County Court *v.* United States, 105 *id.* 733; Memphis *v.* United States, 97 *id.* 293; Siebert *v.* Lewis, 122 *id.* 284.

[2] Louisiana *v.* Pillsbury, 105 U. S. 278.

[3] Rolls County Court *v.* United States, 105 U. S. 733.

HISTORY OF THE CLAUSE. 161

the power of the states is not to be found in either Mr. Pinckney's, Mr. Hamilton's, or Mr. Patterson's *projets* as presented to the convention, nor is it implied in Mr. Madison's resolutions, nor does it appear in the draft reported by the Committee of Five on 6 August, 1787; but when article XIII of the report of that committee was under consideration on 28 August, Mr. King "moved to add in the words used in the ordinance of Congress establishing new states, a prohibition on the states to interfere in private contracts," but, on motion of Mr. Rutledge, as a substitute for Mr. King's proposition, there was adopted a prohibition of state bills of attainder and *ex post facto* laws.[1] The journal of the convention mentions Mr. Rutledge's motion, but omits all reference to Mr. King's proposition. Mr. Madison reports Mr. King's resolution, with the mention of declarations of opinion in favour of it by Messrs. Sherman, Wilson, and Madison, and objections to it by Messrs. Gouverneur Morris, and Mason, on the ground that state laws, limiting the times within which actions might be brought, necessarily interfered with contracts, and ought not to be prohibited, and that there might be other cases in which such interferences would be proper. There does not seem to be any record of any other discussion of this subject in the convention. The Committee of Revision reported on 12 September, 1787, to the convention their revised draft of the Constitution, in which Art. I, Sec. 10, declares "no state shall . . . pass any . . . laws altering or impairing the obligation of contracts." In convention on Friday, 14 September, 1787, the clause was finally amended and put into the form in which it appears in the Constitution, there being, so far as is known, no debate on the subject, save by Mr. Gerry, who

[1] Madison Papers, 5 Elliot's Debates 485.

11

"entered into observations inculcating the importance of the public faith and the propriety of the restraint put on the states from impairing the obligation of contracts," and unavailingly endeavoured to obtain the insertion in the Constitution of a similar restraint upon congressional action.[1]  Mr. Bancroft states,[2] with reference to the Committee of Revision's report, that "Gouverneur Morris retained the clause forbidding *ex post facto* laws —and resolute not 'to countenance the issue of paper money and the consequent violation of contracts,'"[3] he of himself added the words, "no state shall pass laws altering or impairing the obligation of contracts."[4] Mr. Bancroft also quotes from the official report to the Governor of Connecticut made by Roger Sherman and Oliver Ellsworth, the deputies from that state to the Federal Convention, wherein they say, "the restraint on the legislatures of the several states respecting emitting bills of credit, making anything but money a tender in payment of debts, or impairing the obligation of contracts by *ex post facto* laws, was thought necessary as a security to commerce, in which the interest of foreigners, as well as of the citizens of different states may be affected." The clause does not appear to have been made a subject of discussion in any of the state conventions called to ratify the Constitution. Mr. Hamilton, when Secretary of the Treasury, said in his memorandum of 28 May, 1790, to President Washington on the subject of the resolutions of Congress with regard to the arrears of pay due to certain soldiers of the Revolution,[5] "the Constitution of the United States interdicts the states individually from

---

[1] Madison Papers, 5 Elliot's Debates 546.
[2] 2 Hist. of the Constitution 214.   [3] G. Morris by Sparks, III, 323.
[4] Gilpin 1552, 1581.
[5] Works of Hamilton, Lodge's Edition, Vol. II, p. 147.

passing any law impairing the obligation of contracts. This, to the more enlightened part of the community, was not one of the least recommendations of that Constitution. The too frequent intermeddlings of the state legislatures, in relation to private contracts were extensively felt, and seriously lamented; and a Constitution which promised a prevention, was, by those who felt and thought in that manner, eagerly embraced."— Mr. Madison said in the Federalist,[1] "Bills of attainder, *ex post facto* laws, and laws impairing the obligation of contracts, are contrary to the first principles of the social compact, and to every principle of sound legislation. The two former are expressly prohibited by the declarations prefixed to some of the state Constitutions, and all of them are prohibited by the spirit and scope of these fundamental charters. Our own experience has taught us, nevertheless, that additional fences against these dangers ought not be omitted. Very properly, therefore, have the convention added this constitutional bulwark in favour of personal security and private rights; and I am much deceived, if they have not, in so doing, as faithfully consulted the genuine sentiments as the undoubted interests of their constituents. The sober people of America are weary of the fluctuating policy which has directed the public councils. They have seen with regret and with indignation, that sudden changes, and legislative interferences, in cases affecting personal rights, become jobs in the hands of enterprising and influential speculators, and snares to the more industrious and less informed part of the community. They have seen, too, that one legislative interference is but the first link of a long chain of repetitions; every subsequent interference being naturally produced by the effects of the preceding. They very

[1] No. XLIV, Lodge's Edition.

rightly infer, therefore, that some thorough reform is wanting, which will banish speculations on public measures, inspire "a general prudence and industry, and give a regular course to the business of society." In Sturges v. Crowninshield,[1] Marshall, C. J., said "the fair, and, we think, the necessary construction of the sentence requires that we should give these words their full and obvious meaning. A general dissatisfaction with that lax system of legislation which followed the war of our revolution undoubtedly directed the mind of the convention to this subject. It is probable that laws, such as those which have been stated in argument, produced the loudest complaints, were most immediately felt. The attention of the convention, therefore, was particularly directed to paper money, and to acts which enabled the debtor to discharge his debt otherwise than as stipulated in the contract. Had nothing more been intended, nothing would have been expressed. But, in the opinion of the convention, much more remained to be done. The same mischief might be effected by other means. To restore public confidence completely, it was necessary not only to prohibit the use of particular means by which it might be effected, but to prohibit the use of any means by which the same mischief might be produced. The convention appears to have intended to establish a great principle, that contracts should be inviolable. The Constitution, therefore, declares that no state shall pass 'any law impairing the obligation of contracts.'"

67. In 1810 the judgment in Fletcher v. Peck,[2] established the doctrine that contracts, to which a state is a party, are within the protection of the constitutional prohibition. The facts in that case were these: in 1795, the state of Georgia enacted a statute authorizing

[1] 4 Wheat. 205.     [2] 6 Cr. 87.

the issue of a patent to "the Georgia Co." for a tract of land in that state, and on 13 January, 1795, the patent was issued. By sundry *mesne* conveyances before 1796 title in fee to a part of the tract vested in Peck, who had purchased for value and without notice of any matter which could invalidate the title of the state's grantees. In 1796 the state of Georgia enacted a statute repealing the Act of 1795 and annulling the patent to the Georgia Co. On 14 May, 1803, Peck conveyed to Fletcher, covenanting, *inter alia*, that his title had been "in no way constitutionally or legally impaired by virtue of any subsequent act of any subsequent legislature of the state of Georgia." Fletcher brought covenant *sur* deed against Peck in the Circuit Court, declaring, *inter alia*, that the statute of 1796 was enacted by reason of fraud practiced in securing the enactment of the statute of 1795 and was an impairment of Peck's title. Peck pleaded that he was a purchaser for value and without notice, etc. Fletcher demurred, and the court entered judgment thereon for Peck, which judgment was affirmed in the Supreme Court on a writ of error, the ground of decision being, that the constitutional prohibition comprehends contracts executed, including grants, as well as contracts executory, and that the states being prohibited from passing "any bill of attainder, *ex post facto* law, or law impairing the obligation of contracts," and the prohibition of bills of attainder and *ex post facto* laws being a restraint upon governmental action, there is not to be implied "in words which import a general prohibition to impair the obligation of contracts, an exception in favour of the right to impair the obligation of those contracts into which the state may enter." It has, therefore, since 1810, been settled that the term "contract" includes not only contracts between individuals, private and corporate, but also contracts, executed and executory, between the state and individuals, private and corporate. Following in the line of Fletcher v. Peck, it has been held that, a grant of land by a state to a railway corporation is a contract whose obligation is impaired by a subsequent act resuming the land,[1] that a state cannot deprive of his right to recover *mesne* profits from a disseisor one whose title vested under a compact between that state and another state, and who under that compact was entitled to recover *mesne* profits,[2] and that a state cannot, by statute, divest religious corporations of their title to land acquired under colonial laws antecedently to the revolution.[3]

68. When in 1812 the case of New Jersey v. Wilson,[4] came before the Supreme Court, the doctrine of Fletcher v. Peck necessarily required the court to hold that the state was bound by the express contract contained in a statute which authorized the purchase of certain land for the remnant of the tribe of Delaware Indians, and which, in terms, declared that the land so purchased "shall not hereafter be subject to any tax," and that that contract forbade the subsequent taxation of such lands, after their sale to other parties with the state's consent. The legal inviolability of a state's contract to exempt lands from state taxation having been thus established, it followed that a similar contract with regard to corporate franchises or assets was entitled to the like protection, and that contracts of exemption from state taxation, contained in corporate charters, or stipulated by subsequent agreement, if made in express terms and supported by an adequate consideration, constitute contracts so binding upon the state that their obligation cannot be impaired by a subsequent repeal of the charter,

[1] Davis v. Gray, 16 Wall. 203.
[2] Green v. Biddle, 8 Wheat. 1.
[3] Terrett v. Taylor, 9 Cr. 43.
[4] 7 Cr. 164.

or by an imposition of a rate of taxation inconsistent with the state's contract.[1] Thus, the line and rolling stock of a railway cannot be taxed when its charter exempts from taxation its "property" and "shares;"[2] nor can the shares of the capital stock of a corporation be taxed in the hands of the shareholders, when the charter requires the corporation to pay to the state a tax on each share of the stock "in lieu of all other taxes;"[3] nor can the gross receipts of a corporation be taxed when its charter exempts the corporation from taxation;[4] nor can a corporation be taxed in excess of the limits specifically designated in the charter,[5] or other contract.[6] Nor can a municipal corporation in the exercise of authority delegated to it by statute assess a street railway for a new paving of a street, when the railway has contracted with the municipality to keep the street in repair, for the acceptance of that contract limits by necessary implication the obligation of the railway to repairs, and relieves it from liability for betterments;[7] nor can property held by a charitable corporation as an investment be taxed, when its charter exempts from taxation all property of whatever kind or description belonging to or owned by the corporation.[8] An adequate consideration for a charter exemption from taxation is to be found in the exercise by the corporation of the powers conferred by the charter, or, in the

[1] Jefferson Branch Bank v. Skelly, 1 Black 436; W. R. R. v. Reid, 18 Wall. 264; R. & G. R. R. v. Same, ibid. 269; Chicago v. Sheldon 9 Wall. 50; Humphrey v. Pegues, 16 id. 244; P. R. R. v. Magwire, 20 id. 36; New Jersey v. Yard, 95 U. S. 104; University v. People, 99 id. 309; Asylum v. New Orleans, 105 id. 362.
[2] W. R. R. v. Reid, 13 Wall 264.
[3] Farrington v. Tennessee, 95 U. S. 679.
[4] P. R. R. v. Magwire, 20 Wall. 36.
[5] R. & G. R. R. v. Reid, 13 Wall. 269.
[6] New Jersey v. Yard, 95 U. S. 104.
[7] Chicago v. Sheldon, 9 Wall. 50.
[8] University v. People, 99 U. S. 309; Asylum v. New Orleans, 105 id. 362.

case of corporations for charitable purposes, in the contribution of funds to the corporation for the accomplishment of its benevolent purpose.[1] So also the building by a railway corporation of its line, under the terms of a statute amendatory of its charter and granting in express terms an exemption from taxation, constitutes a consideration for the exemption, though the original charter granted a power to the corporation, which it did not exercise, to build the line.[2] Statutory exemptions from state taxation not incorporated in charters and unsupported by a consideration moving to the state, or from the exempted corporation, do not constitute irrepealable contracts of exemption, but are subject to modification or repeal in the exercise of legislative discretion; as, for instance, bounty laws offering such an exemption as an inducement for the organization of corporations to develop a particular industry,[3] or voluntary grants of exemption of the real property of a charity from taxation.[4]

If the Constitution of a state prohibits legislative grants of exemption from state taxation, such a grant, though accepted in good faith by the exempted corporation, cannot constitute a contract whose obligation is impaired by a subsequent imposition of taxation.[5] Such a constitutional prohibition operates to extinguish an exemption made by contract in the case of a railway, which having been exempted before the adoption of the constitutional prohibition, had been after the adoption thereof sold under foreclosure to reorganize the corporation.[6] On the same principle, a statutory consoli-

[1] University v. People, 99 U. S. 309; Asylum v. New Orleans, 105 id. 362.
[2] Humphrey v. Pegues, 16 Wall. 244.
[3] Salt Co. v. East Saginaw, 13 Wall. 273.
[4] Christ Church v. Philadelphia, 24 How. 300.
[5] Railroad Co. v. Gaines, 97 U. S. 697.
[6] Trask v. Maguire, 18 Wall. 391; Morgan v. Louisiana, 93 U. S. 217.

dation of two railways works the dissolution of the original corporation, and subjects the consolidated corporation to the operation of an amended state Constitution, which took effect subsequently to the incorporation of the original corporations, but prior to their consolidation; and, therefore, the state legislature may, without impairment of the obligation of the contract, prescribe rates for the transportation of passengers by the consolidated corporation, though one of the original corporations was by charter protected against such legislative regulation.[1] General statutory prohibitions of the exemption of corporations from state taxation are not binding on subsequent legislatures,[2] unless referred to in, and incorporated with, subsequently granted charters.[3] In the case of a statutory consolidation accepted by two railways, each of whose charters contained a limited exemption from taxation, a reservation by a general statute before the enactment of the consolidating act and incorporated therewith, operates to extinguish the limited exemption contained in the original charters.[4] Of course, if the state in the charter reserves the right to alter, modify, or repeal that charter, that reservation authorizes any such amendment of the charter granted as will not defeat nor substantially impair the obligation of the grant or any rights that may be vested thereunder.[5] The first suggestion of any such reservation is to be found in the judgment of Parsons, C. J., in Wales v. Stetson,[6] which is cited by Miller, J., in Greenwood v. Freight Co.[7] A provision in a charter, or a general statute incorpo-

[1] Shields v. Ohio, 95 U. S. 319.
[2] New Jersey v. Yard, 95 U. S. 104.
[3] Greenwood v. Freight Co., 105 U. S. 13; Tomlinson v. Jessup, 15 Wall 454.
[4] A. & G. R. R. v. Georgia, 98 U. S. 357.
[5] Close v. Glenwood Cemetery, 107 U. S. 466
[6] 2 Mass. 146.    [7] 105 U. S. 13, 19.

rated therewith, that that charter shall not be alterable in any other manner than by an act of the legislature, operates as a reserved power authorizing a statutory amendment of the charter.[1] Express contracts of exemption from state taxation are to be strictly construed. Thus a charter of a railway imposing an annual tax assessed on the cost of the line, reserving the right to impose taxes on the gross earnings of the corporation and stipulating that the above several taxes shall be in *lieu* of other taxation, is not a contract whose obligation is impaired by a subsequent statute taxing lands owned by the railway and mortgaged as security for its bonded debt, but not used in the construction or operation of its line.[2] So a provision in the charter of a ferry company that it "shall be subject to the same taxes as are now or hereafter may be imposed on other ferries," does not exempt the corporation from liability to pay an annual license fee on each of its boats, under the requirements of a municipal ordinance enacted under due legislative authority.[3] So the charter of a street railway requiring the payment to the municipality of such annual license "as is now paid by other railway companies," is to be construed to mean that the company shall not at any future time be required to pay a greater license than that then required to be paid by other companies.[4] A charter granting to a corporation all the rights, powers, and privileges "granted by the charter" of another corporation, confers an exemption from state taxation contained, not in the charter to which reference is made, but in a statute amendatory thereof, and the exemption thus conferred constitutes a contract

---

[1] Pennsylvania College Cases, 13 Wall. 190; Holyoke Company *v.* Lyon, 15 *id.* 500; Miller *v.* State, *ibid.* 478.

[2] Tucker *v.* Ferguson, 22 Wall. 527.

[3] W. F. Co. *v.* East St. Louis, 107 U. S. 365.

[4] U. P. Ry. *v.* Philadelphia, 101 U. S. 528.

whose obligation cannot be impaired by a subsequent repeal of the statute conferring by reference the right of exemption.[1] So a state may make a contract conferring the exclusive right of building a toll bridge by reference to a previously enacted statute.[2] On the other hand, the incorporation of a railway by a charter investing the company "for the purpose of making and using the said road with all powers, rights, and privileges, and subject to the disabilities and restrictions that have been conferred and imposed upon" another railway company, whose charter contained an express exemption from taxation, does not confer that exemption on the former company.[3] So in the case of the merger of a corporation having an exemption from state taxation for a limited period with another corporation having an unlimited exemption, the consolidating statute not granting any exemption, the consolidated corporation cannot claim as to property acquired from the first mentioned corporation any exemption beyond the limits contained in the charter of that corporation.[4]

69. Express stipulations in a charter as to the privileges thereby conferred on the corporation are also within the protection of the constitutional prohibition; thus, a provision in the charter of a toll bridge company that it shall not be lawful for any person to erect another bridge within a specified distance of the bridge thereby authorized, constitutes a contract binding the state not to authorize the construction of such other bridge,[5] but the authorization by the state of the construction of a railway viaduct does not impair the obligation of such

[1] Humphrey v. Pegues, 16 Wall. 244.
[2] Binghamton Bridge, 3 Wall. 51.
[3] R. R. v. Gaines, 97 U. S. 697.
[4] Tomlinson v. Branch, 15 Wall. 460.
[5] Binghamton Bridge, 3 Wall. 51; Bridge Proprietors v. Hoboken, 1 id. 116.

a contract.[1] So, also, a statute forbidding the transfer by any bank of any note, bill receivable, or other evidence of debt, impairs the obligation of a contract created by the grant in a charter of a bank of power to receive, hold, and grant chattels and effects of what kind soever, and to receive deposits and discount notes.[2] On the same principle a state is bound by its express contracts, not including appointments to public office, between the state and an individual for the performance of special services for a stipulated compensation,[3] by its grants of franchises and exclusive privileges, such as the privilege of supplying a municipality with water,[4] or gas,[5] by its contracts conceding peculiar privileges to state obligations, as for instance, stipulating that coupons of state bonds should be receivable for taxes,[6] or that the circulating notes of a bank should be receivable in payment for taxes,[7] or of other debts due to the state,[8] by contracts made by a political subdivision of the state for the payment of the principal of, or interest upon, the public debt of that subdivision,[9] and by the contracts of a corporation, whose sole shareholder is the state, for the payment of the corporate debt.[10] Contracts between two or more states, under which private rights have vested,[11] are so far protected that neither state can

[1] Bridge Proprietors v. Hoboken, 1 Wall. 116.
[2] Planter's Bank v. Sharp, 6 How. 301.
[3] Hall v. Wisconsin, 103 U. S. 5.
[4] New Orleans Water Works v. Rivers, 115 U. S. 674; St. Tammany Water Works v. N. O. Water Works, 120 id. 64.
[5] New Orleans Gas Co. v. Louisiana Light Co., 115 U. S. 650; Louisiana Gas Co. v. C. Gas Co., ibid. 683.
[6] Hartman v. Greenhow, 102 U. S. 672; Virginia Coupon Cases, 114 id. 270; Royall v. Virginia 116 id. 572; Same v. Same, 121 id. 105.
[7] Keith v. Clark, 97 U. S. 454; Furman v. Nichol, 8 Wall. 44.
[8] Woodruff v. Trapnell, 10 How. 190; Pant v. Drew, ibid. 218; Trigg v. Same, ibid. 224.
[9] Murray v. Charleston, 96 U. S. 432.
[10] Curran v. Arkansas, 15 How. 304; Barings v. Dabney, 19 Wall. 1.
[11] Green v. Biddle, 8 Wheat. 1.

annul or modify such contracts to the prejudice of the private rights so vested.

70. There can be no contract between a state and a political subdivision of a state, such as a municipality, giving to the municipality a vested right to property, for all such property rights are held by the municipality in trust for the state, and are subject to revocation at the state's pleasure.[1] Therefore, a statute imposing a pecuniary penalty upon a railway, payable by it to a county of the state for its failure to locate the railway on a certain line, does not constitute a contract between the county and the railway whose obligation is impaired by a subsequent repeal of the statute.[2] On the same principle, a legislative charter of a railway, granting to it power to appropriate public wharves erected by a municipality under a prior legislative grant of authority, does not impair the obligation of any contract, nor infringe upon the rights of the municipality.[3]

71. The next mooted question under this clause of the Constitution was whether or not a charter of incorporation granted by a state constituted an implied contract on the part of the state, whose obligation the state could not be permitted to impair by a subsequent repeal or modification of the charter. The leading case is Trustees of Dartmouth College *v.* Woodward,[4] judgment in which was rendered in 1819, and the facts in which were that, in 1769, the Royal Governor of the Province of New Hampshire, acting in the name of the King, granted to Dr. Wheelock and eleven other persons a charter, whereby they were incorporated under the title of "The Trustees of Dartmouth College," with

---

[1] East Hartford *v.* Hartford Bridge Co, 10 How. 511; Maryland *v.* B. & O. R. R., 3 *id.* 551; R. R. *v.* Ellerman. 105 U. S. 166.
[2] Maryland *v.* B. & O. R. R., 3 How. 534.
[3] R. R. *v.* Ellerman, 105 U. S. 166.       [4] 4 Wheat. 518.

perpetual succession, and with "the whole power of governing the college, of appointing and removing tutors, of fixing their salaries, of directing the course of study to be pursued by the students, and of filling vacancies created in their own body." After the charter had been granted to, and accepted by, the corporation, " property both real and personal, which had been contributed for the benefit of the college, was conveyed to and vested in the corporate body." Acts of the legislature of the state of New Hampshire, passed on 27 June, and 18 December, 1816, increased "the number of trustees to twenty-one," gave "the appointment of the additional number to the executive of the state," and created " a board of overseers, to consist of twenty-five persons, of whom twenty-one are also appointed by the executive of New Hampshire," with " power to inspect and control the most important acts of the trustees." Prior to the enactment of these statutes, one Woodward was the secretary and treasurer of the corporation, and, as such, he had in his possession the charter, corporate seal, records, and certain chattels belonging to the corporation; in 1816 the trustees removed him from office; in 1817 he was appointed Secretary and Treasurer of the new Board of Trustees, which was organized under the statutes of 1816, and, as he refused to surrender to the original corporation the property which was in his hands, that corporation brought an action of trover in a court of the state of New Hampshire against him, in which the facts as stated having been found by a special verdict, judgment was entered in favour of the defendant by the state court of last resort, and the cause was removed by writ of error to the Supreme Court of the United States, which reversed the judgment of the state court, the ground of decision being that the college as incorporated was a private eleemosynary corporation; that its charter, in terms, and by force of the donations of funds made on the faith of it, constituted a contract between the colonial government and the corporation as the representative of the donors of those funds; that it was an implied, but essential, condition of that contract that that charter should not be so modified, without the consent of the corporation, as to substitute governmental control for the will of the donors; that, by the revolution, the duties, as well as the powers, of government devolved on the people of New Hampshire, and the obligations imposed by the charter were the same under the state government, as they had formerly been under the colonial government; and that the effect of the statutes of 1816 was to substitute the will of the state for the will of the donors, and, to that extent, to impair the obligation of the contract between the state and the corporation, as made by the charter. Marshall, C. J., in his judgment,[1] after accepting the suggestion, that "taken in its broad, unlimited sense, the clause would be an unprofitable and vexatious interference with the internal concerns of a state, would unnecessarily and unwisely embarrass its legislation, and render immutable those civil institutions, which were established for purposes of internal government, and which, to subserve those purposes, ought to vary with varying circumstances;" and "that as the framers of the Constitution could never have intended to insert in that instrument a provision so unnecessary, so mischievous, and so repugnant to its general spirit, the term 'contract' must be understood in a more limited sense," expressly conceded, that "the framers of the Constitution did not intend to restrain the states in the regulation of their civil institutions, adopted for internal government, and

[1] 4 Wheat. pp. 628, 629.

that the instrument they have given us is not to be so construed," and that "the provision of the Constitution never has been understood to embrace other contracts, than those which respect property, or some object of value, and confer rights which may be asserted in a court of justice," put his judgment on the ground that the charter of the College constituted a contract as hereinbefore stated. Applying to the Dartmouth College Case, the test so clearly stated by Marshall, C. J., in Ogden v. Saunders,[1] that "the positive authority of a decision is co-extensive with the facts on which it is made," it is obvious that the case is an authority for the proposition, that the grant by a state of a charter of incorporation for private purposes unconnected with the administration of government constitutes a contract between the state and the corporation, whose obligation is not to be permitted to be impaired by a material modification of the terms of the charter, either expressed or implied, and that, in every such charter it is an implied condition of the contract, that the state shall not by subsequent legislation change either the purpose of the corporation, or its system of administration.

72. The later cases have narrowed the doctrine of the Dartmouth College Case with regard to the implied contracts created by charters, and thereby made obligatory on the states granting them. In Providence Bank v. Billings,[2] it was decided, in 1830, that the grant of corporate privileges does not carry with it any implied exemption of either the corporate franchise, or property, from state taxation, and this principle has been re-asserted in the later cases of Memphis Gaslight Co. v. Shelby County,[3] N. M. R. R. v. Maguire,[4] Bailey

[1] 12 Wheat. 333.
[2] 4 Pet. 575.
[3] 109 U. S. 398.
[4] 20 Wall. 46.

*v.* Maguire,[1] and Tucker *v.* Ferguson.[2] Following in the same line, it has been held that the imposition in a charter of a specific form, or rate of taxation, is not to be construed in the absence of an express contract of exemption from other taxation to constitute an implied exemption from such other taxation.[3]

73. On the same principle, it has been held that, legislative grants of exclusive privileges are, in the interests of the public, to be strictly construed, and, therefore, charters of incorporation do not vest in the corporation any powers other than those expressly granted.[4] From this it follows that charters do not grant by implication exclusive privileges or exemptions; thus the creation of a corporation with power to erect a toll bridge, or to operate a ferry, does not impliedly bind the state not to license the establishment of a competing bridge, or ferry, either toll or free.[5] Nor does the charter of a corporation by a state constitute a contract by the state either with the corporation, or with the creditors thereof, that the corporation shall not be subsequently dissolved after due legal proceedings founded upon a forfeiture of the corporate franchises either for misuser or for non-user.[6]

74. There is no implied contract in a charter, that the state will exempt the corporate franchises and prop-

[1] 22 Wall. 215.
[2] 22 *id.* 527.
[3] The Delaware Railroad Tax, 18 Wall. 206; Erie Railway *v.* Penna., 21 Wall. 492; The License Cases, 5 *id.* 462; Home Insurance Co. *v.* Augusta, 93 U. S. 116.
[4] Rice *v.* M. & N. W. R. R., 1 Bl. 358; Charles River Bridge *v.* Warren Bridge, 11 Pet. 544; Mills *v.* St. Clair County, 8 How. 581; R. R. R. *v.* L. R. R., 13 How. 81; O. L & T. Co. *v.* Debolt, 16 How. 435; Perrine *v.* C. C. Co., 9 How. 192; J. B. Bank *v.* Skelly, 1 Bl. 436; The Binghamton Bridge, 3 Wall. 51, 75.
[5] Fanning *v.* Gregoire, 16 How. 524; Turnpike Co. *v.* State, 3 Wall. 210; Wright *v.* Nagle, 101 U. S. 791.
[6] Mumma *v.* The Potomac Co., 8 Pet. 281, 286; Chicago Life Ins. Co. *v.* Needles, 113 U. S. 574, 584.

erty from the operation of the police power of the state. A state, therefore, may limit by subsequent legislation the rates of fare and freight charged by its railways.[1] A state may, in the case of a railway whose charter authorizes it from time to time to fix, regulate, and receive tolls and charges vest in a commission by a subsequent statute the power of fixing those rates.[2] Nor can a state surrender by implication, the right to regulate by subsequent legislation the location of railway stations and the stoppage of trains at such stations.[3] A state may by statute regulate the rates of a water corporation whose charter vested the power of fixing the rates in a board of commissioners, some of whom were appointed by the company.[4] A state may forbid the continued prosecution of their respective trades by corporations organized for the purpose of manufacturing and selling liquors,[5] or selling lottery tickets and drawing lotteries,[6] or rendering dead animals and offal into fertilizers.[7] So also a state may, in derogation of previous grants of exclusive privileges for the conduct of a business,[8] which is necessarily subject to police regulation, such as that of slaughtering cattle, authorize others to conduct the same business.

75. In Dartmouth College v. Woodward,[9] Marshall, C. J., conceded that "the framers of the Constitution did not intend to restrain a state from the regulation of

[1] C., B & Q. R. R. v. Iowa, 94 U. S. 155; Peik v. C. & N. W. Ry., ibid. 164; M. & St. P. R R. v. Atlee, ibid. 179; W. & St. P. R. R. v. Blake, ibid. 180; Stone v. Wisconsin, ibid. 181; Ruggles v. Illinois, 108 U. S. 526.
[2] Stone v. F. L. & T. Co., 116 U. S. 307; Same v. I. C. R. R., ibid. 347.
[3] M. H. & N. R. R. v. Hamersly, 104 U. S. 1.
[4] S. V. Water Works v. Schottler, 110 U. S. 347.
[5] Beer Co. v. Massachusetts, 97 U. S. 25.
[6] Phalen v. Virginia, 8 How. 163; Boyd v. Alabama, 94 U. S. 645; Stone v. Mississippi, 100 id. 814.
[7] Fertilizing Co v. Hyde Park, 97 U. S. 659.
[8] Butchers' Union v. Crescent City, 111 U. S. 746.
[9] 4 Wheat. 629.

its civil institutions adopted for internal government." On this principle, there can be no implied contract on the part of a state that it will not amend its Constitution, in so far as that Constitution deals with the administration of the public concerns of the state.[1] Nor can a state legislature bind subsequent legislatures as to the exercise of the powers of sovereignty over the political subdivisions of the state, and over its municipal corporations with regard to subject-matters of public and not of private interest, as, for instance, the location of a county seat,[2] or the boundaries of its municipalities,[3] or the sale of property held by a municipality for public purposes, such as water works,[4] or the appropriation under state authority of municipal obligations by their holders as a set-off against municipal claims against those holders;[5] nor does the appointment by the state of a public officer for a fixed term for a stipulated compensation constitute a contract between the state and the appointee whose obligation is impaired by either the reduction of his compensation or his removal from office,[6] but after the duties have been performed by the appointee of a municipal corporation during the term of his office there is a contract whose obligation is impaired by a subsequent statute abolishing the power of taxation for the payment of his compensation.[7] Of course, in the case of an officer appointed under a statute which in terms defines the tenure of the office to be according to law, a subsequent statute removing him is not an impairment of the contract.[8]

[1] Church v. Kelsey, 121 U. S. 282.
[2] Newton v. Commissioners, 100 U. S. 548.
[3] U. S. v. Memphis, 97 U. S. 284.
[4] New Orleans v. Morris, 105 U. S. 600.
[5] Amy v. Shelby County, 114 U. S. 187.
[6] Butler v. Pennsylvania, 10 Howard 402.
[7] Fisk v. J. Police Jury, 116 U. S. 131.
[8] Head v. University, 19 Wall. 526.

76. The state's consent to be sued being voluntary and of grace, that consent does not constitute a contract whose obligation can be impaired by a subsequent repeal of the statute permitting such suit,[1] especially where the statute authorizing the suit has provided no means for the enforcement of any judgment that may be rendered against the state. Under such circumstances the state may, by subsequent legislation, withdraw its consent to be sued.[2] In this connection, that which was forcibly said by Mathews, J., in the judgment of the court in the case of *In re Ayres*,[3] may well be borne in mind. The learned judge said : " it cannot be doubted that the XI Amendment to the Constitution operates to create an important distinction between contracts of a state with individuals and contracts between individual parties. In the case of contracts between individuals, the remedies for their enforcement or breach, in existence at the time they were entered into, are a part of the agreement itself, and constitute a substantial part of its obligation.[4] That obligation . . . cannot be impaired by any subsequent legislation. Thus, not only the covenants and conditions of the contract are preserved, but also the substance of the original remedies for its enforcement. It is different with contracts between individuals and a state. In respect to these, by virtue of the XI Amendment to the Constitution, there being no remedy by a suit against the state, the contract is substantially without sanction, except that which arises out of the honour and good faith of the state itself, and these are not subject to coercion. Although the state may, at the inception of the contract, have consented as one of its conditions to

---

[1] Beers *v.* Arkansas, 20 How. 527 ; Bank of Washington *v.* Same, *ibid.* 530.
[2] M. & C. R. R. *v.* Tennessee, 101 U. S. 337 : S. & N. A. R. R. *v.* Alabama, *ibid.* 51.
[3] 123 U. S. 504.
[4] Louisiana *v.* New Orleans. 102 U. S. 203.

subject itself to suit, it may subsequently withdraw that consent and resume its original immunity, without any violation of the obligation of its contract in the constitutional sense." [1]

77. The force and effect of the prohibition, as construed by the court, is, that a state may not, by any law or by any act to which the state, by its enforcement thereof, gives the force of a law, deprive a party of the legal right of enforcing, or obtaining compensation for the breach of, an express contract, executed or executory, between individuals, or between a state and individuals, but a state may regulate or limit the remedies of the contracting parties, provided that it leaves in force a substantial part of the legal remedies which subsisted at the time of the making of the contract.

[1] Beers v. Arkansas, 20 How. 527; Railroad Company v. Tennessee, 101 U. S. 337.

# CHAPTER VI.

### EX POST FACTO LAWS AND BILLS OF ATTAINDER.

78. The constitutional provisions.
79. The distinction between retrospective and *ex post facto* laws.
80. *Ex post facto* laws defined.
81. Illustrations of *ex post facto* laws.
82. Illustrations of laws which are not *ex post facto*.
83. Bills of attainder and bills of pains and penalties.

78. Section 10 of article I of the Constitution declares that "no state shall . . . pass any bill of attainder or *ex post facto* law." Section 9 of article I of the Constitution, restricting the powers of Congress, declares that "no bill of attainder or *ex post facto* law shall be passed."

79. *Ex post facto* laws relate to criminal, and not to civil, procedure. They are necessarily retrospective, but all retrospective laws are not *ex post facto*.[2] State laws which operate retrospectively, or which divest antecedently vested rights of property, are not prohibited by the Constitution of the United States, if they are not *ex post facto* laws, and if they do not impair the obligation of contracts.[3] A state legislature, unless restrained by the Constitution of the state, may, therefore, enact statutes setting aside a decree of a court of probate, refusing to

[1] Calder *v.* Bull, 3 Dall. 386; Watson *v.* Mercer, 8 Pet. 88, 110; Carpenter *v.* Pennsylvania, 17 How. 456.

[2] Calder *v.* Bull, 3 Dall. 386.

[3] Calder *v.* Bull, 3 Dall. 386; Fletcher *v.* Peck, 6 Cr. 138; Ogden *v.* Saunders, 12 Wheat. 266; Satterlee *v.* Matthewson, 2 Pet. 380; Watson *v.* Mercer, 8 Pet. 88, 110; Carpenter *v.* Pennsylvania, 17 How. 456; B. & S. R. R. *v.* Nesbit, 10 How. 395; Livingstone *v.* Moore, 7 Pet. 469.

allow probate of a will, and granting a rehearing by the court of probate with liberty of appeal therefrom, after the time limited by existing laws for an appeal has passed;[1] declaring that the relation of landlord and tenant exists between parties as to whom the courts of the state have decided, that that relation does not exist;[2] curing defective acknowledgments of deeds by *femes covert;*[3] construing by a declaratory statute, after the death of a decedent, existing tax laws so as to subject to a collateral inheritance tax the distributive shares of non-resident distributees;[4] directing a county court to set aside an inquisition condemning certain land for the use of a railway and to order a new inquisition;[5] directing the imposition of a tax according to an assessment theretofore made;[6] and authorizing the sale of lands on which the state has a lien for debts due to it.[7] Upon the same principle, Congress having passed an act for the admission of a territory as a state, and having in that act omitted to provide for the disposal of causes pending in the Supreme Court of the United States, on appeal from the territorial courts, may by a subsequent act properly make provision for such causes, for such legislation is remedial.[8] So also Congress may by statute impose a tax retrospectively.[9]

80. In Fletcher *v.* Peck,[10] Marshall, C. J., defines an *ex post facto* law to be one " which renders an act punishable in a manner in which it was not pun-

---
[1] Calder *v.* Bull, 3 Dall. 386.
[2] Satterlee *v.* Matthewson, 2 Pet. 380.
[3] Watson *v.* Mercer, 8 Pet. 88.
[4] Carpenter *v.* Pennsylvania, 17 How. 456.
[5] B. & S. R. R. *v.* Nesbit, 10 How. 395.
[6] Locke *v.* New Orleans, 4 Wall. 172.
[7] Livingstone *v.* Moore, 7 Pet. 469.
[8] Freeborn *v.* Smith, 2 Wall. 160.
[9] Stockdale *v.* The Insurance Companies, 20 Wall. 223.
[10] 6 Cr. 138.

ishable when it was committed." In Cummings *v.* Missouri,[1] Field, J., defines an *ex post facto* law, as "one which imposes a punishment for an act which was not punishable at the time it was committed; or imposes additional punishment to that then prescribed; or changes the rules of evidence by which less or different testimony is sufficient to convict than was required." In Calder *v.* Bull,[2] Chase, J., classified *ex post facto* laws as follows:—"*first*, those that make an action, done before the passing of a law, and which was innocent when done, criminal, and punish such action; *second*, those that aggravate a crime, or make it greater than it was when committed; *third*, those that change the punishment and inflict greater punishment than the law annexed to the crime when committed; and, *fourth*, those that alter the legal rules of evidence and receive less or different testimony to convict the offender than that required at the time of the commission of the offense." That classification is quoted with approval by Miller, J., in his judgment in Kring *v.* Missouri.[3]

81. Laws have been held to be *ex post facto*, which, after the commission of an act, alter the situation of the accused to his disadvantage, as for instance, by providing that the plea of *autrefois convict* should not at a second trial be a defense in the case of a prisoner convicted of murder in the second degree under an indictment charging murder in the first degree, the law having been at the time of the commission of the crime that such a plea was a defense;[4] or by requiring a clergyman,[5] or a lawyer,[6] as a condition precedent to the practice of his profession, to take an oath that he

---

[1] 4 Wall. 325.
[2] 3 Dall. 386.
[3] 107 U. S. 221.
[4] Kring *v.* Missouri, 107 U. S. 221.
[5] Cummings *v.* Missouri, 4 Wall. 277.
[6] *Ex parte* Garland, 4 Wall. 333.

has not done an act, for the doing of which, when done, deprivation of office was not a legal penalty; or by requiring one who applies to a court to open a judgment rendered against him *in absentia*, to take oath, as a condition precedent to his obtaining the desired relief, that he has not done an act for the doing of which the deprivation of the right to sue in courts of justice was not by law antecedently imposed as a penalty.[1] Upon the same principle, Congress cannot provide, by statute, that an act, which is not an offense against the law at the time of its doing, may become such by a subsequent independent act with which it has no necessary connection; as, for instance, that subsequent bankruptcy, either voluntary or involuntary, shall render criminal and punishable by imprisonment the obtaining of goods with intent to defraud at any time within three months before the commission of the act of bankruptcy.[2]

82. On the other hand, a law of a state changing the *venue* in a criminal case, though passed subsequently to the commission of the offense, is not *ex post facto*;[3] nor is a law open to that objection, which, though passed after the commission of an offense, enlarges the class of persons who may be competent to testify as witnesses at the trial, as, for instance, by repealing a statutory prohibition of the admission of the testimony of convicted felons,[4] nor is a law *ex post facto* which denies the exercise of the right of franchise to bigamists, or polygamists, for "the disfranchisement operates upon the existing state and condition of the person, and not upon a past offense."[5]

83. A bill of attainder is defined by Field, J., in Cummings *v.* Missouri,[6] as "a legislative act which in-

---

[1] Pierce *v.* Carskadon, 16 Wall. 234.
[2] United States *v.* Fox, 95 U. S. 670.
[3] Gut *v.* The State, 9 Wall. 35.
[4] Hopt *v.* Utah, 110 U. S. 574.
[5] Murphy *v.* Ramsey, 114 U. S. 15.
[6] 4 Wall. 323.

flicts punishment without a judicial trial," and he adds, "if the punishment be less than death, the act is termed a bill of pains and penalties. Within the meaning of the Constitution, bills of attainder include bills of pains and penalties." It has been held that a state Constitution, requiring clergymen as a condition precedent to the exercise of their profession, to take oath that they had not committed certain designated acts, some of which were at the time offenses subject to legal penalties, and others of which were innocent acts,[1] and that a state statute requiring one who applied to a court to open a judgment rendered against him *in absentia*, to take oath that he had not committed certain designated public offenses,[2] and that an act of Congress, requiring a lawyer, as a condition precedent to the exercise of his profession, to take an oath that he had not voluntarily borne arms against the United States, etc.,[3] constituted in each case a bill of pains and penalties and was, therefore, subject to the constitutional prohibition against bills of attainder, inasmuch as, by legislative action, and without judicial investigation, the statute imposed a punishment for an act done before the enactment of the statute, the oath being offered to the party incriminated as a means of compelling an admission of guilt.

[1] Cummings *v.* Missouri, 4 Wall. 277.
[2] Pierce *v.* Carskadon, 16 Wall. 234.
[3] *Ex parte* Garland, 4 Wall. 333.

# CHAPTER VII.

## THE PROHIBITION OF STATE BILLS OF CREDIT.

84. Bills of credit defined.
85. What are, and what are not, bills of credit.

84. Section 10 of article I of the Constitution declares that "no state shall .... emit bills of credit." Bills of credit within the meaning of this constitutional provision are promissory notes issued by a state government on its credit "intended to circulate throughout the community for its ordinary purposes as money," and redeemable on demand, or at a day certain in the future.[1]

85. A state, therefore, may not issue interest-bearing certificates in denominations "not exceeding ten dollars, nor less than fifty cents" receivable by the state in payment of taxes, and of debts due to the state, and payable to officers of the state in discharge of salaries and fees of office, and redeemable by the state under an arrangement that there shall be withdrawn "annually from circulation one-tenth part of the certificates."[2] Nevertheless, a state may incorporate a bank, of which that state shall be the sole shareholder, and it may authorize that bank to issue notes as circulation, without contravening the constitutional prohibition, the distinction being that such notes are issued, not on the credit of the state, but on the credit of the capital and

[1] Craig v. Missouri, 4 Pet. 411; Byrne v. Missouri, 8 id. 40; Briscoe v. Bank of Kentucky, 11 id. 257.
[2] Craig v. Missouri, 4 Pet. 410; Byrne v. Missouri, 8 id. 40.

assets of the bank.[1] Coupons of state bonds, though negotiable and receivable for taxes due to the state, are not bills of credit, for they are not intended to circulate as money.[2]

[1] Briscoe *v.* Bank of Kentucky, 11 Pet. 257; Darrington *v.* The Bank of Alabama, 13 How. 12.
[2] Virginia Coupons Case, 119 U. S. 269, 284.

# CHAPTER VIII.

### STATE COMPACTS.

86. What compacts are permitted, and what are forbidden.

86. Section 10 of article I of the Constitution declares, that "no state shall enter into any treaty, alliance, or confederation. . . . . No state shall, without the consent of Congress, . . . . enter into any agreement or compact with another state." This constitutional prohibition forbids compacts between a state and foreign nations, and also compacts between states of the United States, to which the assent of Congress has not been given. It is, therefore, decisive against the validity of the confederation entered into by the insurgent states in 1861.[1] It also forbids a governor of a state to enter into an agreement with a foreign government for the extradition of a prisoner.[2] But states may, with the consent of Congress, enter into agreements touching conflicting boundaries,[3] and, in such cases, the consent of Congress does not necessarily have to be given by congressional legislation expressly assenting to each of the stipulations of the agreement between the states, but that consent may be inferred from the legislation of Congress touching the subject-matter of the agreement.[4]

[1] Williams *v.* Bruffy, 96 U. S. 176; Sprott *v.* U. S., 20 Wall. 459; Ford *v.* Surget, 97 U. S. 594; U. S *v.* Keehler, 9 Wall. 83.
[2] Holmes *v.* Jennison, 14 Pet. 540.
[3] Rhode Island *v.* Massachusetts, 12 Pet. 724; Missouri *v.* Iowa, 7 How. 660; Florida *v.* Georgia, 17 *id.* 478; Alabama *v.* Georgia, 23 *id.* 505; Virginia *v.* West Virginia, 11 Wall. 39; Poole *v.* Fleeger, 11 Pet. 185.
[4] Virginia *v.* West Virginia, 11 Wall. 39.

# CHAPTER IX.

#### FUGITIVES FROM JUSTICE.

87. The constitutional provision.
88. The concurrent jurisdiction of the federal and state courts.

87. Section 2 of article IV of the Constitution declares, that "a person charged in any state with treason, felony, or other crime, who shall flee from justice and be found in another state, shall on demand of the executive authority of the state from which he fled, be delivered up, to be removed to the state having jurisdiction of the crime." The words "treason, felony, or other crime," as Taney, C. J., said in Kentucky *v.* Dennison,[1] "in their plain and obvious import, as well as in their legal and technical sense, embrace every act forbidden and made punishable by a law of the state. The word 'crime' of itself includes every offense, from the highest to the lowest in the grade of offenses, and includes what are called 'misdemeanors,' as well as treason and felony."[2] This constitutional provision imposes on the executive of the state in which the fugitive has taken refuge the duty of surrendering the fugitive upon demand made by the executive of the state from which the fugitive has fled, and upon proof made that he has been legally charged with crime, and this duty has been recognized by the act of Congress of 12 February, 1793,[3] but if the governor of the state to which the

---

[1] 24 How. 99.
[2] See also *Ex parte* Reggel, 114 U. S. 642.
[3] 1 Stat. 302; Rev. Stat., Secs. 5278, 5279.

fugitive has fled refuses to deliver him up to justice, "there is no power delegated to the general government, either through the judicial department or any other department, to use any coercive means to compel him."[1] The Supreme Court of the United States, therefore, will not issue a *mandamus* to compel the performance by a governor of a state of his constitutional duty of surrendering to another state a fugitive from the justice of that state.[2]

88. An alleged fugitive from justice may petition a court of the United States for a writ of *habeas corpus* to inquire into the legality of his detention, but as the responsibility of determining whether or not the alleged fugitive from justice be in fact a fugitive from justice, rests upon the executive of the state to which the fugitive has fled, a court of the United States will not discharge the fugitive upon the hearing of the writ of *habeas corpus*, because, in its judgment the proof that the prisoner is a fugitive from justice is, though satisfactory to the executive, not as complete as might have been required.[3] The alleged fugitive may also apply, by petition for a writ of *habeas corpus*, to a court of the state within which he is detained in custody for the purpose of being delivered to the justice of another state, for the jurisdiction of the courts of the United States over such petitions for writs of *habeas corpus* is not exclusive of the jurisdiction of the courts of the states in such cases, and the agent of the state demanding the surrender of the alleged fugitive is in no sense an officer of the United States, nor otherwise exempt from the process of the courts of the states.[4]

[1] *per* Taney, C. J., in Kentucky *v.* Dennison, 24 How. 109.
[2] Kentucky *v.* Dennison, 24 How. 66.
[3] *Ex parte* Reggel 114 U. S. 642.
[4] Robb *v.* Connolly, 111 U. S. 624.

# CHAPTER X.

### THE JUDICIAL POWER.

89. The necessity for the existence of a judicial department of the United States.
90. The constitutional provisions.
91. The terms of the grant of federal jurisdiction.
92. The exclusive jurisdiction.
93. The original jurisdiction.
94. Removal of causes from state courts to the courts of the United States.
95. The appellate and supervisory jurisdiction.
96. The requisites of a judicial case.
97. Courts-martial.
98. Impeachment.
99. The judicial construction of the Constitution.
100. The XI Amendment.
101. Section 2 of Article III of the Constitution, and the IV Amendment.
102. The V Amendment.
103. The VI Amendment.
104. The VII Amendment.
105. The exemption of federal process from state control.
106. Limitation of federal process by the reserved rights of the states.
107. The limitations of state jurisdiction and process by the federal supremacy.
108. The rule as to conflict of jurisdiction.
109. The XIV Amendment as affecting state jurisdiction.
110. The effect of Section 1 of Article IV of the Constitution.

89. It is, under any form of government, essential to the enforcement of the laws with a due regard to the maintenance of the liberties of the citizens, that a judicial department, independent by reason of the security of the tenure of office and adequacy of compensation of the judges, should be charged with the duty, and entrusted with the power, of construing the laws, and of finally determining issues of fact and of law in prosecutions for crime and in litigations as to

individual rights. Having regard to the relation between the United States and the states, and bearing in mind that the United States cannot impose duties upon officers of the states, and compel the performance by those officers of the duties so imposed,[1] it is, in an especial degree, essential that the United States should have the power of establishing courts of civil and criminal jurisdiction for the punishment of offenses against the laws of the United States, and for the protection and enforcement of rights created by the Constitution, laws, and treaties of the United States. It is also necessary to the enforcement of the declared supremacy of the Constitution, laws, and treaties of the United States, that a court constituted by the United States with jurisdiction co-extensive with the territory subject to the Constitution, should be, so far as regards all subjects of judicial cognizance, the final arbiter by whom the construction of the Constitution of the United States is to be authoritatively determined,[2] for otherwise the Constitution might have one meaning in one state, and a different meaning in another state, and it might be construed in one way in one court and in another way in another court,[3] and if the legislative, executive, and judicial departments of the several states were at liberty to conclusively determine for themselves the construction of that instrument, and the nature and the extent of the restraints upon freedom of state action imposed by it, those restraints would bind any one state only in so far as that state might choose to be bound at any particular time, and the inevitable result would be,

---

[1] Prigg v. Pennsylvania 16 Pet. 539; Kentucky v. Dennison, 24 How. 66.
[2] Cohens v. Virginia, 6 Wheat. 264; Bank of Hamilton v. Dudley's Lessee, 2 Pet. 429, 524; Dodge v. Woolsey, 18 How. 331, 347; Martin v. Hunter's Lessee, 1 Wheat. 304.
[3] Marbury v. Madison, 1 Cr. 137; Van Horne v. Dorrance, 2 Dall. 304; The Mayor v. Cooper, 6 Wall. 253; Norton v. Shelby County, 118 U. S. 443.

as Marshall, C. J., said in Cohens *v.* Virginia,[1] to prostrate the federal "government and its laws at the feet of every state in the Union."

90. In recognition of these principles, and in order to give practical effect to them, the Constitution has created a judicial department of the government of the United States. Section 1 of article III declares, that "the judicial power of the United States shall be vested in one Supreme Court, and in such inferior courts as the Congress may, from time to time, ordain and establish. The judges, both of the Supreme and inferior courts, shall hold their offices during good behaviour, and shall, at stated times, receive for their services a compensation, which shall not be diminished during their continuance in office." Section 2 declares that "the judicial power shall extend to all cases, in law and equity, arising under this Constitution, the laws of the United States, and treaties made, or which shall be made, under their authority; to all cases affecting ambassadors, or other public ministers and consuls; to all cases of admiralty and maritime jurisdiction; to controversies to which the United States shall be a party; to controversies between two or more states; between a state and citizens of another state; between citizens of different states; between citizens of the same state claiming lands under grants of different states, and between a state, or the citizens thereof, and foreign states, citizens, or subjects. In all cases affecting ambassadors, other public ministers, and consuls, and those in which a state shall be a party, the Supreme Court shall have original jurisdiction. In all the other cases before mentioned, the Supreme Court shall have appellate jurisdiction, both as to law and fact, with such exceptions and under such regulations as the Congress shall make."

[1] 6 Wheat. 385.

91. The Constitution has, therefore, conferred upon the courts of the United States jurisdiction in two classes of causes, depending in the one class on the character of the cause, and in the other class on the character of the parties.[1]

[1] Cohens *v.* Virginia, 6 Wheat. 264, 378; Martin *v.* Hunter's Lessee, 1 Wheat. 304, 331, 343; The Moses Taylor, 4 Wall. 411, 429. Jay, C. J., in his judgment in Chisholm *v.* Georgia, 2 Dall. 475, after referring to the declaration in the preamble to the Constitution, that that instrument was ordained, *inter alia*, "to establish justice," added, "it may be asked, what is the precise sense and latitude in which the words '*to establish justice,*' as here used, are to be understood? The answer to this question will result from the provisions made in the Constitution on this head. They are specified in the 2d section of the 3d article, where it is ordained, that the judicial power of the *United States* shall extend to ten descriptions of cases, viz, 1st: to all cases arising under this Constitution; because the meaning, construction, and operation of a compact ought always to be ascertained by all the parties, or by authority derived only from one of them: 2d: to all cases arising under the laws of the *United States;* because as such laws, constitutionally made, are obligatory on each state, the measure of obligation and obedience ought not to be decided and fixed by the party from whom they are due, but by a tribunal deriving authority from both the parties: 3d: to all cases arising under treaties made by their authority; because, as treaties are compacts made by, and obligatory on, the whole nation, their operation ought not to be affected or regulated by the local laws or courts of a part of the nation: 4th: to all cases affecting Ambassadors, or other public Ministers and Consuls; because, as these are officers of foreign nations, whom this nation is bound to protect and treat according to the laws of nations, cases affecting them ought only to be cognizable by national authority: 5th: to all cases of Admiralty and Maritime jurisdiction; because, as the seas are the joint property of nations, whose right and privileges relative thereto, are regulated by the law of nations and treaties, such cases necessarily belong to national jurisdiction: 6th: to controversies to which the *United States* shall be a party; because in cases in which the whole people are interested, it would not be equal or wise to let any one state decide and measure out the justice due to others: 7th: to controversies between two or more states; because domestic tranquillity requires that the contention of states should be peaceably terminated by a common judicatory; and, because, in a free country justice ought not to depend on the *will* of either of the litigants: 8th: to controversies between a state and citizens of another state; because in case a state (that is all the citizens of it) has demands against some citizens of another state, it is better that they should prosecute their demands in a national court than in a court of the state to which those citizens belong; the danger of irritation and criminations, arising from apprehensions and suspicions of partiality, being thereby obviated. Because, in cases where some citizens of one state have demands against all the citizens of another state, the cause of liberty and the rights of men forbid that the latter should be the sole judges of the justice due to the latter; and true republican

"Cases, in law and equity, arising under this Constitution, the laws of the United States, and treaties made, or which shall be made, under their authority" include all subject-matters of litigation, civil or criminal, whose determination requires the application or construction of the Constitution, laws, or treaties of the United States.[1] "Cases affecting ambassadors, other public ministers, and consuls" are cases to which such officers are parties, or so far privies, that the determination thereof will conclude their rights.[2] "Cases of admiralty and maritime jurisdiction" comprehend liti-

government requires that free and equal citizens should have free, fair, and equal justice; 9th: to controversies between citizens of the same state, claiming lands under grants of different states; because, as the rights of the two states to grant the land are drawn into question, neither of the two states ought to decide the controversy: 10th: to controversies between a state or the citizens thereof, and foreign states, citizens, or subjects; because, as every nation is responsible for the conduct of its citizens toward other nations, all questions touching the justice due to foreign nations or people, ought to be ascertained by, and depend on, national authority."

[1] Waite, C. J., said in Starin v. New York, 115 U. S. 257, "the character of a case is determined by the questions involved. If from the questions it appears that some title, right, privilege, or immunity on which the recovery depends will be defeated by one construction of the Constitution, or of a law of the United States, or sustained by the opposite construction, the case will be one arising under the Constitution or laws of the United States, within the meaning of that term . . . otherwise not." In Tennessee v. Davis, 100 U. S. 264, Strong, J., said, "a case arising under the Constitution and laws of the United States may as well arise in a criminal prosecution as in a civil suit. . . . It is not merely one where a party comes into court to demand something conferred upon him by the Constitution or by a law or treaty. A case consists of the right of one party as well as the other, and may truly be said to arise under the Constitution or a law or a treaty of the United States, whenever its correct decision depends upon the construction of either. Cases arising under the laws of the United States are such as grow out of the legislation of Congress, whenever they constitute the right or privilege, or claim, or protection, or defense of the party, in whole or in part, by whom they are asserted." See also Cohens v. Virginia, 6 Wheat. 264, 379; Osborn v. Bank of the U. S., 9 id. 737, 824; The Mayor v. Cooper, 6 Wall. 247, 252; Gold W. & W. Co. v. Keyes, 96 U. S 199, 201; R. R. Co. v. Mississippi, 102 id. 135, 140; Ames v. Kansas, 111 id. 449, 462; K. P. Co. v. A. T. & S. F. R. R., 112 id. 414, 416; P. Savings Co. v. Ford, 114 id. 635, 641; P. R. Removal Cases, 115 id. 1, 11.

[2] U. S. v. Ortega, 11 Wheat. 467; Blyew v. U. S., 13 Wall. 581.

gated cases with regard to acts done and rights created, or contracts to be performed, upon the high seas or inland navigable waters, or with regard to contracts for the transportation of passengers or goods on the high seas or on navigable waters between different states.[1] The phrase "controversies to which the United States shall be a party" requires no elucidation further than to note that the United States, as a sovereignty, cannot be sued without its own consent,[2] and the constitutional provision does not impose upon Congress any duty to constitute tribunals to take cognizance of claims against the United States.

The phrase, controversies "between citizens of different states," vests in the courts of the United States jurisdiction over all proceedings *in personam*, between such parties. As Marshall, C. J., said in Cohens *v.* Virginia,[3] "if these be the parties, it is entirely unimportant what may be the subject of controversy. Be it what it may, these parties have a constitutional right to come into the courts of the Union;" and as Field, J., said in Gaines *v.* Fuentes,[4] "it rests entirely with Congress to determine at what time the power may be invoked, and upon what conditions."[5] But that jurisdiction which is dependent on the character of the parties does not include proceedings *in rem*, or *quasi in rem*, such as questions of probate,[6] or actions for divorce.[7]

[1] *Supra* pp. 45, 46, The Genessee Chief *v.* Fitzhugh, 12 How. 443; The Daniel Ball, 10 Wall. 557; The Montello, 20 *id.* 430; Waring *v.* Clarke, 5 How. 441; Allen *v.* Newberry, 21 *id.* 244; Maguire *v.* Card, *ibid.* 248; The Belfast, 7 Wall. 624; The Eagle, 8 *id.* 15; Fretz *v.* Bull, 12 How. 466; The Moses Taylor, 4 Wall. 411; The Hine *v.* Trevor, *ibid.* 555; N. J. Navigation Co. *v.* Merchants' Bank, 6 How. 344; Hobart *v* Drogan, 10 Pet. 108; The St. Lawrence, 1 Bl. 522.
[2] McElrath *v.* U. S., 102 U. S. 426.
[3] 6 Wheat. 378. [4] 92 U. S. 18.
[5] See also Payne *v.* Hook, 7 Wall. 425; Hyde *v.* Stone, 20 How. 170, 175; Railway Co. *v.* Whitton, 13 Wall. 270, 287; Dennick *v.* R. R. Co., 103 U. S. 11; *Ex parte* Boyd, 105 *id.* 647; Boom Co. *v.* Patterson, 98 *id.* 403.
[6] Fouvergne *v.* New Orleans, 18 How. 470. [7] Barber *v.* Barber, 21 How. 582.

The phrases "controversies between two or more states . . . between citizens of the same state claiming lands under grants of different states" seem to be unambiguous. The cases of suits between states have been mainly controversies as to conflicting boundaries.[1] It has, however, been held that as the United States "has no power to impose on a state officer, as such, any duty whatever, and compel him to perform it," a state cannot, by a suit against the governor of another state, compel the performance of a "duty" by an officer of that other state, for "there is no power delegated to the general government, either through the judicial department, or any other department, to use any coercive means to compel him."[2] It has also been held that since the adoption of the XI Amendment a court of the United States cannot entertain jurisdiction of a cause, in which one state seeks relief on behalf of its citizens, against another state in a matter in which the plaintiff state has no corporate interest, as, for instance, when the plaintiff state has assumed the collection of a debt due to one of its citizens by the defendant state.[3] An Indian tribe within the United States being a "domestic dependent nation," and not a state, cannot bring suit against a state under this clause of the Constitution.[4] But the other clauses of the constitutional provision, those giving jurisdiction to the courts of the United States in "controversies . . . between a state and citizens of another state . . . and between a state or the citizens thereof, and foreign states, citizens, or subjects," were, at an early day in the history of the government,

[1] Rhode Island v. Massachusetts, 12 Pet. 724; Missouri v. Iowa, 7 How. 660; Florida v. Georgia, 17 id. 478; Alabama v. Georgia, 23 id. 505; Virginia v. West Virginia, 11 Wall. 39.
[2] Kentucky v. Dennison, 24 How. 66.
[3] New Hampshire v. Louisiana. 108 U. S. 76.
[4] The Cherokee Nation v. Georgia, 5 Pet. 1.

the subject of much controversy. No one has ever doubted the jurisdiction in causes in which a state[1] was plaintiff, but the jurisdiction was earnestly contested in cases in which a state was defendant and citizens of other states were plaintiffs. In 1792 the Supreme Court of the United States, in Chisholm v. Georgia,[2] the cause being an action of assumpsit brought by a citizen of South Carolina against the state of Georgia, sustained the original jurisdiction of the Supreme Court in suits by a citizen of one state against another state. In consequence of that judgment, and for the purpose of relieving the states from liability to suits to enforce the payment of their obligations,[3] the XI Article of the Amendments to the Constitution was adopted.[4] As the courts of the United States are courts of limited jurisdiction, the record must show affirmatively that the cause is necessarily of federal cognizance, by reason of either the subject-matter of litigation,[5] or the character of the parties.[6] The jurisdiction of the courts of the United States is, in its character, either civil or criminal, and, in its exercise, either exclusive of, or concurrent with, the jurisdiction of the courts of the states, and either original, or appellate. In causes of civil cognizance, where the federal court has acquired original jurisdiction under the Constitution and laws of the United States, it may protect rights and administer remedies

---

[1] Texas v. White, 7 Wall. 700.
[2] 2 Dall. 419.
[3] Cohen v. Virginia, 6 Wheat. 406.
[4] *Infra*, sec. 100.
[5] Lawler v. Walker, 14 How. 149; Mills v. Brown, 16 Pet. 525; R. R. v. Rock, 4 Wall. 177, 180; Osborn v. Bank of the United States, 9 Wheat. 738, 823.
[6] Dred Scott v. Sandford, 19 How. 393; Breithaupt v. Bank of Georgia, 1 Pet. 238; Godfrey v. Terry, 97 U. S 171; Hornthall v. The Collector, 9 Wall. 560; Grace v. American Ins. Co., 109 U. S. 278, 283; Robertson v. Cease, 97 id. 646; Brown v. Keene, 8 Pet. 115; Bingham v. Cabot, 3 Dall. 382; Capron v. Van Noorden, 2 Cr. 126.

not only under the Constitution, laws, and treaties of the United States, but also under the common law, as adopted by the state within which the court sits,[1] the principles of equitable jurisprudence, "as distinguished and defined in that country from whence we derive our knowledge of those principles,"[2] and the statutes of the state.[3] In causes of criminal cognizance, the original jurisdiction of the federal courts is limited in two respects. In the first place, those courts cannot take cognizance of an act alleged to be criminal, which has not been declared to be such by an act of Congress.[4] In the second place, Congress cannot, under the Constitution, declare an act to be criminal, unless, as Field, J., said,[5] that act has "some relation to the execution of a power of Congress, or to some matter within the jurisdiction of the United States." Thus, a murder committed on board a vessel of the navy of the United States, while at anchor in navigable waters within the jurisdiction of a state, is not cognizable in a court of the United States;[6] Congress cannot make it a misdemeanor to sell within the territory of a state illuminating oil inflammable at a less than specified temperature;[7] while Congress may legislate with regard to bankruptcy, and may prohibit and declare to be punishable the commission of a fraud in contemplation of

---

[1] Parsons v. Bedford, 3 Pet. 433; Wheaton v. Peters, 8 id. 591; Parrish v. Ellis, 16 id. 451; Ex parte Bollman and Swartwout, 4 Cr. 75.

[2] Robinson v. Campbell, 3 Wheaton 222; Pennsylvania v. W. & B. Bridge Co., 13 How. 563; Livingston v. Story, 9 Pet. 632; Holland v. Challen, 110 U. S. 15.

[3] Edwards v. Elliott, 21 Wall. 532; The Lottawanna, ibid. 558; C. & N. W. Ry. v. Whitton, 13 id. 270; Ex parte Gordon, 104 U. S. 515; Ex parte Ferry Co., ibid. 519.

[4] U. S. v. Hudson, 7 Cr. 32; U S. v. Coolidge, 1 Wheat. 415; Bush v. Kentucky, 107 U. S. 110; Sed cf. Tennessee v. Davis, 100 U. S. 257.

[5] U. S. v. Fox, 95 U. S. 570.

[6] U. S. Bevans, 3 Wheat. 336.

[7] United States v. DeWitt, 9 Wall. 41.

bankruptcy, it cannot constitute the obtaining of goods on false pretences without intent to defraud, but not in contemplation of bankruptcy, to be an offense against the United States;[1] Congress cannot by statute provide for the punishment of state election officers for wrongfully refusing to receive the vote of a qualified voter at an election, when that refusal is not based upon a discrimination against the voter on account of his race, colour, or previous condition of servitude.[2] The appellate and supervisory jurisdiction of the courts of the United States over the courts of the states in causes of criminal cognizance is, as explained in Section 95, exercisable only in causes wherein there has been denied to the prisoner a right secured to him by the Constitution or laws of the United States.

92. It is a principle of constitutional construction, as stated by Marshall, C. J., in Sturges v. Crowninshield,[3] that "wherever the terms in which a power is granted to Congress, or the nature of the power require that it should be exercised exclusively by Congress, the subject is as completely taken from the state legislatures as if they had been expressly forbidden to act on it."[4] In conformity with this principle, it has been decided in Martin v. Hunter's Lessee,[5] and in The Moses Taylor,[6] that Congress has power to divest the courts of the states of jurisdiction over all subject-matters which are included within the constitutional grant of judicial power to the United States, or whose determination by

---

[1] United States v. Fox, 95 U. S. 670.
[2] U. S. v. Reese, 92 U. S. 214; U. S. v. Cruikshank, 92 U. S. 542.
[3] 4 Wheat. 193.
[4] See also Houston v. Moore, 5 Wheat. 193; Gilman v. Philadelphia, 3 Wall. 730.
[5] 1 Wheat. 304.
[6] Wall. 411. See also Cohen v. Virginia, 6 Wheat. 314, 315, 325; Slocum v. Mayberry, 2 id. 9; Gelston v. Hoyt, 3 id. 246; Waring v. Clarke, 5 How. 451; Sed. cf. Story's Commentaries, § 1672, note 4.

the judicial power of the United States is necessary to the exercise by Congress of its constitutional power of legislation, and where Congress has expressed its will that, as to any particular subject-matter of federal cognizance the jurisdiction of the courts of the United States shall be exclusive, the courts of the states cannot take cognizance of such subject-matter.[1]

[1] In Martin v. Hunter's Lessee, 1 Wheat. 334, Story, J., referring to the constitutional grant of judicial power to the United States, said: "the first class includes cases arising under the Constitution, laws, and treaties of the United States; cases affecting ambassadors, other public ministers, and consuls and cases of admiralty and maritime jurisdiction. In this class the expression is, that the judicial power shall extend to *all* cases; but in the subsequent part of the clause which embraces all the other cases of national cognizance, and forms the second class, the word '*all*' is dropped seemingly *ex industria*. Here the judicial authority is to extend to controversies, not to *all* controversies, to which the United States shall be a party, etc. From this difference of phraseology, perhaps a difference of constitutional intention may, with propriety, be inferred. It is hardly to be presumed that the variation in the language could have been accidental. It must have been the result of some determinate reason; and it is not very difficult to find a reason sufficient to support the apparent change of intention. In respect to the first class, it may well have been the intention of the framers of the Constitution imperatively to extend the judicial power either in an original or appellate form to *all* cases; and in the latter class to leave it to Congress to qualify the jurisdiction, original or appellate, in such manner as public policy might dictate. The vital importance of all the cases enumerated in the first class to the national sovereignty might warrant such a distinction. In the first place as to cases arising under the Constitution, laws, and treaties of the United States. Here the state courts could not ordinarily possess a direct jurisdiction. The jurisdiction over such cases could not exist in the state courts previous to the adoption of the Constitution, and it could not afterwards be directly conferred on them; for the Constitution expressly requires the judicial power to be vested in courts ordained and established by the United States. This class of cases would embrace civil as well as criminal jurisdiction, and affect not only our internal policy, but our foreign relations. It would, therefore, be perilous to restrain it in any manner whatsoever, inasmuch as it might hazard the national safety. The same remarks may be urged as to cases affecting ambassadors, other public ministers, and consuls, who are emphatically placed under the guardianship of the law of nations; and as to cases of admiralty and maritime jurisdiction, the admiralty jurisdiction embraces all questions of prize and salvage, in the correct adjudication of which foreign nations are deeply interested; it embraces also maritime torts, contracts, and offenses, in which the principles of the law and comity of nations often form an essential inquiry. All these cases, then, enter into the national policy, affect the

Of course, the Constitution, having granted the power, and not having commanded Congress to exercise

national rights, and may compromise the national sovereignty. The original, or appellate, jurisdiction ought not, therefore, to be restrained, but should be commensurate with the mischiefs intended to be remedied, and, of course, should extend to all cases whatsoever. A different policy might well be adopted with reference to the second class of cases; for, although it might be fit that the judicial power should extend to all controversies to which the United States should be a party, yet this power might not have been imperatively given, lest it should imply a right to take cognizance of original suits brought against the United States as defendants in their own courts. It might not have been deemed proper to submit the sovereignty of the United States, against their own will, to judicial cognizance, either to enforce rights or to prevent wrongs; and as to the other cases of the second class, they might well be left to be exercised under the exceptions and regulations which Congress might, in their wisdom, choose to apply. It is also worthy of remark, that Congress seems, in a good degree, in the establishment of the present judicial system, to have adopted this distinction. In the first class of cases, the jurisdiction is n t limited except by the subject-matter; in the second, it is made materially to depend upon the value in controversy. We do not, however, profess to place any implicit reliance upon the distinction which has here been stated and endeavoured to be illustrated. . . . At all events, whether the one construction or the other prevail, it is manifest that the judicial power of the United States is unavoidably, in some cases, exclusive of all state authority, and in all others, may be made so at the election of Congress. No part of the criminal jurisdiction of the United States can, consistently with the Constitution, be delegated to state tribunals. The admiralty and maritime jurisdiction is of the same exclusive cognizance; and it can only be in those cases where, previous to the Constitution, state tribunals possessed jurisdiction independent of national authority, that they can now constitutionally exercise a concurrent jurisdiction. Congress, throughout the judicial act, and particularly in the 9th, 11th, and 13th sections, have legislated upon the supposition that in all the cases to which the judicial powers of the United States extended, they might rightfully vest exclusive jurisdiction in their own courts." In The Moses Taylor [4 Wall. 411], Field, J., in the judgment of the court, quoted the constitutional grant of judicial power to the United States, and said [p. 428], "how far this judicial power is exclusive, or may, by the legislation of Congress, be made exclusive, in the courts of the United States, has been much discussed, though there has been no direct adjudication upon the point;" and after referring to the judgment of Story. J., in Martin v. Hunter's Lessee, he added [p. 429], "we agree fully with this conclusion. The legislation of Congress has proceeded upon this supposition. The Judiciary Act of 1789, in its distribution of jurisdiction to the several federal courts, recognizes and is framed upon the theory that, in all cases, to which the judicial power of the United States extends, Congress may rightfully vest exclusive jurisdiction in the federal courts. . . . The constitutionality of these provisions cannot be seriously questioned and is of frequent recognition it, it is for Congress to determine when and to what extent it will exercise it. Therefore, the jurisdiction of the courts of the United States within the limits imposed by the Constitution is either exclusive of, or concurrent with, that of the courts of the states, as Congress may, from time to time, determine.[1] As the law now is, the jurisdiction of the courts of the United States is exclusive of that of the states in cases of crimes and offenses cognizable under the authority of the United States; in suits for penalties and forfeitures incurred under the laws of the United States; in civil causes of admiralty and maritime jurisdiction, saving to suitors in all cases the right of a common law remedy, where the common law is competent to give it; in seizures under the laws of the United States on land or on waters not within admiralty and maritime jurisdiction; in cases arising under the patent right or copyright laws of the United States; in all matters and proceedings in bankruptcy; in all controversies of a civil nature, where a state is a party, except between a state and its citizens, or between a state and citizens of other states, or aliens; and in all suits or proceedings against ambassadors, or other public ministers, or their domestics, or domestic servants, or against consuls or vice-consuls.[2]

93. The original jurisdiction of the courts of the United States is exercised in some cases by the Supreme Court, and, in other cases, by the inferior courts. As

by both state and federal courts." In Claflin v. Houseman, 93 U. S. 136, Bradley, J., said, the general principle is, "that, where jurisdiction may be conferred on the United States courts, it may be made exclusive where not so by the Constitution itself; but, if exclusive jurisdiction be neither express nor implied, the state courts have concurrent jurisdiction whenever, by their own Constitution, they are competent to take it."

[1] Martin v. Hunter's Lessee, 1 Wheat. 304, 331, 333; The Moses Taylor, 4 Wall. 411, 429.
[2] Rev. Stat. Sec. 711.

Johnson, J., said in United States *v.* Hudson,[1] "only the Supreme Court possesses jurisdiction derived immediately from the Constitution, and of which the legislative power cannot deprive it. All other courts created by the general government possess no jurisdiction but what is given them by the power that creates them, and can be vested with none but what the power ceded to the general government will authorize them to confer."

The original jurisdiction of the Supreme Court is limited by the Constitution to "cases affecting ambassadors, other public ministers, and consuls, and those in which a state shall be a party." Congress cannot confer upon the Supreme Court any original jurisdiction other than that so conferred by the express terms of the Constitution.[2] Whether or not Congress can authorize other courts of the United States to exercise concurrent original jurisdiction in the cases, original jurisdiction over which is vested by the Constitution in the Supreme Court, was for a long time an unsettled question. In U. S. *v.* Ortega,[3] the question was raised, but not decided, but in Bors *v.* Preston,[4] it was determined, that the Congress might confer a concurrent original jurisdiction upon the circuit courts of the United States in actions against consuls of foreign states.[5] The original jurisdiction of the courts of the United States concurrent with that of the state courts, is regulated by the acts of Congress.[6]

[1] 7 Cr. 32.
[2] Marbury *v.* Madison, 1 Cr. 137.
[3] 11 Wheat. 467.
[4] 111 U. S. 252.
[5] Rev. Stat., sec. 687. See, also, Ames *v.* Kansas, 111 U. S. 449. *Sed. cf.* Curtis's Jurisdiction of the Courts of the U. S., p. 10.
[6] Rev. Stat. U. S., Sections 563, 629, and 711. The Act of 3 March, 1887, declares that "the Circuit Courts of the United States shall have original cognizance, concurrent with the courts of the several states, of all suits of a civil nature, at common law or in equity, where the matter in dispute exceeds, exclusive of interest and costs, the sum or value of $2,000, and arising under the Constitution or laws of the United States, or treaties made, or which shall

**94. The removal of civil causes from the courts of the states to the courts of the United States is now regulated by the Act of 3 March, 1887.**[1]

be made, under their authority, or in which controversary the United States are plaintiffs or petitioners, or in which there shall be a controversary between citizens of different states, in which the matter in dispute exceeds exclusive of interest and costs, the sum or value aforesaid, or a controversary between citizens of the same state, claiming land under grants from different states, or a controversary between citizens of a state and foreign states, citizens, or subjects in which the matter in dispute exceeds, exclusive of interest and costs, the sum or value aforesaid, . . . and no civil suit shall be brought before either of said courts against any person by any original process of proceeding in any other district than that whereof he is an inhabitant; but where the jurisdiction is founded only on the fact that the action is between citizens of different states, suit shall be brought only in the district of the residence of either the plaintiff or the defendant; nor shall any Circuit or District Court have cognizance of any suit except upon foreign bills of exchange, to recover the contents of any promissory note or other chose in action in favour of any assignee, or of any subsequent holder of such instrument be payable to bearer, and be not made by any corporation, unless such suit might have been prosecuted in such court to recover the said contents if no assignment or transfer had been made." Section 3 of the act subjects to liability to suit receivers appointed by any court of the United States. Section 4 of the act declares national banking associations to be, for purposes of jurisdiction citizens of the states in which they are located, and provides that the federal courts shall not have, in cases brought by such associations, any "jurisdiction other than such as they would have in cases between individual citizens of the same state," saving the federal jurisdiction "in cases commenced by the United States, or by any officer thereof, or cases for winding up the affairs of any such bank "

[1] That act declares, "Sec. 2, that any suit of a civil nature, at law or in equity, arising under the Constitution or laws of the United Sta es, or treaties made, or which shall be made, under their authority, of which the C rcuit Courts of the United States are given original jurisdiction by the preceding section, which may now be pending, or which may hereafter be brought, in any state court, may be removed by the defendant or defendants therein to the Circuit Court of the United States for the proper district any other suit of a civil nature, at law or in equity, of which the Circuit Courts of the United States are given jurisdiction by the preceding section, and which are now pending, or which may hereafter be brought, in any state court, may be removed into the Circuit Court of the United States for the proper district, by the defendant or defendants therein being non-residents of that state; and when in any suit mentioned in this section there shall be a controversy which is wholly between citizens of different states, and which can be fully determined as between them, then either one or more of the defendants actually interested in such controversy may remove said suit into the Circuit Court of the United States for the proper district. And where a suit is now pending, or may be hereafter brought, in any state court, in which there is a contro-

## CONCURRENT JURISDICTION. 207

versy between a citizen of the state in which the suit is brought and a citizen of another state, any defendant, being such citizen of another state, may remove such suit into the Circuit Court of the United States for the proper district, at any time before the trial thereof, when it shall be made to appear to said Circuit Court that from prejudice or local influence he will not be able to obtain justice in such state court, or in any other state court to which the said defendant may, under the laws of the state, have the right, on account of such prejudice or local influence, to remove said cause: provided, that if it further appear that said suit can be fully and justly determined as to the other defendants in the state court, without being affected by such prejudice or local influence, and that no party to the suit will be prejudiced by a separation of the parties, said Circuit Court may direct the suit to be remanded, so far as relates to such other defendants, to the state court, to be proceeded with therein. 'At any time before the trial of any suit which is now pending in any Circuit Court, or may hereafter be entered therein, and which has been removed to said court from a state court on the affidavit of any party plaintiff, that he had reason to believe and did believe that, from prejudice or local influence, he was unable to obtain justice in said state court, the Circuit Court shall, on application of the other party, examine into the truth of said affidavit and the grounds thereof, and, unless it shall appear to the satisfaction of said court that said party will not be able to obtain justice in such state court, it shall cause the same to be remanded thereto.' Whenever any cause shall be removed from any state court into any Circuit Court of the United States, and the Circuit Court shall decide that the cause was improperly removed, and order the same to be remanded to the state court from whence it came, such remand shall be immediately carried into execution, and no appeal or writ of error from the decision of the Circuit Court so remanding such cause shall be allowed."

"Sec. 3. That whenever any party entitled to remove any suit mentioned in the next preceding section, except in such cases as are provided for in the last clause of said section, may desire to remove such suit from a state court to the Circuit Court of the United States, he may make and file a petition in such suit in such state court at the time, or any time before the defendant is required by the laws of the state or the rule of the state court in which such suit is brought, to answer or plead to the declaration or complaint of the plaintiff, for the removal of such suit into the Circuit Court to be held in the district where such suit is pending, and shall make and file therewith a bond, with good and sufficient surety, for his or their entering in such Circuit Court, on the first day of its then next session, a copy of the record in such suit, and for paying all costs that may be awarded by the said Circuit Court if said court shall hold that such suit was wrongfully or improperly removed thereto, and also for their appearing and entering special bail in such suit if special bail was originally requisite therein. It shall then be the duty of the state court to accept said petition and bond. and proceed no further in such suit, and the said copy being entered as aforesaid in said Circuit Court of the United States, the cause shall then proceed in the same manner as if it had been originally commenced in the said Circuit Court; and if, in any action commenced in a state court, the title of land be concerned, and the parties are citizens of the same state, and the matter in dispute exceed the sum or value

The removal of causes of criminal cognizance is likewise regulated by statute.[1]

95. As the Constitution has declared, that in all cases, other than those in which original jurisdiction has been by its terms vested in the Supreme Court, that court "shall have appellate jurisdiction, both as to law and fact, with such exceptions and under such regulations as the Congress shall make," Congress may define and limit the appellate jurisdiction of the Supreme Court,[2] but the Supreme Court cannot be

of $2,000, exclusive of interest and costs, the sum or value being made to appear, one or more of the plaintiffs or defendants, before the trial, may state to the court, and make affidavit if the court require it, that he or they claim and shall rely upon a right or title to the land under a grant from a state, and produce the original grant, or an exemplification of it, except where the loss of public records shall put it out of his or their power, and shall move that any one or more of the adverse party inform the court whether he or they claim a right or title to the land under a grant from some other state, the party or parties so required shall give such information, or otherwise not be allowed to plead such grant, or give it in evidence upon the trial; and if he or they inform that he or they do claim under such grant, any one or more of the party moving for such information may then, on petition and bond, as hereinbefore mentioned in this act, remove the cause for trial to the Circuit Court of the United States next to be holden in such district; and any one of either party removing the cause shall not be allowed to plead or give evidence of any other title than that by him or them stated as aforesaid as the ground of his or their claim." The Act of 1887 is, indeed, a legal curiosity.

[1] Rev. Stat., secs. 641 and 642. The Act of 3 March, 1887, declares: Sec. 5. That nothing in this act shall be held, deemed or construed to repeal or affect any jurisdiction or right mentioned either in sections 641, or in 642, or in 643, or in 722, or in Title 24 of the Revised Statutes of the United States, or mentioned in Section 8 of the act of Congress of which this act is an amendment, or in the act of Congress, approved March 1, 1875, entitled "An act to protect all citizens in their civil or legal rights." Sec. 6. That the last paragraph of section 5 of the act of Congress, approved March 3, 1875, entitled "An act to determine the jurisdiction of Circuit Courts of the United States, and to regulate the removal of causes from state courts, and for other purposes," and section 640 of the Revised Statutes and all laws and parts of laws in conflict with the provisions of this act, be and the same are hereby repealed. *Provided*, That this act shall not affect the jurisdiction over or disposition of any suit removed from the court of any state, or suit commenced in any court of the United States, before the passage hereof, except as otherwise expressly provided in this act.

[2] Wiscart *v.* Dauchy, 3 Dall. 321; Durosseau *v.* U. S., 6 Cr. 307, 314; The Francis Wright, 105 U. S. 381.

required to review the actions of officers of the United States under legislative or executive references.[1] In the exercise of its appellate jurisdiction the Supreme Court of the United States may review the final judgments and decrees of the inferior courts of the United States under the restrictions stated in the acts of Congress,[2] and it may review the final judgments or decrees of the courts of last resort of the states in causes either civil or criminal, "where is drawn in question the validity of a statute of, or an authority exercised under, any state, on the ground of their being repugnant to the Constitution, treaties, or laws of the United States, and the decision is in favour of their validity; or where any title, right, privilege, or immunity is claimed under the Constitution, or any treaty or statute of, or commission held or authority exercised under, the United States, and the decision is against the title, right, privilege, or immunity specially set up or claimed by either party, under such Constitution, treaty, statute, commission, or authority."[3] The courts of the United States also exercise a supervisory jurisdiction over the courts of the states by a removal from a court of a state to a federal court of a cause, either civil or criminal, depending but not yet finally adjudicated in the state court,[4] or by the issue of a writ of *habeas corpus* in cases of a restraint of personal liberty under process of a court of a state, void by reason of the offense with

---

[1] Hayburn's Case, 2 Dall. 409; U. S. v. Ferrera, 13 How. 40; Hunt v. Pallas, 4 How. 589; McNulty v. Batty. 10 id. 72; Gordon v. U. S., 2 Wall. 561.

[2] Rev. Stat. Sec. 690 et seq.

[3] Rev. Stat. 709. See also Cohens v. Virginia, 6 Wheat. 264; Worcester v. Georgia, 6 Pet. 515; Twitchell v. Pennsylvania, 7 Wall. 321; Spies v. Illinois, 123 U. S. 131.

[4] West v. Aurora City, 6 Wall. 139; Ames v. Kansas, 111 U. S. 449; Philadelphia v. The Collector, 5 Wall. 720; The Mayor v. Cooper, 6 id. 247 Tennessee v. Davis, 100 U. S. 257; The Removal Cases, ibid. 457.

which the prisoner is charged being a matter of federal, and not of state, cognizance, or by reason of the restraint of a prisoner in violation of the Constitution, or of any treaty, or law of the United States.[1] The right of appeal, or of removal, or to the writ of *habeas corpus* is in any case dependent, not only on the federal character of the question involved, or the right of the party to sue in the federal court, but also on the terms of the act of Congress authorizing the exercise by the court of the United States of its supervisory jurisdiction in the particular case. The Constitution does not expressly authorize the removal of causes of federal cognizance from the courts of the states to the courts of the United States before final judgment, nor does it expressly authorize the review of such causes in the Supreme Court of the United States after the entry of final judgment in a court of a state, nor does it expressly authorize the release by a court of the United States after a hearing on *habeas corpus* of a prisoner indicted in a state court for doing that which under the Constitution and laws of the United States he may rightfully do, but the right of removal, the right of appeal, and the right to a discharge after hearing on *habeas corpus*, alike result from the constitutional decla-

[1] Harlan, J., said, in *Ex parte* Royall, 117 U. S. 252, if "a person is in custody, under process from a state court of original jurisdiction, for an alleged offense against the laws of such state, and it is claimed that he is restrained of his liberty in violation of the Constitution of the United States, the Circuit Court [of the U. S.] has a discretion, whether it will discharge him upon a *habeas corpus* in advance of his trial in the court in which he is indicted; that discretion, however, to be subordinated to any special circumstance requiring immediate action. When the state court shall have finally acted upon the case, the Circuit Court has still a discretion whether, under all the circumstances as then existing, the accused, if convicted, shall be put to his writ of error from the highest court of the state, or whether it will proceed by writ of *habeas corpus*, summarily to determine whether the petitioner is restrained of his liberty in violation of the Constitution of the United States." See also *Ex parte* Fonda, 117 U. S. 516. Rev. Stat. Sec. 751, *et seq.*

ration of the supremacy of the Constitution and laws of the United States.

96. Whatever be the form in which the jurisdiction of the courts of the United States is invoked, it is essential to the exercise of the jurisdiction that there should be a "case" before the court, that is, a subject-matter of litigation contested by competent parties.[1] It is also essential that the question for decision be judicial in character, for the courts cannot decide political questions, such as whether or not the people of a state have altered their form of government by abolishing an old government and establishing a new one in its place,[2] nor whether or not, in a foreign country, a new

---

[1] In Osborn v. The Bank of the United States, 9 Wheat. 818, Marshall, C. J., said, "the legislative, executive, and judicial powers of every well constructed government, are co-extensive with each other, that is, they are potentially co-extensive. The executive department may constitutionally execute every law which the legislature may constitutionally make, and the judicial department may receive from the legislature the power of construing every such law. All governments which are not extremely defective in their organization, must possess within themselves the means of expounding, as well as enforcing, their own laws. If we examine the Constitution of the United States, we find that its framers kept this great political principle in view. The II Article vests the whole executive power in the President, and the III Article declares, 'that the judicial power shall extend to all cases in law and equity arising under this Constitution, the laws of the United States, and treaties made, or which shall be made, under their authority.' This clause enables the judicial department to receive jurisdiction to the full extent of the Constitution, laws, and treaties of the United States, when any question respecting them shall assume such a form that the judicial power is capable of acting on it. That power is capable of acting only when the subject is submitted to it by a party who asserts his rights in the form prescribed by law. It then becomes a case, and the Constitution declares, that the judicial power shall extend to all cases arising under the Constitution, laws, and treaties of the United States." In Cohens v. Virginia, 6 Wheat. 379, Marshall, C. J., said, "a case in law or equity consists of the right of one party, as well as of the other, and may be truly said to arise under the Constitution or a law of the United States whenever its correct decision depends on the construction of either. Congress seems to have intended to give its own construction of this part of the Constitution in the 25th Section of the Judiciary Act; and we perceive no reason to depart from that construction."

[2] Luther v. Borden, 7 How. 147.

government has been established,[1] nor can the courts by injunction restrain a state from the forcible exercise of legislative power over an Indian tribe "asserting their independence, the right to which the state denies,"[2] nor enjoin the executive department of the government of the United States from carrying into effect acts of Congress alleged to be unconstitutional.[3] Such questions can only be decided by the political power, "and when that power has decided, the courts are bound to take notice of its decision and to follow it."[4] Upon this principle, the recognition by Congress and the executive of the state governments of the then lately rebellious states as reconstructed after the suppression of the rebellion was held to be binding upon the judicial department of the government.[5] But the courts may compel the performance of a ministerial and non-discretionary duty by an executive officer, as, for instance, the delivery of a signed and sealed commission to an officer who has been appointed, nominated, and confirmed,[6] or the crediting to a government creditor of a sum of money found by the Treasury to be due under the express terms of an act of Congress.[7]

[1] Rose v. Himely, 4 Cr. 272; Hoyt v. Gelston, 3 Wheat. 324; Kennett v. Chambers, 14 How. 38.
[2] The Cherokee Nation v. Georgia, 5 Pet. 120.
[3] Mississippi v. Johnson, 4 Wall. 475; Georgia v. Stanton, 6 id. 50.
[4] Luther v. Borden, 7 How. 147.
[5] Texas v. White, 7 Wall. 700, 701.
[6] Marbury v. Madison, 1 Cr. 137.
[7] Kendall, Postmaster General, v. Stockton, 12 Pet. 527.

[In the courts of the United States, laws of foreign countries may be proved as facts, C. & A. R. R. v. W. F. Co., 119 U. S. 615, 622; Talbot v. Seeman, 1 Cr. 1; Strother v. Lucas, 6 Pet. 763; Armstrong v. Lear, 8 id. 52; Church v. Hubbart 2 Cr. 187, by the official publications thereof, satisfactorily certified, Ennis v. Smith, 14 How. 400, or by written copies thereof attested by the oath of an United States Consul, Church v. Hubbart, 2 Cr. 187. Unwritten foreign laws may be proved by the testimony of experts, Ennis v. Smith, 14 How. 400; Livingston v. M. Ins. Co., 6 Cr. 274; Pierce v. Indseth, 106 U. S. 546. The courts of the United States take notice, without proof, of the laws

97. The judicial jurisdiction of the United States, except as regards offenses of soldiers and sailors against the Articles of War, and crimes punishable by impeachment, can only be exercised by courts duly constituted under the Constitution and the laws. Congress, therefore, cannot invest military commissions with jurisdiction to try, convict, or sentence for any offense, a citizen not being a resident of a state in rebellion, nor a prisoner of war, nor in the military or naval service of the United States.[1] Courts martial may exercise judicial jurisdiction with regard to offenses against the Articles of War by soldiers, sailors, and militiamen when called out for service.[2]

98. That which may be termed the extraordinary judicial power of the United States is exercised only in the trial of impeachments. The relevant provisions of the Constitution are that, "the House of Representatives shall . . . have the sole power of impeachment;"[3] "the Senate shall have the sole power to try all impeachments. When sitting for that purpose, they shall be on oath or affirmation. When the President of the United States is tried, the Chief Justice shall preside; and no person shall be convicted without the concurrence of two-thirds of the members present. Judgment in cases of impeachment shall not extend

---

of the several states, C. & A. R. R. *v.* W. F. Co., 119 U. S. 615, 622; Owings *v.* Hull, 9 Pet. 607, and of the laws governing territory subsequently acquired by the United States, U. S. *v.* Perot, 98 U. S. 430; Fremont *v.* U. S., 17 How. 542, 557. But the Supreme Court of the United States, in the exercise of its appellate jurisdiction, does not take judicial notice of the laws of foreign countries, nor of the laws of the several states of the United States, if such laws have not been found as facts in the courts of the first instance, Hanley *v.* Donaghue, 116 U. S. 1; C. & A. R. R. *v.* W. F. Co., 119 U. S. 615, 623.]

[1] *Ex parte* Milligan, 4 Wall. 2.
[2] Wise *v.* Withers, 3 Cr. 331; Houston *v.* Moore, 5 Wheat. 1; Martin *v.* Mott, 12 *id.* 19; Dynes *v.* Hoover, 20 How. 65; *Ex parte* Mason, 105 U S. 696; Keyes *v.* U. S., 109 *id.* 336; Wales *v.* Whitney, 114 *id.* 564.
[3] Art. I, Sec. 2.

further than to removal from office and disqualification to hold and enjoy any office of honour, trust, or profit, under the United States; but the party convicted shall, nevertheless, be liable and subject to indictment, trial, judgment, and punishment, according to law."[1] "The President, Vice-President, and all civil officers of the United States, shall be removed from office on impeachment for, and conviction of, treason, bribery, or other high crimes and misdemeanors."[2] "The President shall . . . have power to grant reprieves and pardons for offenses against the United States except in cases of impeachment."[3] "The trial of all crimes except in cases of impeachment shall be by jury."[4] "No bill of attainder or *ex post facto* law shall be passed."[5] The Supreme Court of the United States has never decided any question as to impeachment, but a consideration of the constitutional provisions shows clearly that, under them, the House of Representatives is the prosecutor; any civil officer of the United States may be the defendant; the Senate of the United States is the court, its members being first sworn or affirmed, the Chief Justice of the Supreme Court of the United States presiding in the case of a trial of the President, and a concurrence of two-thirds of the members present being necessary to a conviction; the offences for which an impeached officer may be tried being "treason, bribery, or other high crimes and misdemeanors," as defined by laws of the United States enacted before the commission of the offense; the punishment extending only "to removal from office and disqualification to hold and enjoy any office of honour, trust, or profit under the United States," but without prejudice to indictment,

---

[1] Art. I, Sec. 3.
[2] Art. II. Sec. 4.
[3] Art. II, Sec. 2.
[4] Art. III, Sec. 2.
[5] Art. I. Sec. 9.

trial, and conviction at law for the same offense; and a presidential pardon not being pleadable in bar of the impeachment nor efficacious in satisfaction of a conviction after impeachment, or in mitigation of the punishment.

99. The most important function of the Supreme Court of the United States is that of construing the Constitution authoritatively and finally, so far as regards subject-matters of judicial determination. The rules, which are applied by the court in the construction of the Constitution, are few and simple. (1). The construction is neither lax nor rigorous, but such as to effectuate the purpose of the instrument as "an establishment of a frame of government and a declaration of that government's fundamental principles intended to endure for ages and to be adapted to the various crises of human affairs."[1] (2). The antecedent history of the country and the state of the public affairs at the time of the adoption of the Constitution are considered, in order that the old law, the mischief, and the remedy may have their relative weight.[2] (3). A contemporaneous legislative exposition acquiesced in for a long term of years fixes the construction.[3] (4). The words are read in their natural sense,[4] departing from and varying by construction the natural meaning of the words only where different clauses of the instrument bear upon each other and would conflict, unless the words were construed otherwise than by their natural and common import.[5] (5). An exception from a

[1] Juilliard v. Greenman, 110 U. S. 421; Gibbons v. Ogden, 9 Wheat. 1; Martin v. Hunter's Lessee, 1 Wheat. 304.
[2] Rhode Island v Massachusetts, 12 Pet. 657.
[3] Stuart v. Laird, 1 Cr. 299; Brisco v. The Bank of the Commonwealth of Kentucky, 11 Pet. 317; Cooper Manufacturing Co. v. Ferguson, 113 U. S. 727.
[4] Gibbons v. Ogden, 9 Wheat. 1.
[5] Sturges v. Crowninshield, 4 Wheat. 122.

power, which is granted in express terms, marks the extent of the power and shows that the power necessarily includes other cases which come within the terms of the grant and which might have been, but were not, specifically excepted.[1] (6). The Federalist is not, o course, of binding authority upon the Supreme Court with regard to the judicial construction of the Constitution, but as Marshall, C. J., said in Cohens *v.* Virginia,[2] the "opinion of the Federalist has always been considered as of great authority. It is a complete commentary on our Constitution, and is appealed to by all parties in the questions to which that instrument has given birth. Its intrinsic merit entitles it to this high rank, and the part two of its authors performed in framing the Constitution put it very much in their power to explain the views with which it was framed." (7). The reported proceedings of the convention which framed the Constitution, and of the several state conventions which ratified it, though frequently referred to in the discussions of questions of constitutional construction, are not of binding authority. The views expressed in the debates are merely the views of the individual speakers, and do not necessarily express the view of the subject which induced the federal convention to insert the particular provision in the Constitution as framed by them, or which led the convention of any one state to ratify the Constitution. The votes of the convention on the details of the Constitution are of no greater importance, for an affirmative vote approving a particular section of the Constitution, throws no light on the meaning of the words of the section; and a negative vote rejecting a proposed constitutional provision may with

---

[1] Gibbons *v.* Ogden, 9 Wheat. 1; Rhode Island *v.* Massachusetts, 12 Pet. 657; Brown *v.* Maryland, 12 Wheat. 438.
[2] 6 Wheat. 418.

equal propriety be regarded as an expression of opinion to the effect that the proposed provision is unnecessary because adequately supplied by other provisions of the Constitution, or as a refusal to adopt the particular provision because in the opinion of the convention such a provision ought not to be inserted in the Constitution. It must be remembered that the Constitution derives its whole force and authority from its ratification by the people,[1] and whenever it becomes necessary to determine the meaning of any clause in the Constitution, the real question for decision is not, what did the federal convention, or any member thereof, understand that clause to mean when that convention framed the Constitution, nor what did the members of any particular state convention understand that clause to mean when their convention ratified the Constitution, but what did that clause really mean as ratified by all the conventions, and that meaning can only be determined by the application of the established rules of judicial construction.[2]

100. The Supreme Court having in Chisholm v. Georgia[3] affirmed its original jurisdiction in actions brought by citizens of one state against another state, in 1797 the XI Amendment was adopted, declaring, that "the judicial power of the United States shall not be construed to extend to any suit in law or equity commenced or prosecuted against one of the United States by citizens of another state, or by citizens or subjects of any foreign states." That amendment having taken effect on 8 January, 1798, in that year the Supreme Court decided in Hollingsworth v. Virginia,[4] that the amend-

---

[1] McCulloch v. Maryland, 4 Wheat. 316, 404.

[2] The view as stated in the text has been forcibly put by Mr. McMurtrie in his "Observations on Mr. George Bancroft's Plea for the Constitution," p. 8, et seq.

[3] 2 Dall. 419.    [4] 3 Dall. 378.

ment barred any further proceedings in cases then depending in the courts of the United States in which a citizen of one state was the plaintiff, and another state was the defendant. In Osborne *v.* The Bank of U. S.,[1] Marshall, C. J., said: "The XI Amendment . . . is of necessity limited to those suits in which a state is a party to the record," but he added,[2] "the state not being a party to the record, and the court having jurisdiction over those who are parties on the record, the true question is not one of jurisdiction, but whether in the exercise of its jurisdiction, the court ought to make a decree against the defendants; whether they are to be considered as having a real interest, or as being only nominal defendants." On the other hand he said,[3] "this suit is not against the state of Ohio within the view of the Constitution, the state being no party on the record." The jurisdictional question in the cause was as to the power of the court to take cognizance of a suit in equity brought by the Bank of the United States against the auditor of the state of Ohio to enjoin the collection of a tax on the business of the bank imposed by a statute of Ohio, and to recover a sum of money wrongfully taken out of the vaults of the bank by the state auditor by way of enforcing the payment of the tax, and the court sustained the jurisdiction on the grounds stated by the Chief Justice. In view of the judgment in the cause and the *dicta* of the Chief Justice, it was not unnatural that the presence or absence of a state as a party defendant on the record should have been regarded as the criterion by which to determine whether or not a suit was within the purview of the XI Amendment. Indeed in Davis *v.* Gray,[4] the court went so far as to hold that a

---

[1] 9 Wheat. 738, 857.
[2] p. 858.
[3] p. 868.
[4] 16 Wall. 203.

receiver of a railway could sue in equity the governor of the state incorporating the railway and the land commissioner of the state to restrain the issue of patents to individuals for certain lands theretofore granted by the state to the railway on certain conditions, and resumed by the state for alleged non-performance of the condition, and that it not being possible to make the state a party the plaintiff's rights could be vindicated by a decree against the officers of the state, but the later decisions of the court have tended toward the establishment of a sounder rule on this subject; and it is now settled, that the criterion is not the presence or absence of the state as a party defendant on the record, but the question of fact, is or is not the suit in substance, though not in form, a suit by a citizen of another state against a state? If a state be either a defendant on the record, or the real defendant though not a party on the record, the XI Amendment forbids the court to take jurisdiction of the cause, unless the state by its voluntary appearance, as in Clark v. Barnard,[1] submits itself to the jurisdiction of the court. In conformity with this view it has been held that a suit by, or against, the governor of a state in his representative capacity is a suit against the state;[2] that the XI Amendment prohibits a suit in the federal courts against the officers of a state to enforce the performance of a contract made by the state, where the controversy is as to the validity and obligation of the contract, and where the remedy sought is a performance of the contract by the state, the nominal defendants having no personal interest in the subject-matter;[3] it

[1] 108 U. S. 436, 447.
[2] Georgia v. Brailsford, 2 Dall. 402; The Governor of Georgia v. Madrazzo, 1 Pet. 110; Kentucky v. Dennison, 24 How. 466.
[3] Hagood v. Southern, 117 U. S. 52.

has also been held that where a state had bought a railway from a receiver appointed at its instance, as the holder of the first mortgage bonds of the railway, the holders of junior bonds having filed a bill to foreclose their mortgage and to set aside the sale to the state, making the governor and treasurer of the state parties defendant, the state being a necessary party to the relief sought, the XI Amendment barred the suit;[1] and that state officers cannot be compelled, at the suit of a citizen of another state, to appropriate the public money of the state in a way prohibited by the laws of the state, for such a suit is in fact a suit against the state, and where a state cannot be sued, the court cannot assert jurisdiction over the officers of the state, so as to control them in their administration of the finances of the state.[2] It has also been held that the XI Amendment bars a suit by one state against another state, where the plaintiff state sues, not in its own right, but only for the benefit of certain of its citizens who have assigned to it their claims against the state defendant;[3] that a private person cannot bring a personal suit in the Supreme Court of the United States against a state to recover the proceeds of property in the possession of that state, such as the proceeds of certain slaves alleged to have been illegally seized by the state;[4] and, in the case of *In re* Ayers,[5] that the XI Amendment forbids the court to take jurisdiction of a bill in equity filed by a holder of, and dealer in, coupons of the bonds of the state, the coupons under the statutes of the state and the judgments of the court being receivable in payment

---

[1] Cunningham v. M. & B. R. R., 109 U. S. 446.
[2] Louisiana v. Jumel, 107 U. S. 711.
[3] New Hampshire v. Louisiana, New York v. Louisiana, 108 U. S. 76.
[4] *Ex parte* Madrazzo, 7 Pet. 627; The Governor of Georgia v. Madrazzo, 1 Pet. 110.
[5] 123 U. S. 443.

of state taxes, to enjoin the officers of a state from prosecuting, on behalf of the state, actions against citizens of the state, for collection of taxes, under a statute of the state, directing the prosecution of the actions, and providing that "if the defendant relies on a tender of coupons as payment of the taxes claimed, he shall plead the same specifically and in writing, and file with the plea the coupons averred therein to have been tendered," and "the burden of proving the tender and the genuineness of the coupons shall be on the defendants;" the equity set up by the plaintiffs in the injunction suit being that they had purchased coupons, for the purpose of dealing in them and selling them to taxpayers to use in payment of taxes to the state, and that, unless the action threatened by the state officers were enjoined, the plaintiffs would not be able to sell their coupons at a profit. Matthews, J., said, "the object and purpose of the XI Amendment were to prevent the indignity of subjecting a state to the coercive process of judicial tribunals at the instance of private parties. It was thought to be neither becoming nor convenient that the several states of the Union, invested with that large residuum of sovereignty, which had not been delegated to the United States, should be summoned as defendants to answer the complaints of private persons, whether citizens of other states or aliens, or that the course of their public policy and the administration of their public affairs should be subject to, and controlled by, the mandates of judicial tribunals without their consent, and in favour of individual interests. To secure the manifest purposes of the constitutional exemption guaranteed by the XI Amendment requires that it should be interpreted, not literally and too narrowly, but fairly, and with such breadth and largeness as effectually to accomplish the substance of its purpose. In this spirit it must be held to cover, not only suits brought against a state by name, but those also against its officers, agents, and representatives, where the state, though not named as such, is, nevertheless, the only real property against which alone in fact the relief is asked, and against which the judgment or decree effectually operates." Harlan, J., dissented on the ground that the *dictum* of Marshall, C. J., in Osborn v. The Bank of the United States was conclusive in favour of the jurisdiction, and that [1] "the difference between a suit against officers of the state enjoining them from seizing the property of the citizen in obedience to a void statute of the state, and a suit enjoining such officers from bringing under the order of the state, and in her name, an action which, it is alleged, will result in injury to the rights of the complainant, is not a difference that affects the jurisdiction of the court, but only its exercise of jurisdiction. If the former is not a suit against the state, the latter should not be deemed of that class." On the other hand, it has been held that the amendment does not prohibit the exercise by the court of its appellate jurisdiction over state courts in cases of criminal cognizance, for the purchase or prosecution of a writ of error to reverse a criminal conviction at the prosecution of the state is not the commencement or prosecution of a suit at law against that state; [2] nor does the XI Amendment prohibit the exercise by the court of jurisdiction over a controversy between individuals as to land granted by and claimed under a state; [3] nor does the fact that a state is a, or the sole, shareholder in a banking corporation prevent the courts of the United States from taking cognizance of a suit against such a

---

[1] p. 546.
[2] Cohens *v.* Virginia, 6 Wheat. 264.
[3] Fowler *v.* Lindsay, 3 Dall. 411.

corporation,[1] for, as Marshall, C. J., said,[2] "when a government becomes a partner in any trading company, it divests itself, so far as concerns the transactions of that company, of its sovereign character, and takes that of a private citizen." Nor does the fact that a state claims property, which is not in its own possession but in the possession of an individual, who has been made defendant in an action to recover that property, oust the jurisdiction of the court of the United States, nor forbid the court to give judgment in favour of the plaintiff.[3] It is likewise well settled, that "when a plain official duty, requiring no exercise of discretion, is to be performed" by an officer of a state "and performance is refused, any person who will sustain personal injury by such refusal may have a *mandamus* to compel its performance; and when such duty is threatened to be violated by some positive official act," of an officer of a state, "any person who will sustain personal injury thereby, for which adequate compensation cannot be had at law, may have an injunction to prevent it,"[4] or he may maintain an action at law for damages against the officer as a wrongdoer. "In either case, if the officer plead the authority of an unconstitutional law for the non-performance or violation of his duty, it will not prevent the issuing of a writ. An unconstitutional law will be treated by the courts as null and void."[5] In conformity with this principle, it has been held that the XI Amendment does not forbid the courts of the United States to take cognizance of a

---

[1] L. C. & C R. R. *v.* Letson, 2 How. 497, 550; The Bank of the United States *v.* The Planters' Bank, 9 Wheat. 904, 907; Bank of Kentucky *v.* Wister, 2 Pet. 318, 323; Briscoe *v.* The Bank of Kentucky, 11 Pet. 257, 324; Curran *v.* Arkansas, 15 How. 304, 309.
[2] 9 Wheat. 407.  [3] United States *v.* Peters, 5 Cr. 115.
[4] per Bradley, J., in Board of Liquidation *v.* McComb, 92 U. S. 541.
[5] per Bradley, J., in Board of Liquidation *v.* McComb, 92 U. S. 541.

cause wherein a federal agency, as, for instance, a national bank, brings suit against the officers of a state to enjoin the enforcement of an unconstitutional law of the state taxing that agency.[1] It has also been held that state officers may be enjoined at the suit of a holder of consolidated bonds of the state which had been issued under an agreement for the funding of the debt of the state, from issuing others of the consolidated bonds in violation of the contract between the state and its bondholders;[2] and that an action brought by a taxpayer against an officer of a state to recover possession of property which that officer has wrongfully seized under an unconstitutional law of the state for non-payment of taxes is an action against that officer as a wrongdoer, and not such an action as is prohibited by the XI Amendment.[3]

As the immunity from suit is a personal privilege, the state may waive that privilege, and it does waive it, when, in a cause pending in a court of the United States, in which it has a sufficient interest to entitle it to become a party defendant, it causes an appearance to be entered by counsel on its behalf, for such an appear-

[1] Osborn v. The Bank of the United States, 9 Wheat. 738, 846.
[2] Board of Liquidation v. McComb, 92 U. S. 531.
[3] The Virginia Coupon Cases, 114 U. S. 269, 284. Some of the cases were actions of trespass or detinue; others of them were bills in equity for an injunction. Bradley, J., with whom concurred Waite, C. J., and Miller and Gray, JJ., dissented. Upon a like principle, it has been held, that, officers of the United States being wrongfully in possession of land, the fact that they hold that possession not for themselves but for the government of the United States will not forbid courts to take jurisdiction of the rightful owner's action to recover his land, nor prevent judgment in his favour, if his title be made out: Meigs v. McClurg's Lessee, 9 Cr. 11 ; Wilcox v. Jackson, 13 Pet. 498; Grisar v. McDowell, 6 Wall. 363; Brown v. Huger, 21 How. 305 ; United States v. Lee, 106 U. S. 196. In Mitchel v. Harmony, 13 How. 114, and in Bates v. Clark, 95 U. S. 204, the same rule was applied in actions of trespass against military officers of the United States for the wrongful seizure of certain personal property of the plaintiffs, in obedience to unlawful orders from a military superior.

ance is a voluntary submission to the jurisdiction of the court.[1] It is obvious that the XI Amendment does not affect the jurisdiction granted by the III Article to the courts of the United States in actions wherein a foreign state, or one of the United States is the plaintiff, and one of the United States is the defendant.

101. The exercise of judicial power by the United States is, in some respects, limited by certain other of the provisions of the Constitution and its amendments. In the most important case that ever came before the Supreme Court,[2] it was held that neither the President, nor the Congress, nor the Judicial Department can deny to a citizen any one of the safeguards of civil liberty incorporated into the Constitution, and in that cause a citizen who was held in custody under a sentence of death pronounced by a military commission was released upon *habeas corpus.* The last clause of section 2 of Article III of the Constitution declares that " the trial of all crimes, except in case of impeachment, shall be by jury; and such trial shall be held in the state where the said crimes shall have been committed; but when not committed within any state, the trial shall be at such place or places as the Congress may by law have directed." The IV Amendment declares that " the right of the people to be secure in their persons, houses, papers, and effects, against unreasonable searches and seizures, shall not be violated; and no warrant shall issue, but upon probable cause, supported by oath or affirmation, and particularly describing the place to be searched, and the persons or things to be seized." This amendment forbids Congress to authorize a court in revenue cases to require, on motion of the government's attorney, the defendant, or claimant, to

[1] Clark *v.* Barnard, 108 U. S. 436, 447.
[2] *Ex parte* Milligan, 4 Wall. 2.

produce in court his books, papers, etc., under penalty of admitting the allegations of the government's attorney as to that which those books, papers, etc., would prove if produced.[1]

102. The V Amendment declares, that "no person shall be held to answer for a capital or otherwise infamous crime, unless on a presentment or indictment by a grand jury, except in cases arising in the land or naval forces or in the militia when in actual service in time of war or public danger." This constitional provision forbids a prosecution upon information in the courts of the United States in the cases of crimes punishable by imprisonment for a term of years at hard labour.[2] But the striking of an attorney from the rolls for professional misconduct is within the proper jurisdiction of the court of which he is an attorney and does not violate this constitutional provision.[3] This amendment also forbids the trial or conviction of a prisoner in a case where after presentment made by the grand jury, the indictment is without resubmission to the grand jury, amended by striking out words, even though those words be regarded by the court as surplusage, and a prisoner, after trial, conviction, and sentence on an indictment so amended, is entitled to his discharge on *habeas corpus*.[4] The same amendment also declares, that, no person shall "be deprived of life, liberty, or property without due process of law." In Murray's Lessee *v.* Hoboken Land and Improvement Co.,[5] Curtis, J., said, "the words

---

[1] Boyd *v.* U. S., 116 U. S. 616. The V Amendment is a restraint upon the exercise of powers by the United States, but not by the states: Barron *v.* Baltimore, 7 Pet. 243; Withers *v.* Buckley, 20 How. 84; Davidson *v.* New Orleans, 96 U. S. 97; Kelly *v* Pittsburg, 104 *id.* 78.

[2] *Ex parte* Wilson, 114 U. S. 417; Mackin *v.* U. S., 117 *id.* 348; Parkinson *v.* U. S., 121 *id.* 281.

[3] *Ex parte* Wall. 107 U. S. 265.   [4] *Ex parte* Bain, 121 U. S. 1.

[5] 18 How. 272, 276

'due process of law' were undoubtedly intended to convey the same meaning as the words 'by the law of the land' in *Magna Charta*. Lord Coke, in his commentary on those words,[1] says they mean due process of law. The Constitutions, which had been adopted by the several states before the formation of the federal Constitution, following the language of the great charter more closely, generally contained the words, 'but by the judgment of his peers, or the law of the land.' . . . The Constitution contains no description of those processes which it was intended to allow or forbid. It does not even declare what principles are to be applied to ascertain whether it be due process. It is manifest that it was not left to the legislative power to enact any process which might be devised. The article is a restraint on the legislative as well as on the executive and judicial powers of the government, and cannot be so construed as to leave Congress free to make any process due process of law by its mere will. To what principle, then, are we to resort to ascertain whether this process, enacted by Congress, is 'due process.' To this the answer must be twofold. We must examine the Constitution itself to see whether this process be in conflict with any of its provisions. If not found to be so, we must look to those settled usages and modes of proceeding existing in the common and statute law of England, before the emigration of our ancestors, and which are shown not to have been unsuited to their civil and political conditions by having been acted on by them after the settlement of this country." In Pennoyer *v.* Neff,[2] Field, J., said, that the words, "due process of law," mean "a course of legal proceedings, according to those rules and principles which have been established

[1] 2 Inst. 50.   [2] 95 U. S. 733.

in our system of jurisprudence for the protection and enforcement of private rights. To give such proceedings any validity, there must be a tribunal competent by its Constitution, that is, by the law of its creation, to pass upon the subject-matter of the suit; and, if that involves merely a determination of the personal liability of the defendant, he must be brought within its jurisdiction by service of process within the state, or by his voluntary appearance." In conformity with these principles it has been held, that the trial of a citizen by military commission within a state where the courts are open and the course of justice unobstructed is not due process of law.[1] It has also been held that there is a deprivation of liberty without due process of law when a court by its order, warrant, or commitment, holds a prisoner in custody, when the *prima facie* case against the prisoner does not show that he has committed an offense of which the court committing him can take cognizance, and in any such case of commitment by an inferior court of the United States the Supreme Court will issue a *habeas corpus* and discharge the prisoner.[2]

On the other hand, it has been held that the owner of property distrained and sold for non-payment of taxes due to the United States, is not deprived of his property without due process of law.[3] It has also been held that an officer of the United States, whose accounts, as settled by the auditing officers of the Treasury, show him to have neglected to account for and pay over public moneys received by him, is not deprived of his

---

[1] *Ex parte* Milligan. 4 Wall. 2.

[2] United States *v.* Hamilton, 3 Dall. 17; *Ex parte* Bollman and Swartwout, 4 Cranch 75; *Ex parte* Lange, 18 Wall. 163; *Ex parte* Kearney, 7 Wall. 38; *Ex parte* Wells, 18 How. 307; *Ex parte* Parks, 93 U. S. 18; *Ex parte* Yarbrough, 110 U. S. 651; United States *v.* Waddell, 113 U. S. 76.

[3] Springer *v.* United States, 102 U. S. 586.

property without due process of law, when the Solicitor of the Treasury, in obedience to the act of Congress of 15 May, 1820,[1] has issued a distress warrant under which the defaulting officer's real property has been taken in execution and sold by a marshal of the U. S. without further proceedings, judicial or otherwise.[2] The V Amendment also declares, that no person shall "be subject for the same offense to be twice put in jeopardy of life or limb." Therefore, a second punishment cannot be imposed for the same crime, and hence when a court imposes a fine and imprisonment as a punishment where the statute under which the prisoner was indicted conferred the power to punish by fine or imprisonment, and the fine has been paid, the court cannot modify its judgment by thereafter imposing imprisonment alone, for the judgment of the court having been executed so as to be a full satisfaction of one of the alternative penalties, the power of the court as to that offense is ended, and a second judgment on the same verdict, is, under such circumstances, void for want of power, and the party must be discharged.[3] The V Amendment also declares, that no person "shall be compelled, in any criminal case, to be a witness against himself."

103. The VI Amendment declares that, "in all criminal prosecutions, the accused shall enjoy the right to a speedy and public trial, by an impartial jury, of the state and district wherein the crime shall have been committed, which district shall have been previously ascertained by law, and to be informed of the nature and cause of the accusation; to be confronted with the witnesses against him; to have compulsory process for

---

[1] 3 Stat. 592.
[2] Murray's Lessee v. Hoboken Land and Improvement Co., 18 How. 272.
[3] *Ex parte* Lange, 18 Wall. 163.

obtaining witneses in his favour, and to have the assistance of counsel for his defense."[1]  The requirement that the prisoner "be confronted with the witnesses against him" will not invalidate a conviction in a case where the witnesses are absent by the procurement of the prisoner, or where enough has been proven to throw on him the burden of showing, and he having full opportunity therefor, fails to show, that he has not been instrumental in concealing or keeping away the witnesses, and ground having been thus laid, evidence is admissible against him of that which the witnesses testified at a previous trial on the same issue between the United States and the prisoner.[2]

104. The VII Amendment declares, that, "in suits at common law, where the value in controversy shall exceed twenty dollars, the right of trial by jury shall be preserved."[3]  This amendment does not affect equity causes in the federal courts, for the determination by a court of equity, according to its own course and practice of issues of fact, does not impair the right of trial by jury, because that right does not extend to causes of equitable jurisdiction.[4]  Nor does this amendment affect proceedings upon claims against the United States heard in the Court of Claims without the intervention of a jury, for the government being suable only by its own consent, may declare in what court it will be sued, and may prescribe the forms of pleading and rules of practice in that court, and such claims so prosecuted are not suits at common law.[5]  Nor does this amend-

[1] This amendment is a restraint upon the judicial action of the United States, and not of the states: Twitchell v. The Commonwealth, 7 Wall. 321.

[2] Reynolds v. United States, 98 U. S. 145.

[3] This amendment is a restraint upon the exercise of powers by the United States, but not by the states: Edwards v. Elliott, 21 Wall. 532; Walker v. Sauvinet, 92 U S. 90; Pearson v. Yewdall, 95 id. 294.

[4] Barton v. Barbour, 104 U. S. 726; Parsons v. Bedford, 3 Pet. 433, 446.

[5] McElrath v. United States, 102 U. S. 426.

ment relieve a party from the consequences of his antecedent voluntary relinquishment of a right of trial by jury in any particular cause, as, for instance, in the case of a banking corporation whose state charter stipulates that the bank should have a summary remedy by execution without jury trial for the collection of notes indorsed to it, and in express terms made negotiable at the bank.[1] The VII Amendment also declares that "no fact tried by a jury shall be otherwise re-examined in any court of the United States than according to the rules of the common law." As Story, J., said in Parsons *v.* Bedford,[2] "this is a prohibition to the courts of the United States to re-examine any facts tried by a jury in any other manner. The only modes known to the common law to re-examine such facts, are the granting of a new trial by the court where the issue was tried, or to which the record was properly returnable; or the award of a *venire facias de novo* by an appellate court, for some error of law which intervened in the proceedings." The amendment obviously governs both the original and appellate jurisdiction of the courts of the United States, and forbids the reversal of a verdict of a jury save as above indicated. Congress cannot by statute provide for the removal from a state court into a federal court of causes tried by jury in the state court, and for a retrial in the federal court of the facts and law in such action in the same manner as if the same had been originally commenced in the federal court.[3]

105. The federal supremacy prevents the states from regulating the process or practice of the courts of the United States at law,[4] or in equity,[5] or in causes

---

[1] Bank of Columbia *v.* Okely, 4 Wheat. 235.
[2] 3 Pet. 447.　　　　　　　[3] The Justices *v.* Murray, 9 Wall. 274.
[4] Wayman *v.* Southard, 10 Wheat. 1; Bank of U. S. *v.* Halstead, *ibid.* 51.
[5] Borer *v.* Chapman, 119 U. S. 587.

of criminal cognizance,[1] but "the laws of the several states, except when the Constitution, treaties, or statutes of the United States otherwise require or provide, shall be regarded as rules of decision in trials at common law, in the courts of the United States in cases where they apply."[2] The federal supremacy also forbids the courts of the states to refuse obedience to a mandate of the Supreme Court of the United States, reversing a judgment of a state court in a cause which is of federal cognizance;[3] and it prevents a state legislature from annulling by statute the judgment of a court of the United States in a cause which is within the jurisdiction of the court.[4] While a state cannot confer jurisdiction on a court of the United States, yet a state may by its legislation create legal and equitable rights which can be enforced in a court of the United States in a cause whereof that court has acquired jurisdiction by reason of either the citizenship of the parties or the federal character of the subject-matter of litigation; thus, pilotage being a subject of admiralty and, therefore, of federal jurisdiction, a pilot may sue in a court of the United States to recover pilotage under a state statute;[5] and the right under a state statute to recover damages for a death caused by negligence is enforcible in a cause between proper parties in a court of the United States;[6] and liens created by state laws in favour of material men for supplies furnished to vessels in

---

[1] U. S. *v.* Reid, 12 How. 361.
[2] Act of 24 September, 1789, c. 20, Sec. 34, 1 Stat. 92; Rev. Stat. Sec. 721. See Field's Federal Courts, p. 430.
[3] Martin *v.* Hunter's Lessee, 1 Wheat. 304. [4] U. S. *v.* Peters, 5 Cr. 115.

The general principle that the *lex fori* governs the limitation of actions applies to actions brought originally in the courts of the United States, and also to actions removed thereto from the courts of the states: Arnson *v.* Murphy, 109 U. S. 238; Mitchell *v.* Clark, 110 *id.* 633.

[5] Hobart *v.* Drogan, 10 Pet. 120; *Ex parte* McNeil, 13 Wall. 236.
[6] C. & N. W. Ry. *v.* Whitton, 13 Wall. 270.

their home ports or for materials furnished to ships in process of construction may be enforced in the courts of the United States.[1]

106. A court of the United States cannot enjoin proceedings in a court of a state,[2] save in aid of bankruptcy proceedings pending in a court of the United States, or as a means of preventing the enforcement in a court of a state of a judgment entered therein after a cause has been properly removed to a court of the United States;[3] nor can the courts of the United States issue writs of *mandamus* to courts of the states, by way of original proceedings where such writs are not ancillary to a jurisdiction which has already attached in the federal court,[4] but where the jurisdiction of the federal court has previously attached to a cause, that court may, as process of execution to enforce its judgment, issue a writ of *mandamus*,[5] and enforce obedience thereto, notwithstanding a court of the state may have, by injunction, forbidden the parties defendant to obey the *mandamus*.[6]

Chattels taken in execution under the judgment of a court of a state and delivered to a claimant upon his giving bond therefor cannot be seized by a marshal under the process of a court of the United States.[7] A

---

[1] Edward's v. Elliott, 21 Wall. 532; The Lottawanna. *ibid.* 588. Where the jurisdiction of a court of the United States has attached, a party to the suit, who refuses or neglects to obey its process, will be liable in damages to any party injured by such neglect or refusal (Amy v. Supervisors, 11 Wall. 136), and a trustee of property to which the jurisdiction of a court of the United States has attached will be held personally responsible if, without adequate resistance, he surrender such property to the process of a court of a state. Chittenden v. Brewster, 2 Wall. 191.

[2] Diggs v. Walcot, 4 Cr. 179; Watson v. Jones, 13 Wall. 679; Haines v. Carpenter, 91 U. S. 254; Dial v. Reynolds, 96 *id.* 340; Leroux v. Hudson, 1 9 *id.* 468.

[3] French v. Hay, 22 Wall. 250; Dietzsch v. Huidekoper, 103 U. S. 494.

[4] Bath County v. Amy, 13 Wall. 244.

[5] Riggs v. Johnson County, 6 Wall. 166; Amy v. Supervisors, 11 *id.* 136.

[6] The Mayor v. Lord, 9 Wall. 409; The Supervisors v Durant, *ibid.* 415.

[7] Hogan v. Lucas, 10 Pet. 400.

court of the United States exercising jurisdiction in bankruptcy cannot divest liens upon the bankrupt's property created by the judgments, either interlocutory or final, of the courts of the states;[1] the assets of the estate of an insolvent decedent in process of judicial administration under the order of a Probate Court of a state are not subject to levy under an execution issued by a court of the United States;[2] and the trustee appointed by a court of a state under a state statute to liquidate a corporation whose charter has been forfeited cannot be sued in a court of the United States by creditors of the corporation to compel his allowance of a claim against the corporation.[3]

107. As Catron, J., said in the judgment in the case of The Bank of Alabama v. Dalton,[4] "in administering justice . . . the states of this Union act independently of each other, and their courts are governed by the laws and municipal regulations of that state, where a remedy is sought, unless they are controlled by the Constitution of the United States, or by laws enacted under its authority." The most important of the restraints imposed by the Constitution upon the exercise of judicial jurisdiction by the states result from the grant, in the III Article of the Constitution, of judicial power to the United States over certain subjects of jurisdiction, and from the power of Congress to render that jurisdiction exclusive. Nevertheless, as the Constitution, laws, and treaties of the United States are "the supreme law of the land," the states, wherever Congress has not, by legislation within the limits of its constitutional powers, excepted any subject from

[1] Peck v. Jenness, 7 How. 612.
[2] Williams v. Benedict, 8 How. 107.
[3] Peale v. Phipps, 14 How. 368. See, also, Vaughan v. Northrop, 15 Pet. 1; Wiswall v. Sampson, 14 How. 52; cf. Erwin v. Lowry, 7 How. 181.
[4] 9 How. 527.

the jurisdiction of their courts, may exercise jurisdiction therein, and, in such cases, rights arising under the Constitution, laws, and treaties of the United States may be administered, subject, of course, to the appellate jurisdiction of the Supreme Court of the United States, and to the right of removal to the federal courts of the first instance; thus, a tribunal constituted by a state may enforce the militia laws of the United States;[1] and an assignee in bankruptcy may sue in a court of a state to recover the assets of the bankrupt.[2] But where Congress has expressed its will that the courts of the United States shall exercise exclusive jurisdiction over any subject-matter, which is included within the constitutional grant of judicial power to the United States, the courts of the states cannot directly exercise judicial jurisdiction over such subject-matter. Upon this principle, a court of a state cannot take cognizance of an act declared to be criminal by the statutes of the United States, unless that act be also an offense against the laws of the state.[3] A state court cannot take jurisdiction of a cause of admiralty cognizance,[4] such as a proceeding *in rem* founded upon a contract for the transportation of passengers by sea, or upon a collision,[5] or upon a

[1] Houston v. Moore, 5 Wheat. 1.
[2] Claflin v. Houseman, 93 U. S. 130; Teal v. Felton, 12 How. 284, referred to by Bradley, J., 93 U. S. 142, was an action of trover for a newspaper which a postmaster wrongfully refused to deliver. See also Eyster v. Gaff, 91 U. S. 521; *Ex parte* Christie, 3 How. 318, 319; Nugent v. Bond, *ibid.* 426.
[3] There is a concurrent jurisdiction over crimes, when the criminal act is an offense against the laws of both the United States and of the states; thus, a state may punish the offense of uttering or passing false coin as a fraud practiced on its citizens: Fox v. Ohio, 5 How. 432, and the United States may punish the same act as a crime against it: United States v. Marigold, 9 How. 560. In the same way, a state might have, before the adoption of the XIII Amendment, punished the harbouring of a fugitive slave: Moore v. Illinois, 14 How. 13, while the same act could have been punished in the courts of the United States as an offense against the fugitive slave legislation of Congress.
[4] The Moses Taylor, 4 Wall. 411.
[5] The Hine v. Trevor, 4 Wall. 555.

contract of affreightment,[1] but a state court may take jurisdiction of an action *in personam* for mariners' wages,[2] or of a proceeding *in rem* founded upon a lien given by a state statute for materials supplied in building a ship,[3] for such actions are not necessarily of admiralty cognizance. A state court cannot take jurisdiction of an action at law against a foreign consul.[4] A state court cannot take jurisdiction in patent causes, nor determine the validity of a patent, or a question of infringement,[5] but a state court may incidentally pass upon the validity of a patent, as, for instance, where it is questioned in an action for the price of the patent.[6] The distinction running through the cases is, that, where Congress has excepted from the action of the courts of the states any subject-matter of federal jurisdiction as designated in the Constitution, the courts of the states thenceforth cannot directly, but may indirectly and collaterally, act upon such subject-matter. The courts of the states cannot issue an injunction before final decree, nor an attachment on *mesne* process, against a national bank.[7] The federal supremacy forbids a court of a state to issue a *mandamus* to an officer of the United States,[8] or, by its process, to take in execution goods imported into a port of the United States, but not yet entered at the Custom-House for payment of duties to the United States,[9] or goods, which, having been seized for violation of the revenue laws of the United States, are in the custody of a marshal of the United States.[10] Nor can a court of a state

[1] The Belfast, 7 Wall. 624.
[2] Leon v. Galceran, 11 Wall. 185.
[3] Edwards v. Elliott, 21 Wall. 532.
[4] Davis v. Packard, 7 Pet. 276.
[5] Rev. Stat., Sec. 711. Per Bradley, J., in Claflin v. Houseman, 93 U. S. 140.
[6] See the judgment of Gray, J., in Nash v. Lull, 102 Mass. 60.
[7] Rev. Stat. 5242; Pacific National Bank v. Mixter, 124 U. S. 721.
[8] McClurg v. Silliman, 6 Wheat. 598.
[9] Harris v. Dennie, 3 Pet. 292.
[10] Slocum v. Mayberry, 2 Wheat. 1.

take jurisdiction of a suit to determine whether or not property has been rightfully forfeited under the laws of the United States.[1] Nor can a court of a state by injunction in equity restrain the execution of a judgment of a court of the United States;[2] nor, under a state insolvent law, discharge a defendant held in custody under a *capias ad satisfaciendum* issued by a court of the United States;[3] nor replevy property taken in execution under a judgment of a court of the United States;[4] nor order the release, after a hearing on *habeas corpus,* of a prisoner held in custody by an officer of the United States under a warrant of commitment from a commissioner of a Circuit Court of the United States upon a charge of the commission of an offense against the laws of the United States, or of a prisoner held in custody by the United States after a trial and conviction in a court of the United States of an offense against the laws of the United States;[5] nor release upon *habeas corpus* an enlisted soldier in the army of the United States, detained in custody under the order of his commanding officer.[6] Nor can an attachment of a debt by the process of a state court, after the commencement of a suit upon that debt in a court of the United States bar the plaintiff's recovery in that suit,[7] nor can the pendency of state insolvent proceedings to set up as a bar to suits in the courts of the United

---

[1] Galston v. Hoyt, 3 Wheat. 246.   [2] McKim v. Voorhies, 7 Cr. 279.
[3] Duncan v. Darst, 1 How. 301.
[4] Freeman v. Howe, 24 How. 450; Covell v. Heyman, 111 U. S. 176.
[5] Ableman v. Booth, 21 How. 506.
[6] Tarble's Case, 13 Wall. 397. A state court may, nevertheless, by process of *habeas corpus,* inquire into the legality of the detention of a person, who, having been arrested as a fugitive from the justice of another state, is detained in custody by an agent of that other state under a warrant issued by the governor of the state within whose territory the alleged fugitive has come; Robb v. Connolly, 111 U. S. 624.
[7] Wallace v. McConnell, 13 Pet. 136.

States brought by parties who are constitutionally entitled to sue therein.[1]

108. In the cases of persons who, or of property which, may be subject to the jurisdiction of the courts of the United States, and also to that of the courts of the states, that jurisdiction, which first actually attaches either to the person or the property, will retain control and cannot be divested by process issued from the other jurisdiction.[2] An officer who, in executing the process issued by a court in a cause within its jurisdiction, seizes property which that process specifically designates, is not liable to action therefor in a court of another jurisdiction; but an officer who, under a judgment *in personam*, seizes property not specifically designated in the process is liable, and may be sued therefor in a court of another jurisdiction,[3] and the party injured by such a

[1] Suydam *v.* Broadnax, 14 Pet. 67; Hyde *v.* Stone, 20 How. 170; Green *v.* Creighton, 23 *id.* 90.

[2] Smith *v.* McIver, 9 Wheat. 532; Taylor *v.* Carryl, 20 How. 583; Pulliam *v* Osborne, 17 *id.* 471; Herdritter *v.* Elizabeth Oil Cloth Co, 112 U. S. 294; Slocum *v.* Mayberry, 2 Wheat. .; Freeman *v* Howe, 24 How. 450; Covell *v.* Heyman 111 U. S. 176; Wallace *v.* McConnell, 13 Pet. 136; Hagan *v.* Lucas, 10 Pet 400; Peck *v.* Jenness, 7 How. 612; Williams *v* Benedict, 8 How. 107; Peale *v* Phipps, 14 *id.* 368; Wiswall *v.* Sampson, *ibid.* 52; Erwin *v.* Lowry, 7 *id.* 81. In Covell *v.* Heyman, 111 U. S. 182, Matthews, J., said. "the forbearance which courts of co-ordinate jurisdiction, administered under a single system, exercise toward each other, whereby conflicts are avoided, by avoiding interference with the process of each other, is a principle of comity, with, perhaps, no higher sanction than the utility which comes from concord; but between state courts and those of the United States it is something more. It is a principle of right and of law, and, therefore of necessity. It leaves nothing to discretion or mere convenience. These courts do not belong to the same system, so far as their jurisdiction is concurrent; and although they coexist in the same space, they are independent, and have no common superior. They exercise jurisdiction, it is true, within the same territory, but not in the same plane; and when one takes into its jurisdiction a specific thing, that *res* is as much withdrawn from the judicial power of the other as if it had been carried physically into a different territorial sovereignty. To attempt to seize it by a foreign process is futile and void. The regulation of process, and the decision of questions relating to it, are part of the jurisdiction of the court from which it issues."

[3] Slocum *v.* Mayberry, 2 Wheat. 1; Day *v.* Gallup, 2 Wall. 97; Buck *v.* Colbath, 3 *id.* 334.

wrongful act by a marshal of the United States may sue on the marshal's official bond;[1] or, he may file a bill in the federal court to restrain or regulate its judgment.[2]

109. The exercise of judicial jurisdiction by the states is also restricted by that provision of the XIV Amendment which declares, "nor shall any state deprive any person of life, liberty, or property, without due process of law, nor deny to any person within its jurisdiction the equal protection of the laws." Field, J., in Pennoyer v. Neff[3] defined the words "due process of law" to mean "a course of legal proceedings according to those rules and principles which have been established in our systems of jurisprudence for the protection and enforcement of private rights;" and he added, "to give such proceedings any validity, there must be a tribunal competent by its constitution, that is, by the law of its creation, to pass upon the subject-matter of the suit; and, if that involves merely a determination of the personal liability of the defendant, he must be brought within its jurisdiction by service of process within the state, or his voluntary appearance."[4] Of course, as Field, J., concedes in his judgment, and as is well settled by other authority, a court may by a proceeding *in rem*, and without any service of personal process, determine the rights of an absent party to a specific *res*, which is within the territorial jurisdiction of the court; a court may so determine the *status* of one of its citizens as to conclude, within the territorial jurisdiction of the court, persons who have not been served with process; and an appellate court may regulate, in its discretion, notice of the removal to it of a cause depending in a court of the

---
[1] Lammon v. Feusier, 111 U.S. 17.
[2] Krippendorf v. Hyde, 110 U. S. 276.   [3] 95 U. S. 733.
[4] Boswell's Lessee v. Otis, 9 How. 336; Harris v. Hardeman, 14 How. 334.

first instance, and in which the parties have in the court below either voluntarily appeared, or been duly served with process.[1] It has been held, under the XIV Amendment, that the exercise of the right of eminent domain[2] and the procedure for the collection of assessments and taxes,[3] cannot be said to deprive of property without due process of law, if provision be made "for a mode of confirming and contesting the charge, thus imposed, in the ordinary courts of justice, with such notice to the person, or such proceedings in regard to the property, as is appropriate to the nature of the case."[4] It has also been held that a state statute, directing the abatement of, as a nuisance, the manufacture of liquors does not deprive of property without due process of law.[5] It has also been held, that a statute of a state, which, as construed by its courts, provides that the fact that a person called as a juror in the trial of a criminal cause is not to be disqualified because he has formed an opinion or impression based upon rumor or newspaper statements, if he shall upon oath state that his verdict will be based only on the evidence at the trial, does not deprive the prisoner tried by such jurors of life, liberty, or property without due process of law.[6] A state may also by statute make water rates a lien on land prior to the lien of a mortgage of date subsequent to the statute;[7] it may require a purchaser of land under a sale for non-payment of taxes to bring his possessory action within five

[1] Nations v. Johnson, 24 How. 195.
[2] Pearson v. Yewdall, 95 U. S. 294.
[3] Kelly v. Pittsburgh, 104 U. S. 78; McMillen v. Anderson, 96 U. S. 37; Hagar v. Reclamation District, 111 U. S. 701; Kentucky R. R. Tax Cases, 115 U. S. 321; Davidson v. New Orleans, 96 U. S. 97; Wurts v. Hoagland, 114 U. S. 606; Head v. A. Manufacturing Company, 113 U. S. 9.
[4] per Miller, J., in Davidson v. New Orleans, 96 U. S. 97.
[5] Mugler v. Kansas, 123 U. S. 623.
[6] Spies v. Illinois, 123 U. S. 131.
[7] Provident Institution v. Jersey City, 113 U. S. 506.

years after the sale;[1] and it may, without depriving a debtor of his property, repeal a statute of limitations after the debt is thereby barred.[2] Nor does the XIV Amendment restrain state action in the regulation of its judicial proceedings, provided there be no discrimination therein as against classes of citizens. A state may, therefore, without violating the amendment, restrain or take away the right of trial by jury in civil cases,[3] or it may permit the prosecution of crimes by information after examination and commitment by a magistrate.[4] So also a state may freely prescribe the jurisdiction of its several courts, both as to their territorial limits and the subject-matter, amount, and finality, of their respective judgments and decrees, and it may vest in one court final appellate jurisdiction over the courts of certain counties, and in another court the like jurisdiction over other counties.[5] Nor does the amendment interfere with a state's regulation of the remedies afforded to creditors of its municipalities for the collection of their debts.[6] Nevertheless, a state may not to the prejudice of a coloured man, who is put upon his trial for an offense against its laws, refuse to other coloured men the privilege of serving upon the jury, nor compel such a prisoner to submit to a trial by a jury from which citizens of African descent are by reason of their race excluded, for to do so is to deny to the prisoner the equal protection of the laws.[7] And a judge, in whom there is vested by a state statute a discretion in the selection of jurors, and who, in the exercise of that

---

[1] Barrett v. Holmes, 102 U. S. 651.  [2] Campbell v. Holt, 108 U. S. 477.
[3] Walker v. Sauvinet, 92 U. S. 90; Church v. Kelsey, 121 U. S. 282.
[4] Hurtado v. California, 110 U. S. 517.
[5] Missouri v. Lewis, 101 U. S. 22.
[6] Louisiana v. New Orleans, 109 U. S. 285; Commissioners of Tippecanoe v. Lucas, 93 id. 108.
[7] Strauder v. West Virginia, 100 U. S. 303; Bush v. Kentucky, 107 U. S. 110.

discretion, excludes coloured jurors, by reason of their colour, is liable to indictment in a federal court therefor.¹ But a prisoner cannot insist upon having a jury composed, either in part or in whole, of his own race, for all that he can rightfully demand is a jury from which men of his race are not excluded because of their colour.² Nevertheless, the amendment being directed against state legislation and not against a judicial misconstruction of such legislation by the courts of the state, when a state legislature has enacted laws for the government of its courts, which, if followed, will furnish all parties with the needed protection to life, liberty, and property, it has performed its constitutional duty, and if one of its courts, acting within its jurisdiction, makes an erroneous decision, the state cannot be deemed guilty of violating the amendment; thus, where a state statute required of all guardians the giving of a bond before selling their wards' real estate, the fact that a court permitted a sale to be made without requiring the giving of such a bond is not a violation of the Amendment.³

110. The judicial action of the states is also restrained by Section 1 of Article IV of the Constitution, which declares that, "full faith and credit shall be given, in each state, to the public acts, records, and judicial proceedings of every other state. And the Congress may, by general laws, prescribe the manner in which such acts, records, and proceedings shall be proved, and the effect thereof." Under this constitutional grant of authority Congress has enacted,⁴ that "the acts of the legislature of any state or territory, or of any country subject to the jurisdiction of the United

---

¹ *Ex parte* Virginia, 100 U. S. 339.
² Virginia *v.* Rives, 100 U. S. 313; Bush *v.* Kentucky, 107 U. S. 110.
³ Arrowsmith *v.* Harmoning, 118 U. S. 194.
⁴ Act of 26 May, 1790, 1 Stat. 122; Section 905, Rev. Stat.

States, shall be authenticated by having the seals of such state, territory, or country affixed thereto. The records and judicial proceedings of the courts of any state or territory, or of any such country, shall be proved or admitted in any other court within the United States by the attestation of the clerk, and the seal of the court annexed, if there be a seal, together with a certificate of the Judge, Chief Justice, or presiding magistrate, that the said attestation is in due form. And the said records and judicial proceedings so authenticated, shall have such faith and credit given to them in every court within the United States as they have by law or usage in the courts of the state from which they are taken." Legislative acts of a state are, under the terms of the Act of 1790, authenticated by the seal of the state, and in the absence of contrary proof, the seal will be presumed to have been affixed by the officer having its custody and duly authorized to affix it to the record.[1] Such acts will "be given the same effect by the courts of another state that they have by law and usage" in the state of their enactment;[2] and, as the courts of every state and country have the exclusive power of construing its local statutes, their construction thereof will be followed in the courts of other countries and states.[3] It is essential to the enforcement in the courts of the states of the legislative acts[4] and records of judicial proceedings in the courts[5] of another state, that they be certified in strict compliance with the directions of the act of Congress. But a judgment of a state court, though certi-

[1] United States v. Amedy, 11 Wheat. 392.
[2] C. & A. R. R. v W. F. Co , 119 U. S. 615, 622.
[3] Elmendorf v. Taylor, 10 Wheat. 152; Smith v. Condry, 1 How. 28.
[4] United States v. Amedy, 11 Wheat. 392.
[5] Caperton v. Ballard, 14 Wall. 238; Ferguson v. Harwood, 7 Cr. 408; Owings v. Hull, 9 Pet. 607, 627.

fied in accordance with the act of Congress, does not operate *proprio vigore* in another state, and in order to give it the force of a judgment in that other state, suit must be brought upon it there, and the period of limitation as prescribed by the *lex fori* may be pleaded as against such a judgment.[1] When so certified and sued upon, such judgments must be given the same effect that is given to them in the jurisdiction in which they have been rendered. Therefore, to an action on a judgment so certified, *nil debet* cannot be pleaded;[2] nor can fraud be pleaded to an action on such a judgment.[3] When the record of a judgment falsely recites an appearance by counsel, it cannot be collaterally impeached, when sued upon in another state, for it might have been set aside by *audita querela*, in the jurisdiction wherein it was rendered.[4] But no greater effect can be given in a state court to a judgment of a court of another state than would be given to that judgment in the state where rendered. Therefore, a personal judgment which has been rendered in one state against several parties jointly, service of process having been made on some of them, or they having voluntarily appeared, and service having been made by publication as to the others, is not evidence outside of the state of any liability on the part of those not personally served.[5] Nor will a judgment rendered in one state against two joint debtors,

---

[1] McElmoyle *v.* Cohen, 13 Pet. 312; Bacon *v.* Howard, 20 How. 22; The Bank of Alabama *v.* Dalton, 9 How. 522.

[2] Armstrong *v.* Carson, 2 Dall. 303; Mills *v.* Duryee, 7 Cr. 481; Hampton *v.* McConnell, 3 Wheat. 234.

[3] Christmas *v.* Russell, 5 Wall. 290; Maxwell *v.* Stewart, 22 *id.* 77.

[4] Landes *v.* Brant, 10 How. 348, 371. A judgment conclusive in the state in which it has been rendered is conclusive in the courts of the United States. Christmas *v.* Russell, 5 Wall. 302; Cheever *v.* Wilson, 9 Wall. 108; Pennoyer *v.* Neff, 95 U. S. 714; Caldwell *v.* Carrington, 9 Pet. 86; C. & A. R. R. *v.* W. F. Co., 108 U. S. 18.

[5] Board of Public Works *v.* Columbia College, 17 Wall. 521.

only one of whom has been served with process, support an action in a court of another state against the party not served, nor avail as the foundation of a judgment against him.[1] A judgment recovered in one state against two joint defendants, one of whom has been duly summoned and the other has not, and which is valid and enforcible by the law of that state against the party served with process, will support an action against that party in another state.[2] It is an essential prerequisite to the enforcement in any court of a judgment, either *in personam* or *in rem*, rendered in any court, that the court rendering the judgment had by law jurisdiction of the subject-matter of the suit;[3] and, if the judgment was *in personam*, that the defendant either was served with process within the territorial jurisdiction of the court, or voluntarily appeared in the suit;[4] and, if the judgment was *in rem*, that the *res* was within the territorial jurisdiction of the court acting upon it, and was properly brought under its control;[5] for process issued by any court, and served personally on a defendant out of its territorial jurisdiction, and process published within that territorial jurisdiction, are equally unavailing in a proceeding to establish a personal liability on the part of the defend-

[1] D'Arcy v. Ketchum, 11 How. 165.
[2] Hanley v Donoghue, 116 U. S. 1; Renaud v. Abbott, *ibid.* 277.
[3] Thompson v. Whitman, 18 Wall. 457; Rose v. Himely, 4 Cr. 241, 269; Elliott v. Piersol, 1 Pet. 328, 340; Voorhees v. Bank of the U. S., 10 Pet. 449, 475; Wilcox v. Jackson, 13 Pet. 498, 511; Shriver's Lessee v. Lynn, 2 How. 43, 59; Lessee of Hickey v. Stewart, 3 How. 750, 762; Williamson v. Berry, 8 How. 495, 540; Glass v. Sloop Betsy, 3 Dall. 7; Thompson v. Whitman, 18 Wall. 457; Maxwell v. Stewart, 22 Wall. 77.
[4] Pennoyer v. Neff, 95 U. S. 714; St. Clair v. Cox, 106 U. S. 350; D'Arcy v. Ketchum, 11 How. 165; Mayhew v. Thatcher, 6 Wheat. 129; La Fayette Ins. Co. v. French, 18 How. 404; Harris v. Hardman, 14 How. 334 Bischoff v. Wethered, 9 Wall. 812; Board of Public Works v. Columbia College, 17 Wall. 521.
[5] Boswell v. Otis, 9 How. 336; Cooper v. Reynolds, 10 Wall. 308; Ennis v. Smith, 14 How. 400, 430.

ant, and while, where property is by seizure or some equivalent act brought within the control of a court, substituted service by publication is sufficient to inform a non-resident owner of the property of the object of the proceeding, such publication is not effectual to ground a personal liability upon.[1] But if a non-resident defendant has by attorney voluntarily appeared in the action, and judgment has been rendered in his favour in the court of the first instance, he may, after the withdrawal of his attorney's appearance, be notified, by publication, of a writ of error or appeal, by means of which the cause is removed to an appellate tribunal, and a judgment of reversal in that tribunal will be binding on him as a judgment *in personam*, and as such enforcible against him in the court of another state.[2] And a judgment *in personam* may be rendered in a proceeding *in rem* against a defendant out of the jurisdiction, who has by his voluntary appearance made himself a party to the litigation, and such a judgment is enforcible by an action thereon in another state against that defendant.[3] Where a corporation chartered by one state is permitted by another state to transact business therein upon condition that service of process upon a resident agent of the corporation should be considered as service upon the corporation, a judgment rendered in the latter state against the corporation, and based upon such service of process upon the agent, must be received in the state chartering the corporation with the same faith and credit that is given to it in the state wherein it is rendered.[4] But a judgment

---

[1] Pennoyer *v.* Neff, 95 U. S. 714; Cooper *v.* Reynolds, 10 Wall. 308; Webster *v.* Reid, 11 How. 437; Phelps *v.* Holker, 1 Dall. 261; Freeman *v.* Alderson, 119 U. S. 185.
[2] Nations *v.* Johnson, 24 How. 195.
[3] Maxwell *v.* Stewart, 22 Wall. 77.
[4] Lafayette Ins. Co. *v.* French, 18 How. 404.

*in personam* rendered against a foreign corporation in a suit begun in a state court by an attachment of property, and, as incident thereto, a service of a copy of the writ and an inventory of the attached property on a resident agent, without appearance by the corporation, is not conclusive in another action to which the corporation is a party in a court of the United States.[1] The record of a judgment rendered in another state may be contradicted as to the facts necessary to give the court jurisdiction, and its recital of the existence of such facts is not conclusive, and want of jurisdiction may be shown either as to the subject-matter or as to the person, and, in proceedings in *rem*, as to the *res*. Therefore, in an action of trespass *de bonis*, etc., in a court of the United States against a county sheriff of New Jersey for taking the plaintiff's oyster boat, the defendant having pleaded in justification the record of a forfeiture of the boat under a New Jersey statute, authorizing a summary conviction on a hearing by two justices of the county in which the seizure was made, it was held, that the recital in the record of a seizure of the boat in the county in which the justices exercised jurisdiction was open to contradiction by evidence that the seizure was not made within the territorial limits of that county.[2] On the same principle, a recital in a record of a personal service of a summons upon a defendant, may be contradicted by proof that the defendant was not served.[3] Administrators in different jurisdictions of the personal estate of the same decedent are not privies in estate to the extent that a judgment in one jurisdiction against one administrator is enforcible in the other jurisdiction against the administrator therein.[4] An objection to the

[1] St. Clair *v.* Cox, 106 U. S. 350.
[2] Thompson *v.* Whitman, 18 Wall. 457.
[3] Knowles *v.* The G. & C. Co., 19 Wall. 58.
[4] Stacy *v.* Thrasher, 6 How. 44.

informality of the authentication of a record cannot be made by a party who has antecedently offered that identical record in another proceeding.[1] A state statute of limitations, providing that suits upon judgments rendered in other states, if not brought within two years shall be barred, is a bar to an action on such a judgment against one who only became a citizen of the state on the day on which suit was brought.[2] Wherever a state court refuses in a cause to give due effect to a judgment rendered in a court of the United States, or in a court of another state, having by law jurisdiction of the subject-matter of litigation, and having acquired by due service of process, or otherwise, jurisdiction of the person of the party against whom judgment has been rendered, the action of the state court in so refusing is subject to review in the Supreme Court of the United States under the 25th Section of Judiciary Act of 1789, and the Act of 5 February, 1867.[3] The record of a court of the United States is sufficiently proved when certified by the clerk of the court under its seal.[4] And the judgments of the courts of the United States, when sued upon, or set up by way of defense in state courts, are, if rendered in a cause of which the court of the United States had jurisdiction both as to the subject-matter and the *res* or the person of the defendant, conclusive upon the parties and privies thereto, and enforcible in the state courts to the same extent as in courts of the United States.[5] Judgments rendered in courts of the United States in causes, jurisdiction of which was obtained by reason of the citizenship of the parties, and in which the law of

[1] Urtetiqui *v.* D'Arbel, 9 Pet. 692.
[2] Bank of the State of Alabama *v.* Dalton, 9 How. 522.
[3] 14 Stat. 385. Rev. Stat. Sec. 709.
[4] Turnbull *v.* Payson, 95 U. S. 418.
[5] Embry *v.* Palmer, 107 U. S. 3.

the state within which the court sat was administered, have only that validity and effect which is due to a judgment of a court of the state in such a cause,[1] and, therefore, a court of a state which refuses to give a greater effect to such a judgment of a court of the United States cannot be said to decide against a title or right claimed under an authority exercised under the United States.

[1] Dupasseur v. Rochercau, 21 Wall. 130.

# CHAPTER XI.

### RIGHTS OF PERSON AND OF PROPERTY.

111. Citizenship of the United States.
112. Citizenship of a state.
113. The right of suffrage.
114. The right of serving on juries.
115. Congressional regulation of the election of senators and representatives.
116. Personal and property rights.
117. The rights within a state of citizens of other states.
118. Foreign corporations.
119. The XIII Amendment.
120. The XIV Amendment.
121. The police power.

111. As Miller, J., pointed out in the judgment in the Slaughter House Cases,[1] the Constitution, as originally adopted, did not define citizenship of the United States, although it did, by Section 2 of Article IV, provide that "the citizens of each state shall be entitled to all privileges and immunities of citizens in the several states," and, by Section 2 of Article I, declare citizenship of the United States to be a necessary qualification for election as a representative in Congress. In view of that which the Constitution said, and of that which it left unsaid, upon this subject, it might well be concluded that citizenship of the United States was dependent upon and only incident to citizenship of a state, but the point was never judicially determined. The 1st Section of the XIV Amendment declares, that "all persons born or naturalized in the

[1] 16 Wall. 72.

United States, and subject to the jurisdiction thereof, are citizens of the United States and of the state wherein they reside." From and after the adoption of that amendment, therefore, the birth within the United States of a person subject to its jurisdiction, or the naturalization of an alien, makes the person so born, or naturalized, a citizen of the United States;[1] and that right of citizenship is entitled to protection under such laws as Congress may enact in execution of the powers conferred by the XIV and XV Amendments. Section 8 of Article I of the Constitution authorizes Congress "to establish an uniform rule of naturalization." It is, therefore, beyond the power of any state to prescribe the conditions of naturalization, or to admit to citizenship any alien other than those whom the acts of Congress permit to be naturalized;[2] nevertheless aliens may be naturalized by proceedings in courts of the states in conformity with the acts of Congress.[3]

112. In Dred Scott v. Sandford,[4] the court determined that a free negro could not be a citizen of a state, but, in his dissenting judgment, Curtis, J., showed that it was an historical fact, that in five of the thirteen original states negroes were not only recognized as citizens, but also admitted to the exercise of the right of suffrage, and that many acts of Congress had, by necessary implication, recognized negroes as citizens; and the weight of authority supports the position, that each state may, so far as the Constitution of the United States does not restrain it, determine the *status*, and consequently the citizenship, of the persons

---

[1] The Slaughter House Cases, 16 Wall. 73; United States v. Cruikshank, 92 U. S. 548.
[2] Chirac v. Chirac, 2 Wheat. 269; Dred Scott v. Sandford, 19 How. 405.
[3] Collet v. Collet, 2 Dall. 294.   [4] 19 How. 393.

domiciled within its territory.¹ By the terms of the XIV Amendment, "all persons born or naturalized in the United States, and subject to the jurisdiction thereof, are citizens of the United States and of the state wherein they reside." Therefore birth, or naturalization, in the United States, followed by residence within the territory of any state, makes the person so born, or naturalized, and so residing, a citizen of that state.

113. All citizens are not necessarily entitled to the exercise of the right of suffrage, for the term "citizen," in the constitutional sense of the term, means one who owes the duty of allegiance and is entitled to the correlative right of protection, and it, therefore, includes persons, who, by reason of sex, or age, may not be qualified to vote. The right of suffrage is a subject of state regulation, and not a privilege, or immunity, of citizenship protected by the Constitution of the United States. A state may, therefore, without contravening any constitutional provision, deny the suffrage to women,² but by force of the XV Amendment a state may not, in its limitations on the exercise of the right of suffrage, discriminate against citizens of the United States on account of their "race, colour, or previous condition of servitude." A state, therefore, cannot limit the right of suffrage to the white race.³ Nevertheless, the power of Congress to legislate for the protection of the rights conferred by that amendment being limited by the terms of the amendment, Congress cannot by statute provide for the punishment of state election officers for wrongfully refusing to receive the vote of a qualified voter at an election, when that refusal is not based upon

---

[1] Strader v. Graham, 10 How. 93; Holmes v. Jennison, 14 Pet. 540; Groves v. Slaughter, 15 *id.* 449; Prigg v. Pennsylvania, 16 *id.* 539.

[2] Minor v. Happersett, 21 Wall. 162.   [3] *Ex parte* Yarbrough, 110 U. S. 665.

a discrimination against the voter on account of his race, colour, or previous condition of servitude;[1] nor can a conviction in a court of the United States be sustained under an indictment which charges the defendant in general terms with an intent to hinder and prevent citizens of the United States, of African descent, therein named, in the free exercise and enjoyment of the rights, privileges, immunities, and protection, granted and secured to them as citizens of the United States and of a state, without specifying any particular right, the enjoyment of which the conspirators intended to hinder or prevent.[2]

114. The right of serving as a juror being incident to citizenship, a state cannot so regulate the selection of jurors in its courts as to prevent citizens of African descent from serving as jurors.[3]

115. Section 4 of Article I of the Constitution declares that, "the times, places, and manner of holding elections for senators and representatives shall be prescribed in each state by the legislature thereof; but the Congress may, at any time, by law, make or alter such regulations, except as to the places of choosing senators." Under this clause of the Constitution, Congress without question provided for the election of its members by separate districts, composed of contiguous territory, and required the election in every district throughout the United States to be held on the Tuesday after the first Monday of November in every second year. In other respects, however, the exercise of power by Congress on this subject has been contested in the courts. In the several cases it has been held, that Congress, having a supervisory control over the election of its members,

[1] U. S. v. Reese, 92 U. S. 214.  [2] U. S. v. Cruikshank, 92 U. S 542.
[3] XV Amendment, Neal v. Delaware, 103 U. S. 307 ; Strauder v. West Virginia, 100 U. S. 303 ; Virginia v. Rives, ibid. 315 ; Ex parte Virginia, ibid. 339.

and being authorized to make regulations of its own, or to alter regulations made by any state, can by statute impose duties on state officers of election, punish the non-performance by such officers of their duties, whether imposed by laws of the state or by acts of Congress, and provide for the appointment of officers of the United States to execute the regulations as made by Congress or by the states.[1] It has also been held that Congress can, for the protection of the voters at congressional elections, punish acts of violence or intimidation, done in furtherance of a conspiracy to prevent a voter from exercising the franchise at such elections.[2]

116. The states retain full control over the personal and property rights of their citizens and of residents within their territory, subject to the restraints imposed by the Constitution.[3] The states retain the power of regulating the tenure of real property within their respective limits, including the mode of its acquisition and transfer, the rules of its descent, and the extent to which a testamentary disposition may be made of such land by its owner, and a state may forbid the United States, by reason of its not being a corporation created by the laws of that state, to take by devise lands within

[1] *Ex parte* Seibold, 100 U S. 371; *Ex parte* Clarke, 100 U. S. 399.
[2] *Ex parte* Yarbrough, 110 U. S. 651.
[3] As Waite, C. J., said in Spies *v.* Illinois, 123 U. S. 166, "that the first ten articles of amendments were not intended to limit the powers of the state governments in respect to their own people, but to operate on the national government alone, was decided more than half a century ago, and that decision has been steadily adhered to since: Barron *v.* Baltimore, 7 Pet. 243, 247; Livingston *v.* Moore, *ibid.* 469, 552; Fox *v.* Ohio, 5 How. 410, 434; Smith *v.* Maryland, 18 *id.* 71, 76; Withers *v.* Buckley, 20 *id.* 84, 91; Pervear *v.* The Commonwealth, 5 Wall. 475, 479; Twitchell *v.* The Commonwealth, 7 *id.* 321, 325; The Justices *v.* Murray, 9 *id* 274, 278; Edwards *v.* Elliott, 21 *id.* 532. 557; Walker *v.* Sauvinet, 92 U. S. 90; United States *v.* Cruikshank, *ibid.* 542, 552; Pearson *v.* Yewdall, 95 *id.* 294, 296; Davidson *v.* New Orleans, 96 *id.* 97, 101; Kelly *v.* Pittsburg, 104 *id.* 78; Presser *v.* Illinois, 116 *id.* 252, 265."

the state.¹ The states may legislate specially for the sale or investment of the estates of infants and other persons not *sui juris*.² The shores of navigable waters, and the soil under those waters, were not granted by the Constitution to the United States, but were reserved to the riparian states respectively, and new states have the same rights, sovereignty, and jurisdiction over this subject as the original states.³ The United States having no proprietary titles to lands on the shore of a state, under navigable waters and below high-water mark, can grant no valid title thereto.⁴ A state may, therefore, prohibit, or license under regulation, the taking of oysters and fish in the navigable waters within its limits.⁵ The states may determine what classes of persons shall come and remain within their territory,⁶ provided, of course, that they do not thereby impair the rights of intercourse and traffic secured by the Constitution to citizens of other states.⁷ The Constitution makes no provision for the protection of the citizens of the several states in their religious liberty, and imposes no restraints on the states in that respect. Therefore, a judgment of a state court imposing a fine upon a clergyman for violation of a municipal ordinance regulating the place and manner of conducting funeral services, is not subject to review in the Supreme Court of the United States.⁸

117. Section 2 of Article IV of the Constitution de-

---

[1] U. S. *v.* Fox, 94 U. S. 315. [2] Hoyt *v.* Sprague, 103 U. S. 613.
[3] Pollard *v.* Hagan, 3 How. 212; Webber *v.* Harbour Commissioners, 18 Wall. 57.
[4] Pollard *v.* Hagan, 3 How. 212; Goodtittle *v.* Kibbe, 9 *id.* 471; Doe *v.* Beebe, 13 *id.* 25.
[5] Smith *v.* Maryland, 18 How. 71; McCready *v.* Virginia, 94 U. S. 391.
[6] Holmes *v.* Jennison, 14 Pet. 540; Groves *v.* Slaughter, 15 *id.* 449; Prigg *v.* Pennsylvania, 16 *id.* 539.
[7] *Infra*, Sec. 117.
[8] Permoli *v.* First Municipality, 3 How. 589.

clares that "the citizens of each state shall be entitled to all privileges and immunities of citizens in the several states." As Miller, J., said, in the Slaughter House Cases,[1] the "sole purpose" of this constitutional provision "was to declare to the several states, that whatever those rights, as you grant or establish them to your own citizens, or as you limit, or qualify, or impose restrictions on their exercise, the same, neither more nor less, shall be the measure of the rights of citizens of other states within your jurisdiction." Washington, J., said, in Corfield v. Coryell,[2] the privileges and immunities in question are those "which are fundamental, which belong of right to all citizens of all free governments, and which have at all times been enjoyed by citizens of the several states which compose this Union, from the time of their becoming free, independent, and sovereign," including "protection by the government, with the right to acquire and possess property of every kind, and to pursue and obtain happiness and safety, subject, nevertheless, to such restraints as the government may prescribe for the general good of the whole." In Paul v. Virginia,[3] Field, J., said, "the privileges and immunities secured to citizens of each state in the several states . . . are those privileges and immunities which are common to the citizens in the latter states under their Constitutions and laws by virtue of their being citizens. Special privileges enjoyed by citizens in their own states are not secured in other states by this provision. It was not intended by the provision to give to the laws of one state any operation in other states. They can have no such operation, except by the permission, express or implied, of those states. The special privileges which they confer must, therefore, be enjoyed at home, unless the assent of

[1] 16 Wall. 77.    [2] 4 Wash. C. C. 371.    [3] 8 Wall. 180.

other states to their enjoyment therein be given." It is clear that this provision guarantees the privileges and immunities of citizens of other states, and has no reference to action by a state in respect to its own citizens;[1] nor does this constitutional provision vest the citizens of one state with any interest in the common property of citizens of another state. Therefore, a statute of a state by which other than its own citizens are prohibited from planting or taking oysters from the soil which is covered by the tide-waters of that state, is not a violation of any privilege or immunity of citizens, for, subject to the paramount right of navigation, the regulation of which in relation to foreign and interstate commerce has been granted to Congress by the Constitution, each state owns the soil of all tide-waters within its jurisdiction, and may appropriate them to be used by its citizens as a common for cultivating and taking fish, etc., if navigation be not thereby obstructed.[2] Nor does this constitutional provision require a state to confer upon citizens of other states peculiar privileges granted to its own citizens; thus, the privilege of community of *acquets* or gains as between married persons in Louisiana, as regards lands in Louisiana acquired by a citizen of Mississippi, who, while living in that state has married a woman born in Louisiana, cannot be claimed as a constitutional right, for the wife by her marriage became a citizen of Mississippi.[3] On the same principle, a state may enact

---

[1] Bradwell v. State, 16 Wall. 130.    [2] McCready v. Virginia, 94 U. S. 391.

[3] Conner v. Elliott, 18 How. 593; Curtis, J., said, " we do not deem it needful to attempt to define the word 'privileges' in the clause of the Constitution. It is safer and more in accordance with the duty of a judicial tribunal, to leave its meaning to be determined in each case, upon a view of the particular rights asserted and denied therein, and especially is this true, when we are dealing with so broad a provision, involving matters not only of great delicacy and importance, but which are of such a character that any merely abstract definition could scarcely be correct; and a failure to make it so would

a statute of limitations, discriminating, as regards suits against non-resident defendants, against creditors, if citizens of other states, and in favour of creditors who are citizens of the state.[1] On the other hand a state cannot, without contravening this constitutional provision, so discriminate by taxation against either the natural products of, or the goods manufactured in, another state, as to hinder the citizens of that other state in their exercise of the rights of freely transporting and selling their goods manufactured or unmanufactured.[2] Nor can a state by taxation, or otherwise, restrict the exercise by the citizens of other states of their right of free transit from place to place within the United States, in order to approach the seat of government of the United States and the federal offices in the various states.[3]

118. Foreign corporations are, in the states of the United States, corporations created by any other state, or by a foreign government. A joint stock partnership organized under the laws of a foreign country, with a statutory recognition of the distinctive entity of the

certainly produce mischief." In McCready *v.* Virginia, 94 U. S. 375, Waite, C. J , after referring to the view thus expressed by Curtis. J., added "this clearly is the safer course to pursue." These *dicta*, of course, mean only that in the decision of a cause, the court ought to confine themselves to the case at bar and ought not to so generalize as to prejudge cases that have not yet arisen for determination, but they do not mean that the court. in order to arrive at a decision should reason empirically, and should avoid a clear statement of the general principles whose application must necessarily determine the particular case. If they did mean that, they would establish a "rule" which is not "salutary," and they would lay down a "course" which is not the "safer" one to pursue.

[1] Chemung Canal Bank *v.* Lowery, 93 U. S. 72; Strong, J., dissented.
[2] Ward *v.* Maryland, 12 Wall. 418; Welton *v.* Missouri, 91 U. S. 275; Webber *v.* Virginia, 103 *id.* 344; Guy *v.* Baltimore, 100 *id.* 434; Corson *v.* Maryland, 120 *id.* 502; Robbins *v.* Shelby County, *ibid.* 489; Walling *v.* Michigan, 116 *id.* 446; *sed cf.* Hinson *v.* Lott, 8 Wall. 148; Machine Co. *v.* Gage, 100 U. S. 676; Tiernan *v.* Rinker, 102 *id.* 123; Downham *v.* Alexandria Council, 10 Wall. 173.
[3] Crandall *v.* Nevada, 6 Wall. 35.

association and with powers of transfer of shares and succession of members, and the right to sue and be sued as an aggregation, is regarded in the United States as a foreign corporation.[1] A corporation is not, in its corporate capacity, a citizen, within the meaning of the Constitution.[2] It, therefore, cannot, when the jurisdiction of the court is dependent on the citizenship of the parties, sue "the citizen of a state, other than that by which it was chartered, unless the persons who compose the corporate body are all citizens of that state," but it may in such a case sue in its corporate name, averring that its members are citizens of the state incorporating it,[3] and, for purposes of jurisdiction, there is a conclusive presumption of law that the members of a corporation are citizens of the state creating it.[4] A foreign corporation is not a citizen within the meaning of Section 2 of Art. IV of the Constitution, which declares that "the citizens of each state shall be entitled to all privileges and immunities of citizens in the several states."[5] While corporations are, so far as regards the legislation of the state creating them, persons to be protected within the meaning of the XIV Amendment,[6] a corporation chartered by one state is not, within the meaning of that amendment, a "person" within the jurisdiction of a state, denying to it "the equal protection of the law" by the discriminating conditions on which it is permitted to do business in the state.[7] A

[1] Liverpool Ins. Co. v. Massachusetts, 10 Wall. 566.
[2] The Bank of the United States v. Deveaux, 5 Cr. 61; Paul v. Virginia, 8 Wall. 168.
[3] The Bank of the U. S. v. Deveaux, 5 Cr. 61.
[4] L. C. & C. R. R. v. Letson, 2 How. 497; Marshall v. B. &O. R. R., 16 id. 314; C. D Co. v. Shepherd, 20 id. 232; O. & M. R. R. v. Wheeler, 1 Bl. 286; Express Co. v. Kountze, 8 Wall. 342; R. R. v. Whitton, 13 Wall. 277.
[5] Paul v. Virginia, 8 Wall. 168.
[6] Santa Clara County v. S. P. R. R., 118 U. S. 394, 396.
[7] Phila. Fire Association v. New York, 119 U. S. 110.

corporation exists only in contemplation of law and by force of law, and it can have no legal existence beyond the bounds of the sovereignty creating it, unless it be, by comity, permitted to exist within the bounds of some other sovereignty.[1] A corporation, therefore, cannot exercise, in any other sovereignty within whose bounds it may be by comity permitted to act, any power which its charter does not authorize it to exercise,[2] nor can it exercise therein any power the exercise of which is not, either expressly or impliedly, permitted by the laws of the sovereignty within whose bounds it is exercised, saving rights, if any, secured to the corporation by the Constitution of the United States.[3] Of course, if there be no prohibitory legislation, it is not competent for an individual citizen, not personally interested in the corporation, to object to the doing of business within a state by a foreign corporation.[4] Unless the local law prohibit, a foreign corporation, if its charter so authorizes, may sue and be sued in the courts of a state,[5] make contracts,[6] acquire and hold real estate,[7] buy and sell bills of exchange,[8] and negotiate and issue policies of life and fire insurance.[9] Corporations, by

[1] The Bank of Augusta v. Earle, 13 Pet. 512; O. & M. R. R. v. Wheeler, 1 Bl. 286; Runyan v Coster. 14 Pet. 112.

[2] Runyan v. Coster, 14 Pet. 112, 130; Bank of Augusta v. Earle, 13 Pet. 519, 587.

[3] Runyan v. Coster, 14 Pet. 122, 130.

[4] Waite, C. J., said, in P. T. Co. v. W. U. T. Co., 96 U. S. 1, 13, "no citizen of a state can enjoin a foreign corporation from pursuing its business. Until the state acts in its sovereign capacity, individual citizens cannot complain. The state must determine for itself when the public good requires that its implied assent to the admission shall be withdrawn."

[5] Bank of Augusta v. Earle, 13 Pet. 519, 587; Cowles v. Mercer County, 7 Wall. 118.

[6] Bank of Augusta v. Earle, 13 Pet. 519, 591; Runyan v. Coster, 14 id. 122, 129.

[7] Runyan v. Coster, 14 Pet. 122.   [8] Bank of Augusta v. Earle, 13 Pet. 519.

[9] Paul v. Virginia, 8 Wall. 168; Ducat v. Chicago, 10 id. 410; Liverpool Ins. Co. v. Massachusetts, ibid. 566; Phila. Fire Association v. New York, 119 U. S. 110

doing business within the bounds of a sovereignty, other than that which has created them, do not become corporations of that other sovereignty, nor lose privileges, which are incident to their citizenship in the sovereignty which created them. Therefore, a railway corporation of Maryland does not, by becoming lessee of a railway in Virginia, forfeit its right to remove into the Circuit Court of the United States a suit brought against it in the courts of Virginia by a citizen of that state.[1] A state may discriminate in favour of its own corporations and against foreign corporations;[2] it may tax foreign corporations,[3] it may arbitrarily refuse to foreign corporations permission to do business within its territory, or it may give its consent on any conditions which "are not repugnant to the Constitution or laws of the United States, nor inconsistent with those rules of public law which secure the jurisdiction and authority of each state from encroachment by all others, or that principle of natural justice which forbids condemnation without opportunity for defense;"[4] it may impose on a foreign corporation a condition that service of process on the resident agent representative of the corporation on reasonable notice shall be considered a service upon the corporation,[5] and it may prohibit the transaction of the business of insurance within its bounds by a foreign corporation, or it may impose in its discretion conditions on the performance of such business, for contracts of insurance being covenants for indemnity and not articles of commerce, the negotiation and issue of policies of insur-

---

[1] B. & O. R. R. v. Koontz, 104 U. S. 5.
[2] Paul v. Virginia, 8 Wall. 168; Ducat v. Chicago, 10 id. 410.
[3] Paul v. Virginia, 8 Wall. 168; Ducat v. Chicago, 10 id. 410; Liverpool Ins. Co. v. Massachusetts, ibid. 566.
[4] L. Ins. Co. v. French, 18 How. 404, 407; St. Clair v. Cox, 106 U. S. 350, 356; Paul v. Virginia, 8 Wall. 168.
[5] L. Ins. Co. v. French, 18 How. 404; St. Clair v. Cox, 106 U. S. 350, 356.

ance are not transactions of foreign or interstate commerce.[1] But a state cannot rightfully impose as a condition the non-exercise by a corporation of its right of removing to the courts of the United States actions brought against it in the courts of the state.[2] If, however, a state prohibit a foreign corporation from doing business within its bounds, because the corporation will not forego the exercise of its right of removal of actions, the corporation cannot be protected by an injunction issued by the courts of the United States;[3] and a state statute, requiring foreign corporations as a condition of doing business in a state to stipulate that they will not remove into the courts of the United States, causes which under the laws of the United States they would be entitled to remove, is void, because it makes the right of doing business in the state dependent on the surrender by the foreign corporation of a right secured to it by the Constitution and laws of the United States;[4] and a servant of the corporation[5] cannot be convicted for doing business for a corporation which had not complied with the statute.[6] A substantial compliance by a foreign corporation with the condition on which it is permitted to do business within the bounds of another sovereignty is sufficient; thus, the law of Colorado requiring the filing of a certificate " designating the principal place where the business of such corporation shall

---

[1] Paul v. Virginia, 8 Wall. 168; Ducat v. Chicago, 10 id. 410; Liverpool Ins. Co. v. Massachusetts, ibid. 566; Phila. Fire Association v. New York, 119 U. S. 110.

[2] Ins. Co. v. Morse, 20 Wall. 445; Doyle v. C. Ins. Co., 94 U. S. 535.

[3] Doyle v. C. Ins. Co., 94 U. S. 535.

[4] Home Ins. Co. v. Morse, 20 Wall. 445, followed; Doyle v. C. Ins. Co., 94 U. S. 535, explained to decide only that a court of the United States could not enjoin the arbitrary revocation by officers of a state of a license previously granted to a foreign corporation.

[5] In this case an engine driver of a foreign railway corporation.

[6] Barron v. Burnside, 121 U. S. 186.

be carried on in this state, and an authorized agent or agents, residing at its principal place of business, upon whom process may be served," is sufficiently complied with by a certificate naming the town in which the business is to be carried on and stating "that the general manager of said corporation residing at the said principal place of business, is the agent upon whom process may be served," but not giving the name of the general manager.[1] A foreign corporation does not, by doing a single act of business in another state, as for instance, by contracting to sell machinery, come within the provisions of a statute of that state forbidding foreign corporations to "do any business" within the state.[2] Every one who deals with a foreign corporation impliedly subjects himself to the laws of the foreign government which chartered the corporation, so far as those laws affect the powers and obligations of the corporation or the validity, enforcement, or discharge of its contracts; thus, for instance, a holder in the United States of bonds, issued by a railway corporation of Canada, but negotiated, and stipulated to be paid, in the United States, is bound by the terms of a statutory scheme of arrangement enacted by the Parliament of Canada subsequently to the issue and sale of the bonds.[3] On the same principle, a holder in Louisiana of a policy of life insurance issued in that state by a Missouri corporation is chargeable with notice of the insurance laws of Missouri substituting the insurance commissioner of that state as the representative of insolvent insurance companies.[4]

119. The XIII Amendment declares that "neither slavery nor involuntary servitude except as a punish-

---

[1] Goodwin *v.* C. M. Ins. Co., 110 U. S. 1.
[2] Cooper Manfg. Co. *v.* Ferguson, 113 U. S. 727.
[3] C. S. Ry. *v.* Gebhard, 109 U. S. 527.   [4] Relfe *v.* Rundle, 103 U. S. 222.

ment for crime, whereof the party shall have been duly convicted, shall exist within the United States or any place subject to their jurisdiction," and that "Congress shall have power to enforce this article by appropriate legislation," and being intended to abolish involuntary slavery in all its forms, the word "servitude" is used therein with that signification, and is not to be construed to be a constructive prohibition of the creation of monopolies by a state, such as the exclusive right of providing a place for the slaughtering of cattle.[1] Nor does the amendment warrant congressional legislation declaring it to be a crime to conspire to deprive others of the equal protection of the laws.[2] The amendment invalidates an express warranty made in March, 1861, upon the sale of a slave warranting the chattel sold to be a slave for life and the warrantor's title to him to be clear and perfect. The warrantor's title having been divested under the operation of the amendment by *vis major*, he can recover on a note given for the price of the slave;[3] and a promissory note made before the adoption of the XIII Amendment, the consideration for which note was the price of a slave, is enforcible after the adoption of that amendment, slavery having been lawful by the *lex loci contractus* at the time the note was given.[4]

120. The XIV Amendment declares, that "no state shall make or enforce any law which shall abridge the privileges or immunities of citizens of the United States; nor shall any state deprive any person of life, liberty, or property, without due process of law, nor deny to any person within its jurisdiction the equal protection of the laws." The purposes of the XIV Amendment are

[1] Slaughter House Cases, 16 Wall. 36.
[2] United States *v.* Harris, 106 U. S. 629.
[3] Osborne *v.* Nicholson, 13 Wall. 654.
[4] White *v.* Hart, 13 Wall. 646; Boyce *v.* Tabb, 18 Wall. 546.

to define citizenship of the United States and of the states, to confer citizenship upon negroes, and to protect against hostile legislation of the several states those privileges and immunities of citizenship which are common to citizens of the United States,[1] and the amendment extends its protection to all natural persons within the territorial jurisdiction of the United States, without regard to difference of race, colour, nationality, or citizenship,[2] and, within any state, to corporations created by that state,[3] but not to corporations created by other states.[4] The rights of citizenship which are protected by the amendment being those which are common to the citizens of the United States, it does not confer the right of suffrage on women, for the right of suffrage is not necessarily a privilege or immunity of citizenship;[5] nor does it confer upon women the right to practice law in the state courts.[6] Nor does the amendment interfere with a state's exercise of the police power.[7] A state may, notwithstanding the amendment, prohibit a white and a negro from living together in adultery or fornication under more severe penalties than those to which the parties would be subjected were they of the same race and colour, for there is in such legislation no discrimination against any persons of a particular race or colour, but only a discrimination against the designated offense.[8] A purchaser of premises, under and subject to a legally defective mortgage, cannot complain of an act validating the mortgage on the ground that it deprives him of property without due process of law.[9]

[1] The Slaughter House Cases, 16 Wall. 86.
[2] Yick Wo v. Hopkins; Wo Lee v. Hopkins 118 U. S. 356.
[3] Santa Clara County v. S. P. R. R., 118 U. S. 394, 396.
[4] Philadelphia Fire Association v. New York, 119 U. S. 110.
[5] Minor v. Happerset, 21 Wall. 163.
[6] Bradwell v. The State, 16 Wall. 130.
[7] *Infra* Sec. 121. [8] Pace v. Alabama, 106 U. S. 583.
[9] Gross v. U. S. Mortgage Co., 108 U. S. 477.

The power of enforcement by appropriate legislation vested by the amendment in Congress, does not author-ize congressional legislation with regard to individuals, for the amendment restrains state and not individual action; it has, therefore, been held that Section 5519, Revised Statutes of the United States, declaring it to be a crime punishable by fine and imprisonment for any two or more persons to conspire to deprive any person of the equal protection of the law is unconstitutional.[1] It has also been held that the Civil Rights legislation of Congress[2] declaring that all persons within the jurisdiction of the United States shall be entitled to the full and equal enjoyment of inns, transportation facilities, etc., and subjecting to fine and imprisonment, and also to a liability to damages in an action at law, any person violating the provisions of the statute, is unauthorized by the amendment, the ground of decision being that the amendment is prohibitory of state legislation and action, and that, therefore, it is not in the power of Congress to directly legislate for the protection of individual rights against wrong doing by individuals.[3]

121. The police power is that function of government, by the exercise of which, all persons, who are subject to the sovereignty of the government exercising the power, are, for ends of public policy, restrained in their use or enjoyment of some right of person or of property. The police power may attain its end by absolutely prohibiting the exercise of a particular right, or by so regulating the exercise of that right as to permit its use under conditions, and, if the power exists, the extent to which it may be exercised in any case is limited only by the will of the government, or

[1] United States v. Harris, 106 U. S. 629.
[2] Act 1 March, 1875, 18 Stat. 335. [3] Civil Rights Cases, 109 U. S. 3.

the department thereof, in which the power may be vested, unless further restraint be imposed by the state Constitution. It is clear that the relation between the United States and the states forbids the United States to exercise within the territory of a state any portion of the police power. Thus in United States *v.* DeWitt,[1] the facts were, that Congress, by the statute of 2 March, 1867,[2] having made it a misdemeanour to offer for sale illuminating fluid inflammable at less than a specified temperature, and DeWitt, having been indicted and convicted under that statute in a court of the United States, it being proven that the offense had been committed at Detroit in the state of Michigan, and the cause having been certified on a division of opinion between the judges of the court of the first instance, the court held that the statute, as a police regulation relating exclusively to internal trade, could have no constitutional operation within state limits, and could only have effect in the territories and in the District of Columbia. There are many cases in which the exercise of the police power by the states has been sustained by the court. It has been held, that a state may require, under a penalty, the master of every passenger-carrying vessel, on arriving at any port within the state, to report to the state authorities the name, place of birth, last legal settlement, age, and occupation of every passenger;[3] that a state may prohibit or restrain the sale of wines, or liquors, imported from foreign countries, or brought within its territory from another state, or manufactured within the state;[4] that a state may regulate the

[1] 9 Wall. 41.          [2] 14 Stat. 484.
[3] New York *v.* Miln, 11 Pet. 102.
[4] The License Cases, 5 How 504; Bartemeyer *v.* Iowa. 18 Wall. 129; Beer Co. *v.* Massachusetts, 97 U. S. 25; Foster *v.* Kansas, 112 U. S. 201; Mugler *v.* Kansas, 123 U. S. 623.

exercise of rights of fishing in its navigable waters;[1] that a state may so regulate the operation of draw-bridges over navigable waters, that the traffic on the water and the traffic on the land shall be so conducted as to interfere as little as possible with each other;[2] that a state may grant, and control the exercise of, ferry licenses;[3] that a state may establish port regulations, prescribing where a vessel may lie in harbour, how long she may remain there, and what lights she must show at night;[4] that a state may regulate the rates charged by a private warehouse for the storage of grain, notwithstanding the fact that grain be stored therein in course of interstate transportation;[5] that a state may regulate the rates of fares and freight charged by railways in interstate transportation;[6] that a state may forbid, under a penalty, the driving of an engine on a railway within its limits, by one who has not been licensed by a state Board of Examiners, even though the engine-driver be engaged in moving passengers or freight between points within and points without the state;[7] that a state may require a railway to maintain fences and cattle guards, and, in default thereof, be liable for double damages;[8] that a state may authorize a municipality to forbid the use of steam-power by railways within its municipal limits;[9] that a state may

[1] Smith v. Maryland, 18 How. 71; McCready v. Virginia, 94 U. S. 391.
[2] Escanaba Co. v. Chicago, 107 U. S. 678.
[3] Fanning v. Gregoire, 16 How. 524, 534; Conway v. Taylor, 1 Bl. 603.
[4] The James Gray v. The John Frazer, 21 How. 184.
[5] Munn v. Illinois, 94 U. S. 113.
[6] Railway Co. v. Fuller, 17 Wall. 560; C., B. & Q. R. R. v. Iowa, 94 U. S. 155; Peik v. C. & N. W. Ry., ibid. 164; Sed cf. W. St. L. & P. Ry. v. Illinois, 118 id. 557, wherein Miller, J., said that in Munn v. Illinois, C., B. & Q. R. R. v. Iowa, and Peik v. C. & N. W. Ry., the question of the exclusive power of Congress to regulate interstate transportation charges, though presented, "received but little attention at the hands of the court."
[7] Smith v. Alabama, 124 U. S. 465.   [8] N. P. Ry. v. Humes, 115 U. S. 512.
[9] R. R. Co. v. Richmond, 96 U. S. 531.

forbid washing and ironing in public laundries within definite limits and between prescribed hours;[1] that a state may regulate the organizing, drilling, and parading of military bodies, provided that such legislation does not interfere with the privileges granted by the militia laws of the United States;[2] and that a state may grant a monopoly of the slaughtering of cattle.[3] It has also been held, that a contract cannot be made by a charter, binding the state to exempt the corporate franchises and property from the operation of the police power of the state.[4] It has also been held that a license granted on payment of a fee by the United States under the Internal Revenue Statutes to carry on the business of a wholesale liquor dealer in a state, does not authorize the licensee to carry on the business in violation of laws of the state prohibiting the traffic;[5] nor does it exempt the licensee from state taxation on the business so conducted;[6] and that letters patent granted for an invention do not confer upon the patentee the right of selling the patented article, within the territory of a state, in violation of a police regulation of the state.[7] On the other hand, reference may be made to the *dictum* of Marshall, C. J., in Brown *v.* Maryland,[8]

[1] Barbier *v.* Connelly, 113 U. S. 27; Soon Hing *v.* Crowley, *ibid.* 703. But a state may not, under pretence of regulating public laundries, vest in a municipality an authority arbitrarily and without the exercise of discretion, to grant or refuse permission to conduct a laundry: Yick Wo *v.* Hopkins; Wo Lee *v.* Hopkins, 118 U. S. 356.
[2] Presser *v.* Illinois, 116 U. S. 252.
[3] Slaughter House Cases, 16 Wall. 36; Butchers' Union *v.* C. C. Co , 111 U. S. 746.
[4] C., B. & Q. R. R. *v.* Iowa, 94 U. S. 155; Ruggles *v.* Illinois, 108 *id.* 526; M. H. & N. R. R. *v.* Hamersly, 104 *id.* 1; S. V. Water Co. *v.* Schottler, 110 *id.* 347; Beer Co. *v.* Massachusetts, 97 *id.* 25; Boyd *v.* Alabama 94 *id.* 645; Stone *v.* Mississippi, 100 *id.* 814; Fertilizing Co. *v.* Hyde Park, 97 *id.* 659; Butchers' Union *v.* Crescent City Co., 111 *id.* 746.
[5] McGuire *v.* The Commonwealth, 3 Wall. 387.
[6] Pervear *v.* The Commonwealth, 5 Wall. 475.
[7] Patterson *v.* Kentucky, 97 U. S. 501. [8] 12 Wheat. 447.

where he said, with regard to the right of the states to control the sale of imported goods, "sale is the object of importation, and is an essential ingredient of that intercourse of which importation constitutes a part. It is as essential an ingredient, as indispensable to the existence of the entire thing, then, as importation itself. It must be considered as a component part of the power to regulate commerce. Congress has a right, not only to authorize importation, but to authorize the importer to sell." There are later cases, which seem to fall within the line of that *dictum.* In Sinnot *v.* Davenport[1] and in Foster *v.* Davenport,[2] it was held that a state cannot require the owners of vessels licensed as coasters by the United States to file with the authorities of a state port a statement in writing of the name of the vessel, the names of its owners, their places of residence, and the amount of their respective interests in the vessel, as conditions prerequisite to the navigation of the waters of the state by such vessels. In Hall *v.* De Cuir[3] it was held that a state cannot by statute require "those engaged in the transportation of passengers among the states to give to all persons traveling, within that state, upon vessels employed in such business, equal rights and privileges in all parts of the vessel, without distinction of race and colour," nor subject "to an action for damages the owner of such a vessel, who excludes coloured passengers, on account of their colour, from the cabin set apart for the use of whites during the passage." In R. R. *v.* Husen,[4] it was held, that a state cannot prohibit the driving of certain species of cattle into the state during a specified portion of the year, nor permit the transportation of such cattle through the state at any other time of year

---

[1] 22 How. 227.
[2] 22 How. 244.
[3] 95 U. S. 485.
[4] 95 U. S. 465.

upon condition that the transporting agent "shall be responsible for all damages which may result from the disease called the Spanish or Texan fever, should the same occur along the line of transportation." In W. St. L. & P. Ry. *v.* Illinois,[1] it was held that a state cannot "regulate the charges by railroad companies within its limits for a transportation which constitutes a part of commerce among the states."[2] In Bowman *v.* C. & N. W. Ry.,[3] it was held, that a state cannot forbid a common carrier to bring into the state from another state intoxicating liquors, when the laws of the state forbid the sale of such liquors by unlicensed persons, nor does such state legislation relieve a common carrier from liability in damages to an unlicensed consignee, who has been injured by the refusal to transport such liquors. It is not easy to reconcile the cases. If the question were to be considered upon principle, and apart from authority, it might be said upon the one side, that the autonomy of the states is nothing more than a name if they are not to be permitted to exercise for the protection of the lives, health, and comfort of their citizens the ordinary police powers of government; and that the constitutional grant to the government of the United States of any power which in its exercise may affect the internal concerns of a state must be understood to have been granted on the implied condition that its exercise is to be subject to the police power of the state. In reply to this it might be said, upon the other side, that, as the power of police involves a power not only to control, but also to

---

[1] 118 U. S. 557. The facts in this case are stated in full, *supra*, pp. 128 *et seq.*

[2] This case was decided before the enactment of the Interstate Commerce Act.

[3] To be reported in 125 U. S., and in which cause judgment was entered on 19 March, 1888.

forbid, the constitutional powers granted to the government of the United States would be nugatory if the government of the state might veto, under the pretense of regulating. Perhaps the rule deducible from the cases is, that, while each state did not, by the adoption of the Constitution, surrender its ordinary local powers of self-government ·operative upon all persons and property which exist, or may come, within its territory, and which merge in the mass of persons and property subject to its jurisdiction, yet, nevertheless, the territorial limits of each state's jurisdiction, the grant to the government of the United States of powers conflicting with state sovereignty, and a due regard to the rights of citizens of other states, must be held to limit the exercise by each state of its otherwise illimitable powers of police, by the restriction that those powers are not to be so exercised as to interfere with the full execution of the powers granted to the United States. If this be the rule, persons or property brought within the territory of a state by the exercise of any federal power, must be exempted from obstructive state control until the federal power has ceased to operate, and the persons, or property, on which it acted, have merged in the mass of persons, or property, within the territory of the state. On the same principle, federal agencies are exempted from any such state regulation, as hinders the agent in the full performance of his, or its, duty to the government of the United States. Of course, Congress may so legislate with regard to any subject-matter of federal regulation, as it has heretofore legislated with regard to Quarantine and Pilotage,[1] that the states may be enabled to rightfully regulate that which would otherwise be exempt from their control.

[1] *Supra*, Sections 46 and 47.

# CHAPTER XII.

## THE FEDERAL SUPREMACY AND THE RESERVED RIGHTS OF THE STATES.

122. The constitutional declaration of the federal supremacy.
123. The supremacy of the Constitution.
124. The supremacy of the acts of Congress.
125. The supremacy of treaties.
126. The results of federal supremacy.
127. The constitutional reservation of the rights of the states.
128. The nature and extent of those reserved rights.
129. The importance of the preservation of the rights of the states.

122. Section 2 of Article VI of the Constitution declares, that "this Constitution, and the laws of the United States which shall be made in pursuance thereof, and all treaties made, or which shall be made under the authority of the United States, shall be the supreme law of the land; and the judges in every state shall be bound thereby, anything in the Constitution or laws of any state to the contrary notwithstanding." The supreme authority is, therefore, *first*, the Constitution; *second*, the laws of the United States made in pursuance thereof; and *third*, treaties duly made under the authority of the United States.

123. The Constitution is the Constitution as originally ratified, and as subsequently amended in the manner and under the restrictions contained in the V Article thereof, and as construed by the executive department of the government, so far as regards executive action, and by the legislative department of the government so far as regards legislative action, and by the judicial department of the government so far as

regards all rights and privileges which may properly become subjects of judicial determination. As the three departments of the government of the United States are co-ordinate in authority, and as they are alike bound to obey the Constitution as a paramount rule of action, it follows that each must determine for itself, so far as regards its action in the performance of the duties delegated to it by the Constitution, what the proper construction of that instrument is.

124. The supremacy of any statute of the United States is dependent upon its constitutionality,[1] but an act of Congress will not, on slight implication, or vague conjecture, be judicially determined to be in conflict with the Constitution, for the presumption is always in favour of the constitutionality of a law.[2] Statutes, which are constitutional in part only, will be upheld by the court so far as they are not in conflict with the Constitution, provided that their constitutional, and their unconstitutional, parts be severable;[3] but when the unconstitutional parts of such a statute are so connected with its general scope, that, should they be stricken out, effect cannot be given to the legislative intent, the other provisions of the statute must fall with them.[4]

125. In the order of supremacy, treaties, duly ratified, are of inferior authority to the Constitution, and to constitutional acts of Congress,[5] but they are of

---

[1] Marbury v. Madison, 1 Cr. 137; Norton v. Shelby County, 118 U. S. 442.
[2] Fletcher v. Peck, 6 Cr. 87; The Legal Tender Cases, 12 Wall. 531; U. S. v. Harris, 106 U. S. 629.
[3] Packet Co. v. Keokuk, 95 U. S. 97.
[4] Allen v. Louisiana, 103 U. S. 80; Spraigue v. Thompson, 118 id. 90; U. S. v. Harris, 106 U. S. 629; The Virginia Coupon Cases, 114 id. 289, 305; Baldwin v. Franks, 120 U. S. 678, 685; The Trade-Mark Cases, 100 U. S. 82.
[5] The Cherokee Tobacco, 11 Wall. 616; Foster v. Neilson, 2 Pet. 253, 314; The Head Money Cases, 112 U. S. 580; Baldwin v. Franks, 120 id. 678, 703; U. S. v. McBratney, 104 id. 621, 623.

superior authority to state legislation,[1] and where a treaty declares the rights and privileges, which the citizens or subjects of a foreign nation may enjoy in the United States, it, in general, operates by its own force, and does not require the aid of any congressional enactment.[2] While, as respects the rights and obligations of the contracting governments, a treaty is to be regarded as concluded and binding from the date of its signature,[3] yet as respects the effects of the treaty on the rights of citizens of the United States vested before the ratification of the treaty but subsequently to its signature, the treaty is not to be considered as a part of the supreme law of the land until after its ratifications have been exchanged, for the Senate may in process of ratification amend the treaty,[4] and it cannot be known, until it be ratified, what it may command or prohibit.[5] Treaties do not, unless they be in express terms retroactive, affect rights vested, or liabilities incurred, before their ratification.[6]

126. A consideration of the cases which have been cited in the preceding chapters of this book leads to the conclusion that the supremacy of the government of the United States, within its constitutional sphere of action, involves: *first*, the exercise of judicial power by the government of the United States for the purposes of enforcing the rights created by the Constitution, laws,

---

[1] U. S. v. 43 Gallons of Whiskey, 93 U. S. 188; Hauenstein v. Lynham, 100 id. 483.

[2] Chirac v. Chirac, 2 Wheat. 259; Carneal v. Banks, 10 id. 181; Hughes v. Edwards, 9 id. 489, 496; Hauenstein v. Lynham, 100 U. S. 483; sed cf. Baldwin v. Franks, 120 U. S. 678.

[3] Dana's Wheaton's International Law, 36.

[4] Art. II, Section 2, of the Constitution requires the advice and consent of the Senate, and the concurrence of two-thirds of the Senators present, to the making of any treaty by the President.

[5] U. S. v. Arredondo, 6 Pet. 691, 749; Haver v. Yaker, 9 Wall. 32.

[6] Prevost v. Greneaux, 19 How. 1; Frederickson v. Louisiana, 23 How. 445.

and treaties of the United States, of punishing offenses against the laws of that government, and of finally determining the judicial construction of the Constitution, statutes, and treaties of the United States; *second*, the exemption of all property and agencies of the federal government from state control; and *third*, the nonexercise by the states of powers clashing with the powers granted by the Constitution to the government of the United States.

127. Articles IX and X of the Amendments to the Constitution declare that, "the enumeration in the Constitution of certain rights shall not be construed to deny or disparage others retained by the people." . . . "The powers not delegated to the United States by the Constitution, nor prohibited by it to the states, are reserved to the states respectively, or to the people." If these amendments had never been adopted, the construction of the Constitution as a whole would lead inevitably to the conclusion that, in so far as the states are not controlled by the expressed or implied restrictions contained in the Constitution of the United States, they may severally exercise all the powers of independent governments.[1]

128. The nature and extent of the reserved rights of the states must be determined by a process of reasoning by exclusion, involving a statement of the specific constitutional restraints upon freedom of state action, and a conclusion that any state may, so far as the United States are concerned, rightfully exercise every power of government which is not included within the specific restraints thus enumerated. A consideration of the terms of the Constitution and of the effect of the judgments of the court, which have been cited in the preceding chapters of this book, renders it easy to formulate

[1] *Supra*, Sec. 3.

a statement of the general nature of the constitutional restraints upon the states. By force of those restraints, a state cannot withdraw from the Union, nor deprive itself of its rights as one of the United States, nor emancipate itself from the constitutional limitations upon freedom of state action; it cannot have any international relations with foreign states, nor with any other of the United States; it cannot enter into treaties with foreign powers, nor make interstate compacts; it cannot engage in war, unless actually invaded, or in such imminent danger as will not admit of delay; it cannot grant letters of marque and reprisal; it cannot adopt any other than a republican form of state government, nor grant any title of nobility;[1] it cannot prescribe the conditions of its citizenship, for the birth within the United States of any person subject to their jurisdiction, or the naturalization of any person under the acts of Congress, followed, in either case, by residence within a state makes the person so born or naturalized, and so residing, a citizen of that state; it cannot, in its regulation of the exercise of the right of suffrage by its citizens, discriminate because of race, colour, or previous condition of servitude; it cannot, in its action with regard to its own citizens or with regard to temporary denizens within its territory, abridge those privileges or immunities which are common to citizens of the United States, nor deprive any person of life, liberty, or property, without due process of law, nor deny to any person

[1] Section 4 of Article IV of the Constitution requires the United States to "guaranty to every state in this Union a republican form of government." It rests with Congress to decide what government is the established one in a state, and also to determine upon the means proper to be adopted to fulfil the guaranty of a republican form of government to the states: Luther v. Borden, 7 How. 1, 42. Chase, C. J., pointed out in Texas v. White, 7 Wall. 727, that this constitutional obligation required the United States, after the suppression of the Rebellion, to re-establish the representation in Congress of the states lately in rebellion.

the equal protection of the laws; it cannot deny to citizens of other states those privileges and immunities of citizenship which it allows to its own citizens; it cannot tax the property of the United States, nor the agencies employed by the United States in the execution of its constitutional powers to such an extent as to interfere with the full performance by such agents of their duties to the United States, nor the subjects of foreign or interstate commerce in such a manner as to amount to a regulation of such commerce, nor lay any imposts or duties on imports or exports, except what may be absolutely necessary for executing its inspection laws, nor lay any duty on tonnage; it cannot coin money, nor emit bills of credit, nor make anything but gold and silver coin a tender in payment of debts; it cannot, by any law or by any act to which it, by its enforcement thereof, gives the force of a law deprive a party of the legal right of enforcing, or obtaining compensation for the breach of, an express and valid contract, executed or executory; it cannot regulate commerce, foreign, or interstate, or with the Indian tribes, by obstructing, or burdening, or discriminating against, such commerce; it cannot exercise judicial jurisdiction over persons or subject-matters rightfully withdrawn by the United States from its jurisdiction, and in its exercise of jurisdiction it cannot derogate from the supremacy of the Constitution, laws, and treaties of the United States, nor fail to give full faith and credit to the public acts, records, and judicial proceedings of every other state; it cannot pass any bill of attainder or *ex post facto* law; and it cannot so exercise its powers of police regulation as to interfere with the exercise of the constitutional powers of the United States, or, in other words, in such manner as to operate upon persons or property brought within its jurisdiction in the exercise of powers granted to the United States, before such persons or property shall have lost their distinctive character and merged in the mass of persons or property within the territory of the state. Such are substantially the constitutional restraints upon the powers of the states; and their practical effect is, that, while limiting the powers of each state in that which concerns foreign nations, and in that which affects the interests of other states, and of the citizens of those other states, it yet reserves to each state full powers of self-government in all that affects only the interests of that state, and of its own citizens.

129. The Constitution was the result of a struggle between contending parties, the one fearing a disintegration of the Union as a consequence of the weakness of the confederation, and striving to create a nation, and the other mindful of the contest for the independence of the colonies, and seeking to sacrifice as little as possible of the autonomy of the states. Fortunately for the peace and prosperity of the country, and for the permanency of its free institutions, neither party triumphed, and their conflict of opinion gave birth to a government, which, though national in its relations to foreign powers, and in the directness of its action upon the citizens of the several states, is also federal in its reservation to the states and the people of all powers not expressly, or by necessary implication, granted to the United States. The distinguishing characteristics of the Constitution, thus created, are the limitation in terms of the powers confided to the United States, the reservation to the states of the right of local self-government, and that practical conservatism, which is the necessary consequence of the supremacy of a written Constitution, whose manner of amendment guards it against hasty changes. The government created by

that Constitution has stood the tests of time and growth; its nationality has survived the shocks of foreign, and of civil, war; and its recognition of the principle of home rule has overcome the disintegrating tendencies of the expansion of territory and the increase of population. That in the future as in the past the United States may escape the perils of dissolution and the dangers of consolidation, it is necessary that its Constitution be maintained in its integrity, and that the reserved rights of the states, and the supremacy of the United States within the limits of its delegated powers, be alike jealously guarded. So long as that just equipoise of federal and of state power shall be preserved, the states, united for the promotion of the general welfare, and independent in all matters of merely local concern, will triumph over all that may menace the perpetuity of their free institutions.

# INDEX.

THE REFERENCES ARE TO THE PAGES.

ABOLITION OF SLAVERY.
    By the XIII Amendment, 6.
ADMIRALTY.
    Jurisdiction in, 46, 196.
AGENCIES.
    Of United States, state taxation of, 28.
    Of states, federal taxation of, 23.
ALLEGIANCE.
    Due to United States and to state, 7.
ALLIANCES.
    By states forbidden, 189.
ALIENS. See NATURALIZATION.
AMBASSADORS.
    Jurisdiction as to, 196.
APPELLATE JURISDICTION. See JUDICIAL POWER.
ATTAINDER.
    Prohibition of bills of, 182.
    Bills of, defined, 185.
BANKS, NATIONAL.
    Power of Congress to create, 10.
BILLS OF ATTAINDER. See ATTAINDER.
BILLS OF CREDIT.
    Prohibition of state, 187.
    Definition of, 187.
    Illustrations of, 187, 188.
BILLS OF EXCHANGE.
    Dealing in, taxable by states, 62.
    As instruments of commerce, 40, 41.
BILLS OF LADING.
    State taxation of, 72.

## BRIDGES.
Regulation of, 92.

## CASE.
Requisites of a judicial, 196, 211.

## CHARTERS.
As contracts, 171, 173.
Implied contracts in, 174.

## CITIZENS.
Federal jurisdiction in suits between, 197.
Citizenship of the United States, 250.
Citizenship of a state, 252.
The right of suffrage not a privilege of citizenship, 252.
Discriminations forbidden in state regulation of suffrage, 252.
Immunities of, 256.

## CIVIL RIGHTS.
State regulation of as affecting interstate commerce, 54.
Unconstitutionality of regulation of, by the United States, 266.

## COMMERCE.
Regulation of, 37.
Constitutional provisions as to, 37, 43.
History of commerce clause, 39.
Definition of, 40.
Regulation of, defined, 41.
Taxation, as regulation of, 34, 42.
Distinction between internal, and foreign or interstate, 44.
Federal action in regulation of, 44.
State action in regulation of, 45.
Incidental regulation of, 59.

## COMPACTS. See ALLIANCES.

## CONFLICT OF JURISDICTION.
The rule as to, between state and federal courts, 238.

## CONSTITUTION OF THE UNITED STATES.
By whom ratified, 1.
Effect of ratification of, 1.
Construction of, 215.
Supremacy of, 273.

## CONSTRUCTION.
Of the Constitution by the judicial power, 215.

CONTRACTS.
    Constitutional prohibition of impairment of obligation of, 145.
    "Law" defined, 146.
    Obligation of, defined, 149.
    Regulation of remedies, 149.
    "Contracts" defined, 153.
    Of exemption from state taxation, 159, 166.
    Made by states, 160, 164.
    History of the clause, 160.
    Executory, 165.
    Charters as, 171.
    With political subdivisions, 173.
    Implied, in charters, 175.
    Implied exemption from taxation, 176.
    Implied exemption from police power, 178.
    As affecting suits against states, 180.
    The force and effect of the constitutional prohibition, 181.

COURTS-MARTIAL.
    Jurisdiction of, 213.

CURRENCY.
    Legal tender, 12.

DAMS.
    Regulation of, 92.

DIRECT TAXES.
    Imposition of, by United States, 22.

DUE PROCESS OF LAW.
    Definition of, 226.

EQUAL PROTECTION OF THE LAWS. See XIV AMENDMENT.

EXPORTS.
    State taxation of, 25, 82.
    Term not applicable to interstate commerce, 73.
    Taxation of, by United States, 81.

EX-POST FACTO LAWS.
    Prohibition of, 182.
    Illustrations of, 184, 185.
    Definitions of, 183.

EXPRESSED RESTRAINTS.
    On states, 4.

**FERRIES.**
Regulation of, 99.
**FOREIGN CORPORATIONS.**
Rights and liabilities of, 258.
**FOURTEENTH AMENDMENT.**
As affecting the exercise of judicial power by the states, 239.
As affecting state power over personal and property rights of citizens, 264.
**FUGITIVES FROM JUSTICE.**
State obligations as to, 190.
Jurisdiction as to issue of *habeas corpus* in cases of, 191.
**GOODS.**
Taxation of, in course of interstate transportation, 73.
**GRANTS.**
As contracts, 165.
**GUARANTY.**
Of republican government to the states, 277.
**HABEAS CORPUS.**
In cases of fugitives from justice, 191.
In cases of restraint of liberty in violation of the Constitution, 209.
**HEALTH LAWS.** See QUARANTINE.
**IMMUNITIES OF CITIZENSHIP.** See CITIZENS.
**IMPAIRING CONTRACTS.** See CONTRACTS.
**IMPARTIAL SUFFRAGE.** See CITIZENS.
**IMPEACHMENT.**
Jurisdiction in, 213.
**IMPLIED POWERS.**
Defined, 3.
Necessity of, 8.
Grant of, 9.
Illustrations of, 10, 11, 12.
**IMPLIED RESTRAINTS.**
On states, 4, 5.
**IMPORTS.**
State taxation of, 25, 82.
Term not applicable to interstate commerce, 73.
**IMPOSTS.**
State imposition of, 25, 81.

IMPROVEMENTS OF NAVIGATION. See NAVIGABLE
WATERS.
INCIDENTAL POWERS OF CONGRESS. See IMPLIED
POWERS.
INDIAN.
    Tribes, not states, 143.
    Regulation of commerce with, 144.
INDICTMENT.
    Not amendable after submission to the grand jury, 226.
INFORMATION.
    Prohibition of prosecution upon, for capital or infamous crimes, 226.
INSOLVENT LAWS.
    Effect of state, 155.
INSPECTION LAWS.
    State, 86.
JUDGES.
    Tenure of office of federal, 194.
    Compensation of, not diminishable during continuance in office, 194.
JUDICIAL POWER.
    Necessity of federal, 192.
    Constitutional provisions as to federal, 194.
    Limited grant of federal, 195.
    Federal jurisdiction in criminal causes, 200.
    Exclusive federal jurisdiction, 201, 204.
    Original jurisdiction of the Supreme Court, 205.
    Removal of causes, 206.
    Appellate jurisdiction, 208.
    Jurisdiction in *habeas corpus*, 209.
    Jurisdiction as to political questions, 211.
    Courts-martial, 213.
    Military commissions, 213.
    Impeachments, 213.
    Construction of the Constitution, by, 215.
    Suits against states, 198, 217.
    Limitation of, by the IV, V, VI, and VII Amendments, 225.
    The federal supremacy as affecting, 231.
    The reserved rights of the states as affecting the federal, 233.
    Of the states, 234.

JUDICIAL POWER—*Continued.*
    Of the states as affected by the grant of judicial power to the United States, 234.
    Of the states as affected by the XIV Amendment, 239.
    Of the states as affected by section 1 of Article IV, 242.

JUDGMENTS.
    As contracts, 158.
    Effect of in the states, 242.

JURISDICTION.
    Conflict of. See CONFLICT OF JURISDICTION.

JURISDICTION OF COURTS OF UNITED STATES.
    Under constitutional grants and acts of Congress, 195.

JURISDICTION OF STATE COURTS.
    As affected by the Constitution, 234.

JURY.
    Trial by, not to be taken away, 225, 229, 230, 231.
    Discriminations forbidden in state regulation of jury service, 253.

LANDS.
    Public, state taxation of, 27.

LAWS OF UNITED STATES.
    Supremacy of, 274.

LEGAL TENDER.
    Power of Congress over, 12.

LICENSE LAWS. See POLICE REGULATION.

LIFE, LIBERTY, AND PROPERTY. See RIGHTS OF PERSON AND OF PROPERTY.

MERCHANDISE. See GOODS.

NATIONAL BANKS.
    Power of Congress to create, 10.
    Taxation of, by states, 29.

NATURALIZATION.
    Regulation of by United States, 251.
    Courts of the states may admit to citizenship under acts of Congress, 251.

NAVIGABLE WATERS.
    Defined, 45.
    Title to land under, 47.
    Improvements of, 87.

NAVIGATION.
>Regulation of by United States, 50.
>Regulations of by states, 55.
>Improvements of, 87.

ORDINANCE.
>Of 1787, effect of on regulation of commerce, 98.

ORIGINAL JURISDICTION. See JUDICIAL POWER.

PAINS AND PENALTIES.
>Prohibition of bills of, 182, 186.
>Definition of bills of, 186.

PATENTS.
>Granted by United States, do not exempt from state taxation, 28.
>Nor from state police power, 269.

PERSON, RIGHTS OF. See RIGHTS OF PERSON.

PILOTAGE.
>Regulation of, 107.

POLICE REGULATION.
>As affecting commerce, 175.
>Implied exemption by contract from, 178.
>Definition of, 266.
>By the United States, 267.
>By the states, 267.
>The rule as to, 271.

PORT DUES.
>Imposition of, by states, 120.

PORT REGULATIONS.
>Under state authority, 121.

PORTS.
>Preferences of, 122.

PREAMBLE OF CONSTITUTION.
>Force and effect of, 6.

PRIVILEGES OF CITIZENSHIP. See CITIZENS.

PROCESS OF LAW.
>Definition of due, 226.

PROPERTY, RIGHTS OF. See RIGHTS OF PROPERTY.

PUBLIC LANDS. See LANDS.

QUARANTINE.
>Regulation of, 116.

**RAILWAYS.**
 State regulation of interstate transportation by. 123.
 Tolls for use of improved facilities of transportation, 124.
 State police, regulation of, 125.
 State taxation of, 131.

**RATIFICATION.**
 Of Constitution, effect of, 1.

**RECEIPTS OF TRANSPORTATION.**
 State taxation of, 132, 137, 138.

**RECORDS AND LAWS.**
 Proof of in other states, 242.

**REGULATION.**
 Of commerce. See COMMERCE.
 Of remedy. See CONTRACTS.

**REMEDY.**
 Regulation of. See CONTRACTS.

**REMOVAL OF CAUSES.** See JUDICIAL POWER.

**RESERVED POWERS AND RIGHTS OF THE STATES.**
 See STATES.

**RETROSPECTIVE LAWS.**
 Not prohibited, 182.

**RIGHTS OF PERSON AND OF PROPERTY.**
 Constitutional protection of, 226.
 State control over, 254.
 As affected by XIV Amendment, 264.

**SECESSION.**
 Unconstitutionality of, 1.

**SELF-GOVERNMENT.**
 Reservation of right of, to the states in local matters, 279.

**SHIPPING.**
 Regulation of by United States, 57.
 Regulation of by states, 53.
 State taxation of, 63.

**STATES, THE.**
 Existence of, before the Constitution, 2.
 Foreign to, and independent of, each other, so far as not controlled by Constitution, 2.
 Powers and obligations of new, 2.
 Taxation by, 23.

STATES, THE—*Continued.*
    Suits against, as affected by contracts, 180.
    Suits against as affected by the XI Amendment, 198, 217
    Judicial power of, as affected by the federal supremacy, 231.
    Judicial power of the states as affected by the grant of judicial power to the United States, 236.
    Judicial power of the states as affected by the XIV Amendment, 239.
    Reserved rights of, 276.
    Necessity for maintenance of, 279.

SUITS.
    Against states. See STATES.

SUPREMACY OF THE UNITED STATES.
    State taxation affected by the, 25.
    State regulation of federal judicial process or practice, 231.
    Supremacy of the Constitution, 272.
    Supremacy of the laws of United States, 274.
    Supremacy of the treaties of United States, 274.
    Effects of the, 275.

SUPREME COURT. See JUDICIAL POWER.

TAXATION.
    Defined, 18, 19.
    Power of, in whom vested, 19.
    By United States, 20.
    By United States, constitutional provisions as to, 21.
    Uniformity of, 22.
    By the states, 23.
    Of imports and exports, 25, 81.
    Of state agencies, 23.
    Of federal agencies, 28.
    Of national banks, 29.
    As affected by contracts of exemption, 33.
    As a regulation of commerce, 34.
    Not to be imposed for private purposes, 20.
    Direct, 22.
    Discriminating against products on manufactures of other states, 75.

TELEGRAPHS.
    Regulation of, 140.
    State taxation of, 142.

**THIRTEENTH AMENDMENT.**
  Effect of, 263.
**TITLES OF NOBILITY.**
  Not to be granted by the states, 277.
**TONNAGE.**
  Defined, 66.
  State taxation of, 25, 66.
**TRANSIT.**
  Right of, not limitable by state taxation, 28.
**TRANSPORTATION.**
  By water, taxation of, by United States, 67.
  By water, taxation of, by states, 68.
  By land, taxation of, by states, 131.
**TRADE-MARKS.**
  Regulation of, by United States, 67.
**TREATIES.**
  Supremacy of, 274.
**TRIAL BY JURY.** See Jury.
**TRIBES.** See Indian.
**UNION.**
  Indissolubility of, 1.
**UNITED STATES.**
  Limited powers of, 2.
  Supremacy of, 3.
**WARRANTS.**
  Requisites to issue of search, 225.
**WATER-WAYS.** See Navigable Waters.
**WHARFAGE.**
  Regulation of, 105.
**WITNESSES.**
  Right of accused to be confronted with, 229.
  Right of accused to have compulsory process for obtaining, 230.

www.ingramcontent.com/pod-product-compliance
Lightning Source LLC
Chambersburg PA
CBHW030750230426
43667CB00007B/918